# DEVELOPING INF
# SYSTEMS

MW00634300

## BCS, THE CHARTERED INSTITUTE FOR IT

BCS, The Chartered Institute for IT champions the global IT profession and the interests of individuals engaged in that profession for the benefit of all. We promote wider social and economic progress through the advancement of information technology science and practice. We bring together industry, academics, practitioners and government to share knowledge, promote new thinking, inform the design of new curricula, shape public policy and inform the public.

Our vision is to be a world-class organisation for IT. Our 70,000 strong membership includes practitioners, businesses, academics and students in the UK and internationally. We deliver a range of professional development tools for practitioners and employees. A leading IT qualification body, we offer a range of widely recognised qualifications.

**Further Information**
BCS, The Chartered Institute for IT,
First Floor, Block D,
North Star House, North Star Avenue,
Swindon, SN2 1FA, United Kingdom.
T +44 (0) 1793 417 424
F +44 (0) 1793 417 444
**www.bcs.org/contact**

http://shop.bcs.org/

# DEVELOPING INFORMATION SYSTEMS
## Practical guidance for IT professionals

James Cadle (editor)

© 2014 BCS Learning & Development Ltd
Reprinted November 2016

All rights reserved. Apart from any fair dealing for the purposes of research or private study, or criticism or review, as permitted by the Copyright Designs and Patents Act 1988, no part of this publication may be reproduced, stored or transmitted in any form or by any means, except with the prior permission in writing of the publisher, or in the case of reprographic reproduction, in accordance with the terms of the licences issued by the Copyright Licensing Agency. Enquiries for permission to reproduce material outside those terms should be directed to the publisher.

All trade marks, registered names etc. acknowledged in this publication are the property of their respective owners. BCS and the BCS logo are the registered trade marks of the British Computer Society charity number 292786 (BCS).

Published by BCS Learning & Development Ltd, a wholly owned subsidiary of BCS The Chartered Institute for IT First Floor, Block D, North Star House, North Star Avenue, Swindon, SN2 1FA, UK.
www.bcs.org

Paperback ISBN: 978-1-78017-245-3
PDF ISBN: 978-1-78017-246-0
ePUB ISBN: 978-1-78017-247-7
Kindle ISBN: 978-1-78017-248-4

British Cataloguing in Publication Data.
A CIP catalogue record for this book is available at the British Library.

Disclaimer:
The views expressed in this book are of the author(s) and do not necessarily reflect the views of the Institute or BCS Learning & Development Ltd except where explicitly stated as such. Although every care has been taken by the authors and BCS Learning & Development Ltd in the preparation of the publication, no warranty is given by the authors or BCS Learning and Development Ltd as publisher as to the accuracy or completeness of the information contained within it and neither the authors nor BCS Learning & Development Ltd shall be responsible or liable for any loss or damage whatsoever arising by virtue of such information or any instructions or advice contained within this publication or by any of the aforementioned.

BCS books are available at special quantity discounts to use as premiums and sale promotions, or for use in corporate training programs. Please visit our Contact us page at www.bcs.org/contact.

Typeset by Lapiz Digital Services, Chennai, India.
Printed at Hobbs the Printers Ltd, Hampshire, UK.

# CONTENTS

# LIST OF FIGURES AND TABLES

# AUTHORS

**Tahir Ahmed**
Tahir is a consultant and project manager with more than 30 years' experience, working mainly with UK FTSE 100 companies. Since 2000, Tahir has worked as an independent consultant, typically leading major projects involving the senior management teams of organisations. He has extensive experience of successful project delivery and senior stakeholder management. Tahir has an MSc in Information Systems and is a full Member (MBCS) of BCS, The Chartered Institute for IT (BCS).

**James Cadle (editor)**
James has been involved in the management services field since 1975 and in IT since 1981. He has been a systems analyst, business analyst, project manager, consultant and business manager and, since 1995, he has developed and presented training courses in his chosen fields. Not including the present text, he is the co-author of four books: *Project Management for Information Systems* (5th edition, 2008); *Business Analysis* (3rd edition, 2014); *Business Analysis Techniques* (2nd edition, 2014); and *The Human Touch* (2012). James is a Chartered Fellow (FBCS CITP) of BCS, a full Member of the Association for Project Management (MAPM) and a Fellow of the Royal Society of Arts (FRSA). James is an oral examiner for the BCS Diplomas in Business Analysis and Solution Development.

**Julian Cox**
Julian is an experienced IT developer, consultant and training professional who specialises in system modelling and architectures. He has extensive experience of a variety of development lifecycles across the spectrum from traditional waterfall/linear approaches such as SSADM, through iterative and incremental approaches such as RUP to RAD and Agile approaches. Julian is a full Member (MBCS) of BCS, an oral examiner of the BCS International Diploma in Solution Development and a member of panels for the BCS Solution Development qualifications.

**Lynda Girvan**
Lynda has over 20 years' experience in systems development as a consultant, professional trainer and practitioner in both private and public sector organisations. She has worked in enterprise and strategic modelling and analysis through to product level consultancy and coaching and has experience throughout the product development lifecycle. Lynda is a full Member (MBCS) of BCS, an oral examiner for the BCS International Diploma in Solution Development, a member of the technical and accreditation panels for the BCS Solution Development qualifications and lead examiner for the BCS Systems Development Essentials and Requirements Engineering qualifications. Lynda has spoken at numerous UK and US conferences in the public and private sectors on this topic.

**Alan Paul**
Alan is Qualifications Director for Assist Knowledge Development and is a highly experienced IT professional whose management roles have included change management, programme and project management, strategy definition and service delivery. Project and programme management has covered the full development lifecycle of a number of multi-million-pound developments in the telecoms, financial services, retail and public sectors. Alan has extensive experience of leading large multi-disciplined teams, and in the procurement and management of third party suppliers, including external consultants. Alan contributed several chapters to *Project Management for Information Systems* (2nd edition, 1996).

**Debra Paul**
Debra has over 30 years' experience in the business analysis and IT field, as a consultant, manager and trainer, and is now Managing Director of Assist Knowledge Development Ltd. She has previously co-authored and edited three books in this field: *Business Analysis* (3rd edition, 2014); *Business Analysis Techniques* (2nd edition, 2014); and *The Human Touch* (2012). Debra is a Chartered Fellow (FBCS CITP) of BCS, a Fellow of the Royal Society of Arts (FRSA) and is the Chief Examiner for the BCS International Diploma in Business Analysis.

**Peter Thompson**
Peter has more than 20 years' experience as a software development practitioner and manager covering all aspects of the systems development lifecycle. He has been the managing director of an independent software house and systems development manager for the UK's largest independent recruitment agency. Peter is now a practising information systems consultant, specialising in the pragmatic application of best practice methods, and standards and combines this with a busy training schedule. Peter is a full Member (MBCS) of BCS, and is an oral examiner for the BCS's International Diplomas in Business Analysis and Solution Development.

# FOREWORD

In the rapidly evolving world of technological and business change it has never been more important to understand that high-quality information systems should be developed, acquired, customised and integrated in a consistent and best-practice way.

Getting the right balance between Agile development, linear development and solution procurement is key to this, and due consideration must also be given to the long-term maintenance and enhancement of any systems developed. This leads to the need to employ robust modelling, design, testing and implementation techniques and standards to support rigorous analysis coupled with architectural considerations.

The well respected authors of this book have excelled in their breadth of coverage of the various aspects of information-systems development, and their efforts have resulted in an excellent primer showing the interaction between the key information-systems disciplines, with many useful pointers to where readers can find more detail on any topics that they wish to explore further.

The book will be particularly useful for those studying for the range of BCS qualifications in the areas of systems and solution development, not least those who are sitting the core and specialist modules which lead to the BCS International Diploma in Solution Development, or those wishing to progress to full Chartered professional status.

*Paul Turner* FBCS CITP
BCS Chief Examiner for Solution Development

# PREFACE

The idea for this book came from a realisation that the existing texts on systems development, excellent though they are, have not been updated for some years and that IT professionals (and others) might benefit from a more up-to-date treatment of the subject. An obvious example is the way in which Agile approaches have gained considerable traction in the last decade.

The book has three main objectives:

- to review the way systems are developed, including the underlying philosophies, methods and techniques at the present time;

- to provide a broad overview of systems development for anyone beginning a career in software development or working in a related field;

- to provide people already working in systems development with usable advice on how to go about it.

Writing the book has been a genuine team effort between a group of people who have worked together for many years and have, between them, considerable experience of developing systems, training people in systems development, creating certifications in systems development and conducting examinations in the subject. I would like to take this opportunity to thank the team of authors for their hard work on the book, their friends and families for giving them their support, and the publishing team at BCS for helping us through the endeavour.

*James Cadle*
Editor
April 2014

# 1 INTRODUCTION TO SYSTEMS DEVELOPMENT

**James Cadle**

## CONTENTS OF THIS CHAPTER

This chapter covers the following topics:

- the purpose of systems development;
- the scope of systems development;
- the typical stages in the systems development process;
- the relationship of systems development to other disciplines, such as project management, business analysis and systems architecture;
- how offshoring and outsourcing influences systems development;
- a synopsis of the remaining chapters of this book.

## WHAT IS SYSTEMS DEVELOPMENT?

Systems development is the process of taking a set of business requirements and, through a series of structured stages, translating these into an operational IT system. The stages vary according to the development approach being used – described more fully in Chapter 2, 'Lifecycle types and their rationales' – but typically would include the activities shown in Figure 1.1, including:

- a feasibility study, to see if the project is worthwhile;
- requirements engineering to analyse the business need and specify the users' requirements;
- design of the system to meet the users' needs;
- development of the software needed to meet the requirements;
- testing of the software;
- implementation of the solution.

**Figure 1.1 The main stages of systems development**

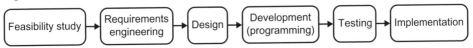

1

Other activities may also be involved, such as the procurement and installation of the hardware on which the system will operate.

At one time, systems development was undertaken in a rather haphazard, ad hoc way, and the result depended to a large extent on the competence and enthusiasm of the individual developers. Today, the core importance of IT systems within most organisations means that more structured and manageable processes have been introduced, to reduce the unpredictable 'human element' and to make possible the construction of larger and more complex systems.

## SYSTEMS DEVELOPMENT AND OTHER DISCIPLINES

Systems development does not take place in isolation; it is part of the intricately connected web of disciplines illustrated in Figure 1.2.

**Figure 1.2  Systems development in a wider context**

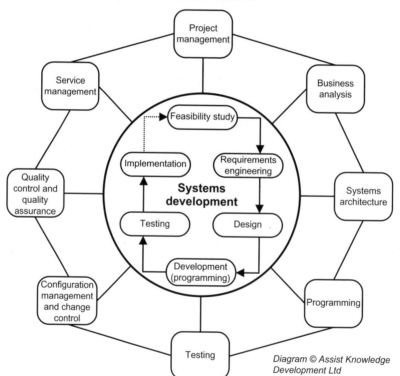

Diagram © Assist Knowledge Development Ltd

The relationship of systems development to other disciplines may be summarised as follows:

**Project management**    If a systems development project is to be successful, technical expertise is not enough; effective project management is also required. The project manager plans the undertaking, mobilises the resources required and controls and coordinates the work. The project manager also ensures that the various stakeholders are kept onside and committed to the project's success. Good project management frees the development team to concentrate on the difficult technical task of devising and implementing the solution.

**Business analysis**    Business analysis is concerned with investigating the business situation and finding out what are the problems to be solved or opportunities to be exploited. It involves developing holistic solutions to business issues, which very often involve the use of IT in some way. Business analysts are also important for eliciting, documenting and managing the requirements for the new or enhanced IT systems and services.

**Systems architecture**    Systems architects are concerned with developing an architecture for the organisation to support and coordinate its systems and provide a coherent platform for expansion and development.

**Programming**    Although within the span of systems development, this is a specialist area which calls for high levels of technical expertise, not least in how to exploit to the full the possibilities offered by the hardware and software available.

**Testing**    The tester's role appears at first to be counter-productive in that he or she is trying to prove that the system does not work. This is an iterative process and, when the tester struggles to identify further defects in any version, it can be stated with some confidence that the system appears to be satisfactory. An important point to realise, though, is that no testing, however thorough, can deliver assurance that the software is one hundred per cent error-free.

**Configuration management and change control**    As systems have become more complex, it has become even more important to know the latest version of the system, the components it is made up of and how these relate to each other. The discipline of managing these components is known as 'configuration management' and it is related to change control, which is a process for managing changes to a system or product in a controlled way.

**Quality control and quality assurance**    Quality control consists of the processes – for example, reviews or code inspections – that are employed within a project team to ensure that the delivered products meet their defined quality

3

criteria. Quality assurance is an external process that ensures that quality control is being exercised; it also puts in place things like standards to assist in quality control.

**Service management**    Service management is concerned with managing and maintaining the services provided by IT systems. It includes, for example, such activities as facilities management – controlling the supporting IT infrastructure – and applications management – supporting and enhancing the applications once they have been delivered initially.

## OFFSHORING AND OUTSOURCING OF SYSTEMS DEVELOPMENT

Two changes that have affected many organisations in recent years have been the offshoring and/or outsourcing of systems development work. These two practices are often referred to together but, in fact, they are separate and one does not necessarily imply the other:

- Offshoring involves using development resources in other countries, usually because high-quality resources can be secured for considerably less cost than in the organisation's home country. For example, India has proved to be a popular place for organisations to establish their development centres because the country's education system produces a large number of high quality IT graduates. Leading firms such as Tesco and HSBC have large development centres in India. More recently, development resources have also been found in ex-communist European countries, such as the Ukraine and the Baltic states.

- Outsourcing means handing over the development work to specialist IT services firms and consultancies. An outsourcing contract may cover just development work or, often, the supplier takes complete responsibility for the organisation's IT systems. Cost may be a driver here too, but often the desire to get control of a spiralling IT budget and to transfer responsibility and risk are also important considerations.

Of course, outsourcing and offshoring are sometimes combined, in that the outsourced supplier chooses to perform its development work overseas, for the reasons already mentioned.

In addition to the claimed benefits, there are of course possible downsides to both offshoring and outsourcing, for example:

- **Offshoring:** there can be delays and communication difficulties associated with working with developers who are a long way away, whose first language is not the same as the customer organisation and whose culture is very different. It could be argued, however, that this just reinforces the need for greater precision in the definition of business requirements, which is a good thing.

- **Outsourcing:** one of the chief dangers here is that the customer organisation loses direct control of systems that are critical to its business objectives. In addition, knowledge of these key systems now resides in the supplier organisation rather than being retained in-house.

## IN THE REST OF THIS BOOK

The chapters that follow explore the elements – the frameworks and models, processes, procedures and techniques – of systems development in more detail, and here we provide a foretaste of what is to come.

### Chapter 2: Lifecycle types and their rationales

A lifecycle provides a framework and structure for undertaking systems development. Over the years, different lifecycles have been developed and employed, ranging from the traditional, linear, step-by-step, 'Waterfall' approach to the currently-popular 'Agile' one. This chapter presents the different lifecycles and assesses their relative strengths and weaknesses.

### Chapter 3: Analysing the business need

Before embarking on any system development project, business analysts should examine the real business need and evaluate the options available to meet it. This analysis should also consider the non-IT issues (changes to organisation structures, to business processes and to people's jobs) that will have to be addressed if the system is to be implemented effectively and provide the expected business benefits.

### Chapter 4: Making a business case

The business case is – or should be – an examination of the justification for undertaking a systems development project and a rigorous analysis of the costs, benefits, impacts and risks of the courses of action available. Assuming that the case is made initially, the business case should be revisited throughout the project's lifecycle to ensure that it has not been invalidated by, for example, rises in costs or changes in the external environment.

### Chapter 5: Requirements engineering

If a system is to be delivered that meets the needs of the organisation, it must be based on well-defined requirements – so that the developers know what is to be produced. Requirements engineering provides a framework and techniques for creating high-quality requirements as a basis for the development work.

### Chapter 6: Programming and development approaches

A major decision to be made is whether, having defined the requirements, the solution should be built from scratch or whether a commercial, off-the-shelf (COTS) solution should be produced. Assuming that at least some development work is to be undertaken, this chapter reviews the different programming and development methods that could be employed.

### Chapter 7: System modelling techniques

Most engineering disciplines make use of models to assist in the conceptualisation and specification of the solution. In the case of systems development, the product can be specified in terms of the functional or processing aspects, the data requirements and the 'dynamic' or event-driven view. This chapter presents approaches to modelling from these three perspectives.

## Chapters 8 and 9: System design

Design is the stage in the development process where decisions are made about how to meet the defined requirements using the hardware and software available. Both the functions/processing and the data need to be designed, and this often involves making compromises between what would be ideal and what is practical given the technology, time and resources available. These two chapters review the challenges of design and conclude with a discussion of the benefits of using defined design patterns to assist in the process.

## Chapter 10: Solution-related architectures

Architecture in IT is similar to architecture in building in that it provides an overall framework and structure for the development of systems. This chapter explains the purpose and approach of architecture, the stakeholders involved and the role of such concepts as Service Oriented Architecture and Service Oriented Development.

## Chapter 11: Quality and testing

Systems must not only be developed on time and within budget, but they must also achieve appropriate levels of quality. This chapter defines what is meant by the term 'quality' in the IT context and presents methods that can be used to assure software quality.

## Chapter 12: Implementation and changeover

The introduction of systems into service is often a very challenging aspect of systems development involving, as it does, moving from manual or older systems to the new ones, training the staff, data conversion and so forth. This chapter reviews these issues and also considers the different approaches to implementation, for example as a 'big bang' or in a phased manner.

## Chapter 13: Maintenance and evaluation

Surveys have shown that, in most cases, the majority of expenditure on IT systems occurs after they have been introduced into service – to fix problems, make enhancements, adapt to changes in other systems and so on. Although live operation follows systems development, this chapter explains the purpose of evaluation and maintenance and shows how decisions made during the development can assist, or hamper, the longevity of the systems.

## Chapter 14: Solution development tools

Systems development can benefit hugely from the development team having at their disposal software support tools to help them do their work. These can range from tools to control the vast amount of documentation that is produced, to aids for the developers, to tools to assist testing. This chapter looks at the pros and cons of software support tools and provides guidance on what to look for in a tool.

## FURTHER READING

Cadle, J. and Yeates, D. (2008) *Project management for information systems* (5th edition). Pearson Prentice Hall, Harlow.

Paul, D., Yeates, D. and Cadle, J. (2014) *Business analysis* (3rd edition), BCS, Swindon.

Skidmore, S. and Eva, M. (2004) *Introducing systems development*. Palgrave Macmillan, Basingstoke.

Various authors (2002) *Best practice for application management*. OGC/TSO, London.

Yeates, D. and Wakefield, T. (2004) *Systems analysis and design* (2nd edition). FT Prentice Hall, Harlow.

# 2 LIFECYCLE TYPES AND THEIR RATIONALES

## Lynda Girvan

**CONTENTS OF THIS CHAPTER**

This chapter covers the following topics:

- introduction to system development lifecycles;
- what we mean by 'system development lifecycle';
- comparing linear and evolutionary approaches;
- lifecycles based on the linear approach;
- lifecycles based on the evolutionary approach;
- the impact of Agile;
- hybrid approaches;
- how to decide on an approach.

**INTRODUCTION TO SYSTEM DEVELOPMENT LIFECYCLES**

A system development lifecycle (SDLC) is a framework describing a process for understanding, planning, building, testing and deploying an information system. The process can apply to both hardware and software systems, as a system can be composed of hardware only, software only, or a combination of both.

---

**Figure 2.1 The main stages of systems development**

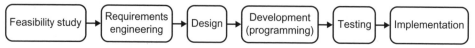

In any system development, there are a number of stages that must be undertaken. Although shown as a set of sequential steps, they do not need to be treated as such. Later in this chapter we will explore when and how often they occur in different lifecycles.

The stages are defined as:

**Feasibility study**

Before system development can commence, funding is required. The feasibility study involves investigation and research in order to evaluate the project's potential for success to support decision-making. Such a study concerns itself with understanding objectively the resources and costs involved and weighing these against the value that will be attained following completion of the project or system. This is called return on investment (ROI) and only those projects and systems that return a reasonable ROI will be supported. The time spent in this stage will depend on how big and complex is the problem that needs to be solved within the organisation or business.

**Requirements engineering**

This stage aims to secure understanding of what the business needs the proposed system to do. To do this, effort is required from business analysts so that requirements can be elicited, analysed, documented and validated. Also, consideration is given to how the requirements will be stored and managed throughout the system development lifecycle, so that they that are accessible to those who need to see or use them and any changes can be managed. The requirements produced during this stage become the input to system design and so it is critical that the requirements can be traced all the way through the system development lifecycle from source to implementation. The amount of requirement detail captured when and where during requirements engineering can be affected by the lifecycle approach to be followed.

**Design**

In the design stage, possible solutions that meet the requirements are considered and weighed against each another. The chosen design is then elaborated in sufficient detail to allow the developers to implement it.

**Development (programming)**

Development is the phase where the technical components (both hardware and software) are created, procured or configured. The developers follow the design to ensure that the system does what is needed for the business or customer.

**Testing**

During testing, the components produced during development are tested to make sure they are working properly and that the system does what it is supposed to do. There are different levels of testing including unit testing, component testing, system testing and acceptance testing.

**Implementation**

Before an IT system is ready to use it must be commissioned into the 'live' or 'operational' environment. Up until this point in a system's development, a reference or test environment may have been used in order to protect other systems from faults within the new system. Moving into the live environment takes careful planning and needs to be understood and managed as part of the overall development lifecycle.

As well as describing how to implement the main stages, a system development lifecycle also describes other elements that together comprise a particular approach that can be used to develop a system. For example, they may describe processes and methods, roles and deliverables, as well as tools and techniques. The elements of a SDLC are illustrated in Figure 2.2.

**Figure 2.2  Elements of the system development lifecycle**

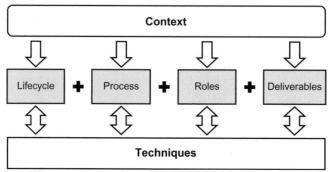

The elements of the system development lifecycle to be considered are:

**Context**  Before beginning to develop a system, it is wise to consider the context in which we are operating. There are many aspects that can affect how we develop a system. Some examples are: Are we expected to deliver one complete system or will the end users expect multiple releases, or phased delivery? What skills and expertise do we currently have within the development team, and what is their preferred delivery style? Are the team and the key stakeholders in the same location? Is there a requirement for audit, quality or regulatory approval? Is our organisation expecting us to move to Agile techniques? How complex is the system we are expecting to deliver? Are the requirements likely to be well understood or could they change? Is this a tried and tested technology, or are we breaking new ground?

Understanding the context we are operating within help us select the right SDLC, and helps us to use it properly.

**Lifecycle**  The lifecycle describes the stages we will typically follow to plan, design, build, test and deliver information systems. Lifecycles are either linear or iterative. The linear lifecycle, often referred to as the 'traditional' or 'step-by-step' approach, takes the form of a sequence of steps, completed in order, with the final step being implementing the system into the operational environment. The 'Waterfall' lifecycle is one well-known example. An alternative to this is the evolutionary lifecycle, often referred to as 'iterative' development, whereby the system evolves through early prototyping and progressive versions of the system.

**Process**

In its simplest form, a process is a set of actions or steps that, if followed, will deliver a particular outcome. Although the lifecycle itself provides key development stages, it is also important to structure, plan and control the processes around those stages. To do this, we adopt methods and standards that apply a framework around managing the processes within the SDLC.

There are many different types of software approach to choose from, some of which lend themselves to a more linear lifecycle and others that are more suited towards an evolutionary lifecycle approach. Some are more prescriptive than others too, in that they mandate which lifecycle they are part of. Some also define specific roles, deliverables, techniques and even the modelling method. Others are more agnostic of lifecycle, and can be used in various types of SDLC.

When deciding upon which system development processes to use, it is important to make sure they are in line with the 'context' and 'lifecycle' that has been chosen or is adopted within the organisation.

Further information about software processes can be found in the section 'How to decide on an approach', where you can find useful tips to help decide which process might best suit your needs.

**Roles**

In order to progress through an SDLC, it is imperative that there are people who can carry out the tasks required. Many system development approaches outline the roles required for us. However, it is worth noting that many of the role titles vary between the different approaches. Below is a generic list of the key roles required within the system development lifecycle:

- business roles;
  - sponsor or senior responsible owner;
  - business analyst;
  - domain expert;
  - end users;
- project roles;
  - project manager;
  - team leader;
  - work package manager;

- technical roles;
  - technical architect;
  - solution developer;
  - solution tester;
- implementation and support roles;
  - release manager;
  - database administrator;
  - system administrator.

**Deliverables**

These are the documents, models, designs and hardware or software components that are required during the different stages of the SDLC. Again, different lifecycles and processes require different deliverables. The important thing to remember is that many of the deliverables are a way of detailing what is understood about the system in terms of what it needs to do, how it needs to do it, how well it does it and how it gets delivered. The deliverables include things such as:

- requirement documents;
- models such as:
  - class or entity relationship models;
  - use case models;
  - process models;
  - state transition diagrams;
  - sequence diagrams;
  - component diagrams;
- test plans;
- test scripts;
- implementation plans;
- system components and working software.

**Techniques**

There is a huge number of techniques that can be adopted during the development of a system. Which specific ones are used varies depending on team and organisation preferences, life cycle choice, and system development approach selected. For example:

- An organisation with a strong military product line may insist on the use of MoDAF (Ministry of Defence Architecture Framework – UK) or DoDAF (Department of Defense Architecture Framework – USA).

- Teams used to rapid prototyping or Test Driven Development may struggle with a linear approach and work better in an Agile model.

- Commercial projects with payment milestones that require formal sign-off and structured review dates may benefit from the rigour provided by a linear 'Waterfall' lifecycle.

- Detailed UML designs may not be appropriate where team members and project sponsors do not understand them.

- Another factor to consider when selecting the techniques is whether there are any formal standards or procedures that need to be adopted within the organisation.

Over the years, many development lifecycles have been created and, in some cases, marketed. They each have their strengths and weaknesses, and some work better for some types of systems and projects than others.

It is important to stress, however, that the lifecycle chosen must not be seen as a recipe to be followed exactly to the letter. Blindly following an SDLC without considering the context or system development approach could actually result in project failure. Each system development project is different in terms of scale and complexity and therefore the lifecycle approach used will often benefit from tailoring.

However, this tailoring must be done with caution, and changing an approach without considering the implications can also result in project failure. Used (and tailored) properly, most lifecycles can be used successfully with most types of system. But it is true that some will be a naturally better fit for some types of system development that for others. This chapter explores the various approaches that have been developed over the years and helps you choose the right one for your project/system.

## WHAT WE MEAN BY 'SYSTEM DEVELOPMENT LIFECYCLE'

There are a great many different system development lifecycles in use today. However, they are underpinned by just five basic lifecycles and two approaches.

The following two sections describe these seven core elements and help us to understand them. This is because understanding and being able to identify the core attributes of a lifecycle is critical to being able to properly evaluate its suitability for a project.

The first fundamental elements describe whether a lifecycle is linear or evolutionary:

- A linear approach describes a sequence of tasks that are completed in order, only moving to the next step once the previous step is complete.

- An evolutionary approach evolves the solution through progressive versions, each more complete than the last, and often uses a prototyping approach to development.

Then, there are five basic system development lifecycles:

- Waterfall;
- 'V' model;
- Incremental;
- Iterative;
- Spiral.

Before we explore these in more depth, we must first consider the scope of a **system development** lifecycle. Earlier in this chapter, we introduced the main stages of systems development, where the final stage is implementation. However, we know that the development of a system doesn't end when it is first released, but rather continues as the system is updated, faults are identified and fixed and improvements are made until, eventually, the system is decommissioned. Throughout this period, the system also requires other maintenance and support activities such as backup, patching, audit and security protection.

However, most SDLCs only cover the development and transition to operating capability and do not include these ongoing activities and costs to support and maintain the system.

The additional costs beyond system development are sometimes referred to as 'through life costs' because they are the costs that will be spent on the system until it reaches its end of life. In most cases, these costs eventually vastly exceed the original development cost.

This is the difference between the whole **system** lifecycle, and the **system development** lifecycle, and can be categorised as follows:

| | |
|---|---|
| **System development lifecycle** | The planning, understanding, analysing, building, testing and implementation of a new system. Delivery is often managed through a project structure, where time and budget are provided to deliver the system. Success is when the system is implemented and transitioned into the 'live' or operating environment. Once implementation occurs, the project is considered complete. |
| **System lifecycle** | The ongoing support and maintenance of a system that has been implemented into the 'live' or operational environment right the way through to its end of life or decommissioning. This is often managed through system managers or service owners and often funded through the business-as-usual (BAU) budget rather than project funding. |

Not surprisingly, through life support often includes adding features and improvements to the system, which require some of the same tasks as developing the initial system. Such updates to the system often come in the form of service pack releases or system enhancements. The main difference is often one of time, budget and scope. Complex or expensive changes might necessitate a new system development phase, whereas smaller, simpler or urgent changes will be applied to the original system.

Since systems can have long lifetimes, particularly in some contexts (such as military), the costs accrued during the system lifecycle can far outweigh the costs spent during system development. Therefore, for many systems it is important to consider the through life costs of the system during the feasibility stage of SDLC and perhaps to modify the design accordingly. More information on this is provided in Chapter 13 'Maintenance and evaluation'.

## Comparing linear and evolutionary approaches

We can categorise SDLCs into whether they are linear or evolutionary.

### Linear approaches

Linear approaches follow the SDLC stages in a defined order. Each step must be completed, understood and agreed before the next step can be started.

In large, complex systems, this agreement between steps requires formal reviews by lots of people before the stage can be signed-off. It also places very definite break points in development that can be linked to project, payment or decision milestones. This rigour and involvement through formal documentation and review leads to a high quality product, as all the mistakes are captured and corrected before the next step starts. This is suitable for developing systems where the requirements are well understood, can be agreed up front and are unlikely to change.

In large, complex systems, where development is distributed or outsourced, a linear approach helps to control cost and scope, and allows development to be split between suppliers.

For smaller projects, a linear approach can be simple to implement, as the steps logically follow one another and can be easily understood by a small team. A smaller team can transition through the steps quite quickly too, so the documentation can be light as the information for each stage will be fresh in the team's minds.

Some of the strengths and weaknesses of a linear approach are:

**Strengths**
- breaks down the problem into distinct stages, each with a clear purpose;
- everything is agreed in advance of being used, with no need to revisit later;
- helps provide structure to complex systems, making distributed or outsourced development easier to manage;

- suits a very detailed design decomposition and detailed specification approach;
- locking down each stage in advance of the next makes it easier to control cost and scope creep;
- simple and intuitive for smaller problems (people who don't think they are using an SDLC are probably taking a linear approach).

**Weaknesses**
- depends greatly on each stage being done properly, as it is hard or impossible to go back and change it later;
- for complex problems, the time required to be thorough at each stage leads to long timescales;
- doesn't cope well with changing requirements;
- customer or business value is not available until the end;
- if the project is stopped early there is little of business value to show for the cost.

### Evolutionary approaches

Evolutionary approaches focus on progressing understanding through delivering early prototypes or iteration releases. The assumption here is that the requirements are not well understood and cannot be well articulated early in the lifecycle, or that early delivery is more important than completeness. Evolutionary approaches are the basis of 'Agile' development today.

Evolutionary development is ideal for new products, which might be innovation projects or green field developments, where the users find it difficult to express their requirements. Using this approach enables the system to evolve, uncovering more and more understanding through the demonstration of working software until the solution is reached. They are also ideal for large, complex systems, where early benefit must be realised in order to justify funding or to get quickly to market. In these examples, high value threads of benefit can be identified for implementation first, with richer functionality following later. This is common in web-based services or products.

An evolutionary approach is also used where there is high business or technical risk. Early versions can focus on exposing or mitigating that risk. If it turns out that the project is not feasible, it can be stopped without having spent much time on it, and all the work delivered so far has value.

Some of the strengths and weaknesses of an evolutionary approach are:

**Strengths**
- early delivery of value to the customer – either working versions or knowledge of project risk;
- copes well with complex requirements – fast changing, uncertain or complicated;
- encourages collaboration with the users throughout, so customer buy-in is higher;

|  | • allows 'just enough' to be done knowing that it can be refined later on. |
|---|---|
| **Weaknesses** | • can be hard to project manage due to multiple iterations; especially hard with multiple iteration teams and complex products; |
|  | • without careful management, the evolving requirements can result in scope creep; |
|  | • overall costs can be higher due to the additional integration and test across multiple teams and iterations; |
|  | • easy to over-promise on early functionality. |

## LIFECYCLES BASED ON THE LINEAR APPROACH

Let us now explore the linear lifecycles. Of the five basic lifecycles, three follow a linear approach and these are:

- Waterfall;
- 'V' model;
- Incremental.

### The Waterfall lifecycle

The most common linear lifecycle is 'Waterfall'. This was one of the first lifecycles introduced back in the 1970s and it still holds much weight and value today. The main stages of the Waterfall lifecycle are illustrated in Figure 2.3, which shows a sequence of steps or stages that cascade down giving it a Waterfall-like look, hence the name.

The principles behind Waterfall are that each step should be completed before moving onto the next step. So, the feasibility study must be completed before the requirements engineering step can be started, and the requirements engineering must be completed before the design can be started, and so on. Completing the steps in this way ensures that the system is well understood through formal documentation and review and therefore should lead to a quality product.

The dotted lines and arrows show that if problems occur in any of the steps, then communication and understanding must also flow backwards to rectify the problems. For example, if during programming a problem occurred whereby a particular requirement could not be satisfied, then the programming would halt whilst the design step was reconsidered in light of the problem and if necessary the requirements engineering step would also be revisited.

Successful Waterfall development requires strong project management, accurate estimation and sound design. This implies that the system must be well understood prior to the start. Otherwise, additional time can be spent in the earlier stages of the lifecycle, getting the requirements and design right and leaving less time in areas in the latter stages, especially testing. Development can take longer than expected due to ambiguity or error in the design, and this can also increase pressure on testing. This tends to result in a poorer quality product; timescales being pushed out, leaving customers to wait even longer for the delivery; or costs increasing as the project goes into overdrive to meet quality and/or timescale demands.

Since requirements are elicited, documented and signed off very early in the lifecycle, Waterfall projects are vulnerable to changes in requirements. Once the requirements stage is complete, changes become increasingly expensive, as the team must revisit the requirements stage and all stages afterwards. To manage this, formal change control procedures and processes are implemented to manage change or, in some cases, even protect the project from change. In fast-moving customer environments, this can present a challenge.

**Figure 2.3 The Waterfall lifecycle**

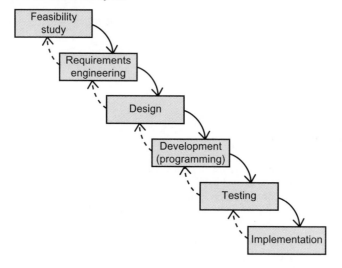

The strengths and weaknesses of the Waterfall lifecycle are:

**Strengths**
- good for developing systems where the requirements and likely solution are well understood and unlikely to change;

- rigour and control around each stage makes it easier to project manage, with obvious hooks for project milestones;

- simple to understand and easy to use due to rigidity of the stages.

**Weaknesses**
- can be costly to manage change, especially if change to requirements is identified during testing;

- working software not delivered until the final stage, implementation;
- poor estimation can severely impact project cost and schedule;
- customer collaboration is limited to requirements and user testing; on long projects this can lead to a lack of customer buy-in, particularly where stakeholders change.

## The 'V' model

The 'V' model was introduced almost as an extension to the Waterfall model to deal with the problem whereby time allocated to testing could often get squeezed during a Waterfall project if time and money started to run out. To address this, the 'V' model, shown in Figure 2.4, changes the way that the development stages are represented from a 'Waterfall' to a 'V'.

This makes a distinction between the activities on the left hand side of the 'V' (project definition) and the right hand side of the 'V' (verification and validation). The bottom of the 'V' is therefore the actual development that takes place to translate the project definition into working software that can be verified and validated.

The dotted lines connecting the left-hand side with the right are a fundamental difference from the Waterfall model, and demonstrate the relationship between each stage of definition with its associated stage of testing. The model is implemented from the top down, meaning that test artefacts are created at the same time as the corresponding requirements, helping ensure that the testing stages will be testing the right things.

This early thought and rigour around testing leads to an approach that focuses on delivering a high-quality system.

## Figure 2.4  The 'V' model

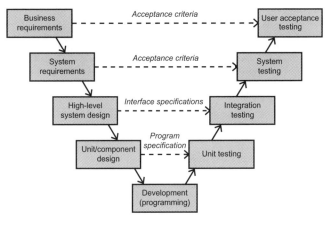

For this reason the 'V' model is particularly good for safety-critical systems where a single release of the system is still anticipated, but high quality and safety are critical. The design of stages, particularly the separation of high-level design and unit/component design, and the inclusion of 'integration testing' lends itself well to complex problems where there are multiple teams or suppliers involved in the development stage.

It is simple to see how system development responsibilities can be split between teams or suppliers in order to divide up a complex or large-scale task.

An extended 'V' model, illustrated in Figure 2.5, was later introduced to include the feasibility and benefits realisation stages. This produces a way of measuring and testing how well the actual business benefits were delivered, as opposed to testing when the requirements were delivered. After all, we could have a system that verifies and validates all the requirements, and yet fails to meet the need of the business because it does not deliver the business benefit.

For example, a system to maximise staff deployment based on skills and experience could easily result in a system that records employees skills and experience. This would probably meet many of the requirements but not the benefit of improved staff deployment.

The extended 'V' model tends to be more popular today than the simple Waterfall, and is used in many system engineering projects. This shows its versatility and ability to scale massively. When used with formal systems engineering frameworks like MoDAF, the 'V' model can be used to manage extremely large and complex systems like aircraft or ships.

**Figure 2.5  The extended 'V' model**

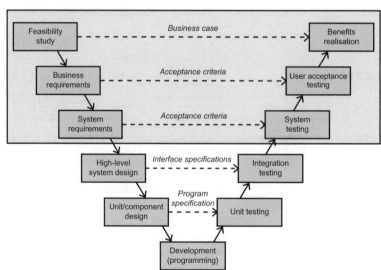

**Strengths**
- additional focus on testing leads to a high quality product;
- ideal for systems with complex or high quality attributes (such as safety critical, challenging to integrate or very large);
- easy to plug in highly complex supply chains and distributed teams due to clear interfaces and boundaries;
- rigour and control around each stage makes it easier to project manage;
- easy to scale.

**Weaknesses**
- heavy testing and integration cost that can be unnecessarily expensive for simpler systems;
- cost and impact of change increases significantly as further progress down and up the 'V' is made;
- early stages take longer to complete as there are test artefacts to complete;
- working system not delivered until the final stage, which could be a long time after the customer was last involved;
- development teams can often omit to put enough effort into planning the right-hand side as they progress down the left; This significantly increases risk, particularly in the integration of complex systems.

## Incremental lifecycle

The Incremental lifecycle, shown in Figure 2.6 is still a linear approach in so much as the first three stages of the SDLC are conducted in sequence, each being completed before the next is started.

Where the Incremental lifecycle differs from the Waterfall or 'V' model is that after fully understanding and designing the system, decisions can then be made to deliver some parts of the system before other parts. This enables high-priority requirements to be delivered first, thus delivering elements of functionality to the customer or business early. Increments can be delivered in parallel, as the core design is complete.

In this way, the customer is able to get a working solution quite early in the development process. This addresses the problem of one final stage delivery, whereby the user has to wait a long time between providing requirements and seeing the results. For this reason this lifecycle is often referred to as Incremental **delivery**.

The Incremental lifecycle is ideal where early capability is required, perhaps for rapid time to market, but where the core architecture is stable. It is also useful where the functionality required is clear, but there are options over what aspect is most important to be delivered first. Because the high-level system design is independent of delivery order, the decision on delivery order can be left until nearer the time.

**Figure 2.6 The Incremental lifecycle**

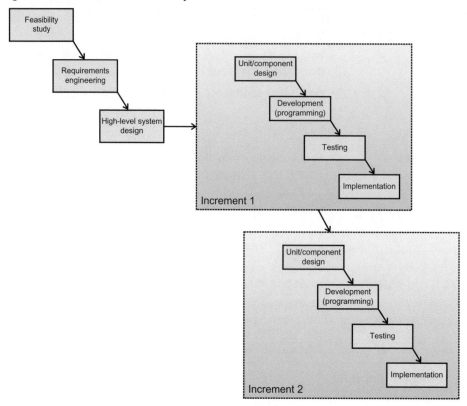

This lifecycle still requires rigorous analysis and design work in the early stages, as these provide the foundation for the last releases, not just the first. The additional releases also add some cost, as release costs (such as user training, deployment, system outages, etc.) are incurred multiple times. Subsequent releases must be regression tested against earlier functionality. This means that features in the first release are re-tested in every subsequent release (to ensure that they still work properly), adding to the test cost. This cost must be weighed up against the value of early and more frequent releases.

However, the Incremental approach can also **reduce** costs. If the organisation decides that the delivered functionality of the earlier increments is sufficient, then the project can be stopped at that point and no further cost is incurred.

| **Strengths** | • delivers working software to users early; |
| | • easier to manage risks because risky pieces can be identified and handled in early increments; |
| | • easier to test and debug smaller increments; |

|  |  |
|---|---|
|  | • increments can be built in parallel, reducing overall time to market. |
| **Weaknesses** | • hard to manage parallel deliveries; |
|  | • still difficult to manage change, as requirements are agreed before increments decided; |
|  | • overall costs can be higher due to additional overheads of parallel implementation and additional 'regression testing'. |

## LIFECYCLES BASED ON THE EVOLUTIONARY APPROACH

The final two core lifecycles we will describe are evolutionary approaches. Evolutionary approaches have been around since the 1980s and underpin the more popular 'Agile' approaches today. Although there are many processes and approaches that follow the evolutionary approach, there are really only two fundamental lifecycles to explore – they are:

• Iterative;

• Spiral.

### Iterative development

Iterative development is a lifecycle whereby the overall project is composed of several small time-boxed developments, called iterations, which take place in sequence.

Each iteration is a self-contained mini project composed of activities such as requirements, analysis, design, development and test; in this respect, they can look a bit like mini-linear projects. Requirements are elicited during each iteration and then developed to produce a working system that delivers some value to the project or customer. On big projects, this could be multiple teams all working on the same iteration.

In doing this, the understanding of the overall solution evolves as the requirements evolve through the iterations. At the end of each iteration, all development across the teams is integrated and tested into an iteration release that may not, initially, be released externally.

As Figure 2.7 illustrates, a minimum of three iterations would typically be required to achieve an external release, and these iterations would consist of:

|  |  |
|---|---|
| **Investigate** | The initial iteration is used to investigate things such as risks around the technology or risks around user functionality. Once this iteration is completed there will be more understanding about what is required to deliver the external iteration or first release. |

**Refine**

During this iteration the requirements are fully detailed and designed and the system is developed to meet the business goal. There are sometimes multiple refinement iterations.

**Consolidate**

The final iteration, prior to external release, ensures that the code and design developed is stabilised and fully integrated with any other components or iterations so that the overall business goal is achieved in the working system, the external release.

**Figure 2.7 The Iterative lifecycle**

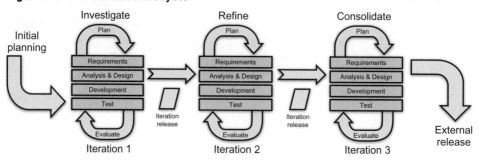

The earlier iterations are mostly for the development team to prove technology or explore and reduce risk and so are not always released. Due to this, the approach is often thought of as Iterative **development**, as delivery can still be through one big final stage release. To avoid this final stage release, Iterative development is often combined with an Incremental delivery approach and is referred to as Iterative Incremental Delivery (IID). Combining Iterative development with Incremental delivery is very common and is widely used today.

Iterative lifecycles are good where the problems or solutions are not clear at the outset, or where the business does not know yet if it wants to fund the project. The early iterations can give greater clarity over what is feasible and how much it may cost. It is also an approach well suited to prototyping, testing the market or proving new technology.

**Strengths**

- requirements evolve through each iteration;
- encourages collaboration with the users throughout so customer buy-in is higher;
- change is easier to manage as requirements are not locked down early;
- cost can be controlled.

**Weaknesses**

- can be hard to project manage due to multiple iterations and multiple iteration teams;
- without careful management, the evolving requirements can result in scope creep;

- if poorly managed, can still appear like a single, final release;
- overall costs can be higher due to the additional integration and test across multiple teams and iterations.

## Spiral

The Spiral lifecycle, shown in Figure 2.8, was developed by Barry Boehm in 1986. The Spiral model combines Iterative development with prototyping to test understanding and evolve the requirements so that risks can be addressed throughout. The Spiral model, like the Iterative approach, does not need requirements to be defined in advance. This approach starts with a concept and repeatedly revisits the four main phases of development until a suitable working product is complete.

The quadrants of the Spiral model are as follows:

**Determine objectives**  In the first stage, the development team and business owners identify the objectives for the development and agree prioritisation of requirements. Throughout the project this understanding is constantly reviewed and revisited.

**Identify and resolve risks**  At this stage, the developers explore technical possibilities to meet the business goal and assess any risks that the technology may bring. An early prototype is a key enabler here and will be produced, in collaboration with the business users, to address the risks.

**Development and test**  Reviewing the prototypes enables the development team to assess how well the requirements and risks were addressed and look at improvements. Designs are then developed for another prototype, which is agreed, developed and tested. After a few iterations this will produce the operational prototype.

**Plan the next iteration**  During this stage, the working system is released into the live operational environment. This may just be an Incremental release and therefore further releases will be planned and developed through subsequent iterations and releases until the complete system is developed and the business objectives are fully met.

**Strengths**
- risks are addressed early so risk avoidance is enhanced;
- requirements evolve, so additional functionality can be added at a later stage;
- collaboration with users throughout is key, so customer buy-in is good;
- a working system is produced early in the development lifecycle.

**Figure 2.8  Boehm's Spiral lifecycle**

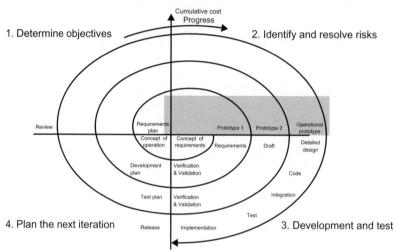

**Weaknesses**

- there is a high chance of scope creep due to evolving nature of requirements;

- overall costs can be higher due to the many implementations of working software into the operational environment;

- as the focus is on a working system, documentation of the system can become de-prioritised, making the system harder to maintain post-project delivery;

- it can seem like a lot of iterations are required, so can be a poor choice for small teams or simple problems.

## THE IMPACT OF AGILE

Agile is a popular term now given to evolutionary development approaches following the 'Agile Manifesto' in 2001. The manifesto was developed by 17 leading IT professionals, who felt that IT system development was failing to meet the growing challenges expected by businesses today. The Agile Manifesto states:

The Agile Manifesto led to a whole new way of thinking about software development and a new craze in Agile development methods, processes and lifecycles emerged, as shown in Figure 2.9.

Linear lifecycles such as Waterfall, 'V' model and Incremental fell out of favour in place of more evolutionary approaches such as Scrum and the Agile Unified Process (AgileUP).

*We are uncovering better ways of developing software by doing it and helping others to do it. Through this work we have come to value:*

**Individuals and interactions** over process and tools

**Working software** over comprehensive documentation

**Customer collaboration** over contract negotiation

**Responding to change** over following a plan

*That is, while there is value in the items on the right, we value the items on the left more.*

(http://agilemanifesto.org/)

For many development teams, this provided a means of throwing out bureaucracy and formal documentation so as to focus more on producing working software. Methods such as Scrum became very popular and lightweight approaches were attractive as they were easy to pick up and start using almost immediately.

**Figure 2.9  Evolution of Agile**

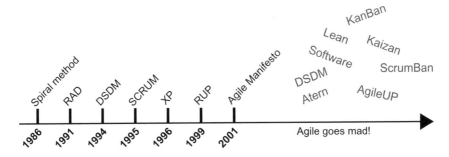

However, like all development methods, the key to success is to understand the method and apply it properly. In order to be successful, many Agile methods depend on high rigour and adherence to rules in order to succeed. While they may not depend on high levels of documentation in advance of development, they do depend on following highly rigorous processes.

Some of the lightweight Agile methods focus purely on the development of the software – and do not cover the stages prior to coding – or on the overarching governance and architecture. Conversely, most lifecycles do not define how the system is developed. This means that, in many cases, Agile approaches can integrate well into more traditional approaches, particularly where the principles of the Agile Manifesto are maintained.

Because the history of many Agile approaches is in small, highly collaborative teams, they work very well in those kinds of environments. However, they are much harder to work well where that environment is challenged. There are a number of factors that can make Agile much harder to work in practice:

- larger teams, particularly where they are geographically distributed;
- complex systems;
- audit, regulatory or safety critical requirements that expect higher quality assurance;
- projects with strict contractual commitments;
- complex user environments, or where the end user is not available;
- sub-contracting into a project being run in a non-Agile way.

In these situations, Agile approaches can still bring considerable benefits, but the additional risk that they also bring must be mitigated in some other way. This can be through the combination of Agile with other approaches, so that the whole scope of the systems development lifecycle is covered and additional rigour can be applied **where necessary**.

## HYBRID APPROACHES

As we have seen, there are many popular lifecycles that are used and followed today and all of them have their roots in one or more of the linear or evolutionary lifecycles already discussed. Some of them are pure versions of one of the core lifecycles described earlier, but there are many more that are a mix of the seven elements already described.

## DEVELOPMENT APPROACHES AND METHODS

This section reviews some of the more popular lifecycles and provides some history and background into each.

### SSADM

The Structured Systems Analysis and Design Method (SSADM) was first released in 1983, although its origins go back as far as 1980. SSADM is a linear Waterfall approach, which focuses on the analysis and design for developing information systems and was produced for the public sector for the Office of Government Commerce. The main difference between SSADM and Waterfall is that SSADM adopts principles from Peter Checkland's Soft Systems Methodology, which considers wider influences on the system than just the IT or application development. The stages of SSADM are:

- stage 0 – feasibility study;
- stage 1 – investigation of the current environment;
- stage 2 – business system options;
- stage 3 – requirements specification;

- stage 4 – technical systems options;
- stage 5 – logical design;
- stage 6 – physical design.

Taking the wider business approach and adding in the additional stages 2 and 3 meant that SSADM provided a more through understanding of the wider business perspective and processes. However, some SSADM projects ran into difficulties as the ever-changing business environment meant that earlier stages had to keep being revisited, causing delays to the later stages and hence delivery. Later versions of SSADM introduced a more dynamic approach to combat this. Modelling is key to SSADM and the three key models are:

- logical model – models the data requirements and business rules;
- data flow model – models how data moves around an information system;
- entity event model – models the behaviour of the entity, or data, and the events that cause the entity to change.

These techniques are prevalent in system development today by the same name or in the form of Object Oriented Analysis and Design (OOA&D).

## DSDM

The Dynamic Systems Development Method (DSDM) is an evolutionary Iterative and Incremental approach that was originally developed in 1994 as an Agile project delivery framework to support the trend towards 'rapid application development'. With its roots in Agile, DSDM was extended in 2003 to support the Agile programming process called 'Extreme Programming' (XP). Shortly afterwards, DSDM recognised that IT projects can often fail because of the people and process changes rather than the IT itself, and this led to the launch of DSDM Atern (now re-named as simply DSDM again).

DSDM has three main phases called pre-project phase, project lifecycle phase, and post-project phase. The project lifecycle phase is further sub-divided into five stages that include: feasibility study, business study, functional model iteration, design and build iteration and implementation. As well as the phases and stages outlined, DSDM also defines eight core principles that are at the heart of the framework which are:

1. focus on the business need;
2. deliver on time;
3. collaborate;
4. never compromise on quality;
5. build Incrementally from firm foundations;
6. develop iteratively;
7. communicate continuously and clearly;
8. demonstrate control.

DSDM is a flexible process that is highly configurable. It doesn't provide guidance on how the development should be done, leaving that to the team to decide. The core elements specify a time-boxing approach and a business focused governance. These make it a good choice for business focused projects, where the implementation methods are less important.

Needless to say, these principles, coupled with the evolutionary and Incremental approach, are what makes DSDM a key player in the Agile lifecycles choice. However, the amount of focus on time-boxing and governance, has led some to believe that DSDM Atern is more a project management framework than a development lifecycle.

## Scrum

Scrum is probably one of the most well known of the Agile approaches used today and was first published in 1995 by Ken Schwaber and Jeff Sutherland. Scrum is an Iterative and Incremental process that follows an evolutionary approach to the development of software systems. It introduces some unique language and concepts that govern how work is planned and monitored by a small team of multi-disciplinary software engineers. Scrum only proposes three roles which are:

- product owner – represents the business and is the voice of the customer;
- development team – cross-functional, self-organising team of 5–9 individuals who deliver the working software;
- Scrum master – person accountable for removing impediments so that the development team can deliver the goals.

The core element of Scrum is a 'Product Backlog', a prioritised list of requirements that the team will be delivering. The 'Product Owner' holds control over the priority of the items on the backlog.

Iterations are called 'Sprints' and will generally be short – perhaps two weeks – and focus on delivering a working version of the product, as defined through agreement with the product owner. The sprint is monitored by the eponymous 'Scrum', a short daily, highly-structured meeting that is focused on removing barriers to success. The team all work together to deliver the items on the Backlog, which could relate to any stage of the development lifecycle (requirements, analysis, design, implementation, etc.).

Scrum works really well for project teams of 5–9 developers, where the team is capable of doing all the work necessary for the product, and where there is often candidate architecture already in mind. Problems can arise, however, if the combined team do not possess all of the skills required. Additionally, as Scrum begins with the Backlog, the wider business approach can sometimes be overlooked, which can lead to innovative products that don't necessarily deliver the expected business benefits.

Scrum can be scaled, but this needs to be done with caution as it can be easy to break. Where Scrum works less well is where there is poor stakeholder engagement – if the team needs to stand in for the Product Owner, then alarm bells should ring.

## Rational Unified Process 1998

The Rational Unified process (RUP), developed originally in 1998 by Rational Software (now IBM), is a software engineering process. It is a risk-driven, evolutionary iterative and Incremental process, built upon the foundations of the Spiral model, that assigns and manages tasks and responsibilities in a disciplined way within a development organisation. RUP is also a process framework that be adapted and tailored to suit the needs of the organisation or project team. RUP consists of four major phases, which are Inception, Elaboration, Construction and Transition as well as six core engineering workflows which are; business modelling, requirements, analysis and design, implementation, test and deployment.

Although the workflows are similar to those within a Waterfall approach, the iterative nature of the process means that the workflows are revisited again and again throughout the lifecycle and across all four major phases of RUP.

Because RUP is a fully-described process that can be used to develop highly complex systems, it is important to tailor it to the scope, risk and size of each project. However, the complexity and flexibility of RUP can make this tailoring hard to do, and some teams end up using more of the process that they really need to, with consequential increases in cost and complexity.

Being a software process, RUP is popular with teams of developers, and makes extensive use of UML (the Unified Modelling Language) for Object Oriented Analysis and Design (OOA&D) and case modelling. This can make it overwhelming to newcomers and business stakeholders, but does encourage strong design and good traceability.

## Lean Software Development

Lean Software Development (LSD) has its roots in lean manufacturing, pioneered by Toyota. This is a set of techniques and tools that can be applied to eliminate waste in manufacturing and hence improve productivity. Lean Software Development was introduced by Mary and Tom Poppendieck in their book *Lean software development: an Agile toolkit* (2003), and translates lean manufacturing into software development principles. These principles are:

- focus on customers;
- energise workers;
- eliminate waste;
- learn fast;
- deliver fast;
- build quality in;
- keep getting better;
- optimize the whole.

Although Lean Software Development does provide tools and techniques, its focus is on reducing waste within the process of developing a product. It does not provide details as to the stages you need to take or the development techniques you should use, as it expects that you already have an approach you are following. Due to this, Lean Software Development is an ideal approach to be combined with other methods or approaches, such as Scrum for instance.

There are more development approaches than the ones mentioned in this chapter. Below is a list of some of the additional approaches you may wish to investigate:

- Kanban;
- Xtreme Programming;
- Agile Unified Process (AgileUP);
- Disciplined Agile Development (DAD);
- Rapid Application Development;
- Crystal Methods;
- Scrumban.

## HOW TO CHOOSE AN APPROACH

This chapter has introduced core elements that can be used to describe any systems development lifecycle. it has also introduced some of the commonly used processes.

So how do we know which approach to follow? Well the answer is 'it all depends!' Used properly, any SDLC should enable us to deliver a successful project; used poorly, none of them will. The trick is to try to identify an SDLC that will give the best chance of the project succeeding.

Some examples of factors to consider are discussed here. Alternatively, we could find someone to discuss the project with, and use the descriptions in this chapter to help us work it out.

| | |
|---|---|
| **Complexity of problem** | For simple problems, choose a simple method such as Waterfall. |
| | For complex problems, choose an approach where the complexity is reduced early, and risk is understood early, such as RUP, 'V' model or spiral. |
| **Team experience** | For risky problems, choosing an approach the team is comfortable with is probably has the best chance of success – unless we think they are failing **because** of the method. For simple problems, we could take the opportunity to pick something new, knowing that the project is likely to still succeed. |

| | |
|---|---|
| **Stability of requirements** | If we are confident the requirements will not change through the life of the development, any approach will work, but those that keep revisiting the requirements stage (like the evolutionary ones) will cause unnecessary re-work. For rapidly changing requirements, choose an iterative approach with short iterations (like Scrum). For less rapidly changing requirements, any of the evolutionary or iterative methods should do. |
| **Delivery speed, and quality** | If the customer needs the system to be complete before delivery, we have a lot of choice. A linear method would work well, but if we have other reasons to prefer an evolutionary approach (to expose technical risk early, for example) then we can use one but not release each iteration to the customer. We should probably avoid an approach, like Scrum, that requires heavy customer involvement unless they are happy with that. If the customer is anxious to see results quickly, then pick one of the evolutionary approaches, or the Incremental approach if there is a stable architecture. |
| **Customer involvement** | For low customer involvement, linear approaches work well, although with an Incremental approach we need to know in what order the customer wants the delivery made. Evolutionary approaches tend to require more customer involvement, particularly Scrum, which needs the customer to be a virtual part of the team – if the customer can't manage that, Scrum probably isn't the best choice. |
| **Uniqueness** | If the project has never been done before, pick an evolutionary approach that allows us to test architectural risk early (and more cheaply), and to re-scope the problem or solution if required. |
| **High regulatory requirements** | More established technologies should work with any approach. If we need to meet regulatory, legal, audit or safety critical requirements, then choose an approach that includes documentation and assurance – Waterfall and 'V' model work well – or for Agile development, perhaps DSDM. |

## REFERENCES

Boehm, B. (1986) 'A spiral model of software development and enhancement'. ACM SIGSOFT Software Engineering Notes, August.

Checkland, P. (1981) *Systems thinking, systems practice*. John Wiley and Sons, Chichester.

Kenneth, R. (2012) *Essential Scrum: A practical guide to the most popular Agile process*. Signature series (Cohn). Addison-Wesley, Boston, MA.

Kruchten, P. (2003) *The rational unified process an introduction* (3rd edition). Addison-Wesley, Boston, MA.

Poppendieck, M. and Poppendieck, T. (2003) *Lean software development: an Agile toolkit*. Addison-Wesley, Boston, MA.

Royce, W. (1970) 'Managing the development of large software systems'. www.cs.umd.edu/class/spring2003/cmsc838p/Process/Waterfall.pdf (accessed 4 June 2014).

## FURTHER READING

Ambler, S. W. and Lines, M. (2012) *Disciplined Agile delivery: a practitioner's guide to Agile software delivery in the enterprise*. IBM Press, Indianapolis, IN.

DSDM Consortium (2008) *DSDM atern: the handbook*. DSDM Consortium, Ashford.

Paul, D., Yeates, D. and Cadle, J. (2014) *Business analysis* (3rd edition). BCS, Swindon.

# 3 ANALYSING THE BUSINESS NEED

Debra Paul

## CONTENTS OF THIS CHAPTER

This chapter covers the following topics:

- the rationale for business analysis;
- the role of the business analyst;
- the place of business analysis in the systems development lifecycle;
- the business analysis process model and activities;
- the potential outcomes from business analysis.

## INTRODUCTION

All organisations can improve how they work. Whether there are opportunities to increase the efficiency of the processes, the capability of the people or to improve the IT systems, possibilities for improvement are many and varied. Sometimes, organisations instigate change initiatives where several of these factors are present. Organisations have to change in order to continue to offer up-to-date products and services, and to ensure they are responsive to customers' needs. Often, change projects address a recognised issue or specific problem. However, it is all too frequent that an organisation sets up a project to replace an IT system – perhaps because a new software package has become available or because there is an assumption that IT will cut costs – without investigating the need before identifying the solution. Inevitably, this leads to problems as with the best will in the world, a project manager can deliver the IT system as specified but this may not address the real underlying issues. Management thinker Peter Drucker provided a most appropriate comment:

Management is doing things right; leadership is doing the right things.

The distinction between 'doing things right' and 'doing the right things' is very important. We can spend a long time following the standards or a selected approach, only to find that what is delivered doesn't meet the need. While there is much discussion about Agile software development at the moment, we also need to think about the most relevant ways of addressing business problems. In some cases, software may not be part of the most appropriate solution as there may be a less expensive and equally valuable process workaround available. In this chapter, we look at the role of the business analyst in ensuring that change projects focus on 'doing the right things' by understanding the real business need and offering relevant solutions.

## BUSINESS ANALYSIS

Business analysis as a specialist discipline emerged in the early 1990s due to a combination of factors:

- The increasing dissatisfaction on the part of business staff (the 'users') with the quality of the IT systems delivered. There were regular project failures but, even where the systems were delivered, many business staff felt that there had been a lack of understanding of their requirements. They felt that the IT staff did not 'speak the business language' and complained that many IT departments delivered what they thought was important without really addressing factors such as how people worked, the environment for the systems and how the less straightforward cases would be handled. On one project from this era, the end users were required to use communal terminals, as it had been assessed that they would only need access to the system a few hours each day. On the first day of live running, it emerged that they all needed access during the **same** few hours in order to fit with other elements in the overall business process. Chaos ensued, as twice as many people as terminals tried to get onto the system.

- The recognition that IT was no longer a department of mystique and wonder and that the systems were actually there to meet the business needs. More and more people were acquiring familiarity with technology and were becoming more insistent on expressing their views. They gained increasing awareness of the potential for the technology and, as a result, were also aware of when this potential was not realised. The business departments gained recognition as the 'owners' of the systems – after all, the IT systems existed to support the work of the business, not the other way around. In line with this, the perception of the IT systems shifted and a realisation developed that they were not an end in themselves but a means to successful business operations.

- The development of the outsourcing business model created an environment where IT systems were developed and supported outside the organisation. This placed additional pressures on the organisation to improve the understanding and specification of the requirements to be met by the systems. A study by David Feeny and Leslie Willcocks (Oxford Institute of Information Management, University of Oxford, 1998) identified a number of key skills required within organisations that have outsourced IT. This report specifically identified business systems thinking, a core element of the business analyst role, as a key skill that needs to be retained within organisations operating an outsourcing arrangement.

- The use of approaches such as systems thinking also helped build an awareness that IT systems may enable, or even be central, to business improvements but they were not the sole element. Other factors such as people and processes were also important if the business changes were to be facilitated successfully by the IT systems and the predicted benefits were to be achieved.

## Rationale for business analysis

Business analysis developed as a response to the issues described above, initially to translate business needs and facilitate communication between the business and IT staff. However, business analysis quickly developed to focus on addressing business problems and opportunities, taking a forward-looking approach rather than just addressing existing issues. Proactivity is an essential part of the business analyst toolkit, as is root cause analysis. There is little point in identifying a solution if we don't understand the problem we are trying to solve.

From the outset, business analysis has been described as a **holistic** discipline, whereby all aspects of a business system, including all of the elements that can contribute to a business problem, are considered. The POPIT™ model in Figure 3.1 is often used both to identify the different elements that form a business system and to support holistic analysis by ensuring that all of these elements – and their interactions - are considered.

**Figure 3.1 POPIT™ model (© Assist Knowledge Development)**

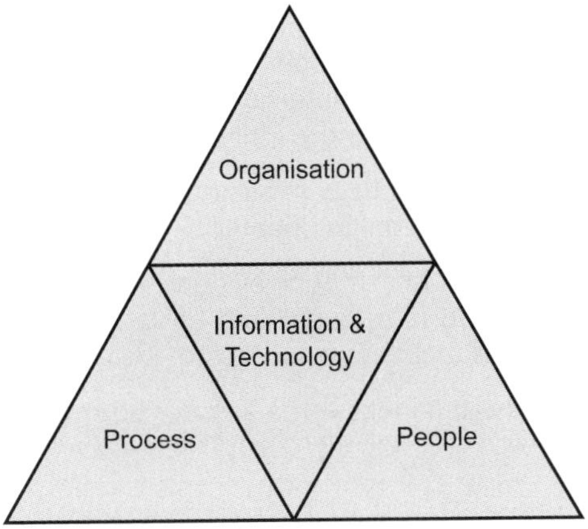

Originally, business analysis provided a link between business and IT, which was sometimes known as 'bridging'. However, it has developed significantly over the last two decades and is now recognised as a discipline that is vital if business needs are to be addressed and business change programmes are to deliver successful outcomes. Many senior business analysts work at an advisory level in the organisation, suggesting or even deciding business change priorities, and identifying how change initiatives can help the organisation develop and improve. Although IT is often a driver for a change project, it is rarely the entire solution. It is the job of the business analyst to understand the business needs and identify what should be changed if these needs are to be addressed. While it is unusual that IT does not form part of the solution, with the economic difficulties faced by many organisations and the need for speedy responses to change, it is important to consider whether a non-IT option would be relevant and valuable.

## Definition of business analysis

BCS, The Chartered Institute for IT, offers the following definition of business analysis:

> An internal consultancy role which has the responsibility for investigating business situations, identifying and evaluating options for improving business systems, defining requirements and ensuring the effective use of information systems in meeting the needs of the business.

It is useful to analyse the component elements of this definition:

- Internal consultancy role – business analysts offer advice and guidance to the organisation. To do this, they need to have an extensive toolkit of skills that will enable them to provide insights and valuable guidance.

- Investigating business situations – the emphasis here is on the business situation not the existing IT system. This involves the consideration of several aspects of the situation; these are described below using the POPIT™ model from Figure 3.1.

- Identifying and evaluating options – the need to consider options is extremely important if an organisation is to gain the most return on any investment. Sometimes, a business analyst may look at a problem and identify a solution that requires only limited or possible no IT change. For example, where a manual workaround is possibly a more efficient and cost-effective solution.

- Defining requirements – a key activity in business analysis which is explored in outline below and in greater detail in Chapter 5.

- Ensuring the effective use of information systems – working with the business to ensure that any solution is relevant and of value, and providing support throughout the lifecycle to facilitate a successful transition to the new system.

- Meeting the needs of the business – the key driver and context for business analysis.

The International Institute for Business Analysis™ (IIBA®), offers a similar definition:

> Business analysis is the practice of enabling change in an organizational context, by defining needs and recommending solutions that deliver value to stakeholders.

## THE PLACE OF BUSINESS ANALYSIS IN THE DEVELOPMENT LIFECYCLE

Business analysis is extremely important when investigating ideas or initiatives for change. However, it is not required just at the outset but across the entire business change and Systems Development lifecycles. Figure 3.2 is an extended version of the 'V' model explained in Chapter 2; this model helps to position business analysis within a Systems Development lifecycle and identifies the major activities conducted by the business analysts (BAs).

**Figure 3.2 The extended 'V' model**

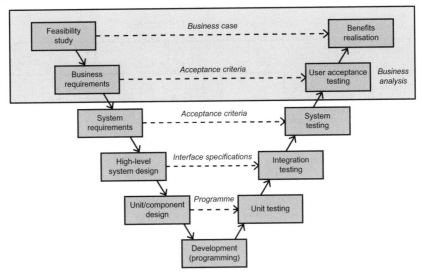

This version of the 'V' model shows the major activities carried out by business analysts, highlighting that business analysis is conducted to investigate the business situation and develop a business case. The business case sets out the options and recommendations that will address any problems and this provides the basis for the benefits management and realisation work. The selected option is then explored further in order to define the business requirements, which then provide the basis for the user acceptance testing. This model is based upon a Waterfall lifecycle, but can be adapted for Agile software development; the activities outside the business analysis area would be undertaken using an Agile approach. So, the business requirements would form the basis for deciding upon the content for each iteration and they would then be elaborated, developed and tested using Agile techniques.

Although this model shows the key areas of work for the business analysts – feasibility study, requirements definition, user acceptance testing and benefits realisation – the work of the business analyst continues throughout the development lifecycle. The core business analysis activities and the stages where business analysis occupies more of a supporting role are discussed below.

**Feasibility study**

The feasibility study stage of the lifecycle is concerned with investigating a situation in order to uncover the issues and then identifying and evaluating possible options to resolve those issues. This stage is essential if the root causes of business problems are to be uncovered – after all, it is important to understand the problem to be solved before identifying solutions. This is a key activity in business analysis, as it is the point where investigation and analysis is vital if the most appropriate way forward is to be determined.

**Figure 3.3  Business analysis process model**

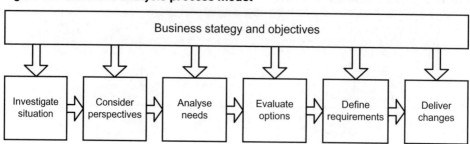

Figure 3.3 identifies some of the key activities conducted by business analysts. The model shows how the organisational strategy and objectives need to provide the context for the business analysis work; there would be little point in recommending a solution that contradicted the defined strategy and direction of the organisation. The four initial activities shown in the model comprise the feasibility study work and are concerned with investigating business situations and analysing stakeholders' needs.

The analysts need to find out exactly where any problems may be found and locate the root causes of those problems. They need to ensure that any stated issues are not just symptoms of an underlying problem but the actual cause. They also need to engage with stakeholders to ensure that they understand different perspectives on the situation – one person's problem could be another person's minor irritation or, even, non-issue. One of the approaches used by business analysts when analysing business needs is to identify stakeholders' perspectives – based around their 'world view' of the system – and they use these perspectives to consider what the system would need to do and what value it would need to deliver in order to fulfil each world view. This provides the basis for developing an overview model, that sets out the high-level activities required by a business system in the light of a particular perspective. This is a conceptual model, which is useful for identifying areas that are problematic or even absent.

The business analysts sometimes investigate activities in detail by considering the business processes required to perform the work. They may develop models of the existing processes – known as the 'as is' processes – and the new processes to be adopted in the future – the 'to be' processes. Using the high level model of business activities and the more specific business process models, the business analysts can analyse the needs by conducting 'gap analysis', identifying where there are deficiencies that need to be addressed or changes that need to be made, if the organisation is to move to a new business system and address the current issues.

This work is essential if there is to be a focus on the delivery of value, both by the project and by the business, and if relevant options for change are to be identified. While many options may be identified initially, they need to be reduced to a manageable number as it is unlikely that the BAs would have sufficient time to thoroughly evaluate more than three options. The evaluation of options forms part of the business case where the shortlisted options are assessed from the financial, business and technical perspectives.

- **Financial feasibility** involves examining the costs and benefits associated with a particular option in order to ensure that the financial return makes the option worthwhile. Techniques such as payback (break-even), discounted cash flow and internal rate of return are used to determine the level of financial return likely to be delivered by the proposed option. These techniques are described further in Chapter 4.

- **Business feasibility** involves considering each option to determine whether or not it will 'fit' with the organisation. This may require checking the alignment of the option with the business architecture or considering whether the option is in line with the culture and management style of the organisation. For example, an option may propose that some work is outsourced but the business architecture may incorporate that work within the internal processes and capabilities; alternatively, an option may be predicated on an empowered team, but this may be contrary to the more directive nature of the organisation and its management style.

- **Technical feasibility** checking is important; first, to ensure that the technology exists to support a proposed option, and second to ensure that the technology will meet the needs of the organisation. Even if the desired technology is available, it is also important to confirm that it does align with the organisation's technical strategy – for example, the technology may only be available on a particular hardware platform, whereas the organisation has standardised on a different platform. Further, there may be requirements that specify non-functional aspects such as processing speed, capacity or robustness and it is important to check that they can be delivered by the technology.

While the business analyst will contribute to the business case by suggesting how the business needs might be met, the business case is the responsibility of the project sponsor, whose role is to ensure that there is a return on the investment made by the business. The feasibility stage is where the business situation is thoroughly investigated to ensure that the most relevant solution is selected – that the project is 'doing the right things'. Without this stage, a systems development project might be defined without due consideration and a solution may be selected that is at best less relevant than an alternative and at worst fails to meet the business need at all.

## Define requirements

Once the solution has been selected by the business decision-makers, the project moves into the define requirements stage of the process model. This is when the business analysts again undertake vital work. The high-level, outline requirements that have been gathered during the feasibility study are explored further. One of the key aspects of business analysis is ensuring that the business receives the solution that will best meet its need. In order to do this, the business requirements must be known and must be defined in sufficient detail to ensure that any development work will address business requirements. After all, if a detailed system requirement does not support a business requirement, there is little point in delivering it. Technical requirements also need to be defined to ensure that any IT solution is aligned with the technical policies and architecture adopted by the organisation.

A hierarchy of requirements may be developed, showing the links between the business and technical high-level requirements with the more detailed solution requirements. The solution requirements fall into two categories: functional requirements define what functions the system is to deliver; non-functional requirements define the level of service the system is to provide in areas such as processing speed and availability. So, we could have a business requirement that states the need to comply with data protection legislation, which is linked to a functional requirement to enable customers to keep their data up-to-date, and is also linked to a non-functional requirement to ensure that access to personal data is restricted to the relevant person.

In the course of eliciting the requirements, the business analysts may interview business managers and staff, examine documentation, run workshops or utilise a range of other elicitation techniques. These techniques are explained in further detail in Chapter 5. Requirements analysis is core to the business analyst role and is vital if an IT system is to be of value to the organisation.

The requirements need to be defined in sufficient detail to meet the needs of the adopted project approach. Should the project adopt a linear approach – for example using the 'V' model, where the stages are performed in sequence – the requirements will need to be defined in detail, with the definitions being supported by models such as use case diagrams and class models; these models are discussed in Chapter 7. Alternatively, where an evolutionary approach, possibly using Agile techniques, is adopted, the requirements may be defined in less detail as they are then explored further when the business analysts work alongside the staff and developers during the development of the system. Chapter 2 discusses the range of lifecycles and approaches available to the project team.

The business analysts perform the majority of the requirements analysis work, eliciting, analysing, modelling and documenting requirements. Requirements Engineering is the standard framework used here; this framework is described in Chapter 5.

## Deliver solution

This stage of the business analysis process involves the acquisition of the solution (including the IT solution, which may be built or bought off-the-shelf) and its implementation. If an off-the-shelf software solution is required, the requirements document provides the basis for evaluating the acceptability of a particular software package and the business analysts may be involved in this evaluation. With regard to the development of the IT solution, business analysts have specific involvement as described below.

### Design, development and testing

During the design, development and testing of a system, business analysts typically need to support the work as follows: by ensuring that any changes to requirements are analysed for impacts, for example on other requirements, on costs or on benefits; by helping the business staff explain their detailed requirements such that the development team can understand what is needed. Business analysts may also need to support these stages by clarifying the requirements or revisiting them where there are inconsistencies. They should have a constant eye on the original business needs defined and on the link to the detailed development work. If an Agile approach such as Scrum is to be used, the business analysts may be needed to support the development work by ensuring that communication between the business staff (end users) and the development team is clear; it is often a problem when jargon or organisational business language is used and the business analyst is invaluable in helping to overcome this. If this approach is used, the business analyst may be needed to maintain the requirements in the product backlog, for example by helping with prioritisation, defining the content to be delivered in the development sprints, and so on.

### User acceptance testing

Although a system is tested by the software testing team, it is important that the stakeholders who will be using the system in their daily work – the business users – also test the system. When the business users test the system, they want to ensure that the data entered produces the expected results. To do this they undertake user acceptance testing (UAT) where they enter pre-defined sets of data that are designed to follow pathways, known as scenarios, through the software system. This approach is followed to ensure that the system behaves as required and expected, and helps the users confirm that the system has delivered their requirements and that they are happy to accept it. As the UAT is based upon the requirements, the business analysts assist the users both in defining the different scenarios to be tested and identifying the data to be used to test each scenario. The analysts may use techniques such as activity diagrams or flow charts, decision trees and decision tables, to define the scenarios and the different combinations of data. These techniques can be particularly useful where there are a lot of business rules to be applied within the system. They can also help to identify exception situations, where the standard process is not followed or an unusual set of data occurs. UAT requires analysis if it is to be conducted thoroughly so the involvement of the business analysts is extremely important. UAT is explored in further depth in Chapter 11.

### Implementation

The implementation of the system has to be planned carefully, and at an early stage in the project, in order to minimise disruption and ensure maximum adoption. The business analysts are often heavily involved in this work, as they can help to ensure that the new ways of working are defined clearly. The users may require training in the new working procedures and may need support as they begin to adopt the new processes, practices and systems. The business analysts, having been instrumental in uncovering the business needs and identifying the means of achieving them, often define and deliver the training, and provide ongoing support for the users during the implementation stage.

### Post-implementation review/benefits realisation

Each project should be reviewed once it has delivered the solution in order to identify where the work has gone well, the lessons to be learned and any outstanding issues. This is known as a post-implementation review. Achieving the business needs is a key part of the context for assessing project success, as this was the initial justification for conducting the project and should have formed the ongoing rationale for its continuation. While the post-implementation review is the responsibility of the project manager and project sponsor, the business analysts may be required to provide information to support the review.

It is also important to carry out a benefits review, although this is typically at a later point in time. This review revisits the benefits defined in the business case for the project and evaluates whether or not they have been realised. Delivering the business benefits predicted for business change projects has become increasingly important. IT projects may require significant investment and organisations need to ensure that there has been a return on that investment. When analysing the business needs, the business analysts will have contributed to the development of the business case and may have been involved in identifying and quantifying the benefits. During the lifetime of the projects, they will have been required to assess any change requests in order to determine the impact on the project and the business case. When the benefits are reviewed, the business analyst may need to help identify actions that may be taken to help deliver benefits where they have not yet been realised. In the light of this, it is important that the business analysts are involved in the benefits review.

Post-implementation and benefits reviews are discussed further in Chapter 13.

## OUTCOMES FROM BUSINESS ANALYSIS

Business analysis offers a holistic approach to addressing business needs. This means that a problem situation is investigated to identify the root causes and the different elements that will need to be changed to address the problem. While it is likely that an IT system will be required as part of the solution, it is unlikely that it will form the entire solution; other changes will be required to the business system. As shown in Figure 3.1 above, there are four major elements of change: information and technology, people, processes and organisation. These are described below.

### IT/IS change

Information technology provides the means of delivering information systems. The systems deliver functionality and information to enable the work of the organisation to be conducted. Often the new software is the core of a larger business change initiative, but sometimes there may just be a need to introduce a later version of a software product or change to a new system in order to align with organisational technical standards and architecture. The early work by the business analysts in identifying the business needs and analysing how they might be addressed is vital if the technological solution is to support the business as required. For example, a system must provide the information needed to run the organisation at the operational, tactical and strategic levels. To do this, early analysis is needed in order to understand the business requirements to be met including the management information requirements. There have been many cases where an IT system has been delivered yet has failed to meet the needs of the business. In some cases, these systems have been abandoned or used to only a limited extent. The only way to avoid this is to ensure that the business need to be addressed is understood at the outset and kept in mind throughout the development process.

### Process change

The introduction of a new IT system also necessitates changes to the business processes. They may need to be redesigned to work with the new software in order to ensure that the aims of the change, typically improved efficiency and accuracy, are achieved. The changes to the processes may include removing some of the individual tasks (possibly because they are performed automatically by the software), changing the sequence of the tasks and reducing the number of times the documents in the process are exchanged between different actors. The revised processes need to be documented in a clear manner so that they can be communicated to the staff required to carry out the work. Any changes to a business process are likely to necessitate changes to the skills of the staff, the technology support and the organisation.

## People change

When a new IT system is to be introduced, there is inevitably an impact upon the processes and, correspondingly, on the work the staff carry out. At the very least, the staff need to adapt from using one system to using another. However, it is rarely a simple transition, as a new IT system should provide additional support for the processes and tasks and, as a result, the people need to do their work differently. It is important to consider the changes and the impact upon the staff. For example, do they require additional skills in order to carry out their job? Will there be an effect upon staff motivation? Will the communication channels change? Have the business objectives changed and do the staff need to be made aware of this? Whatever the impacts on the people, the business analysts need to identify what should happen to ensure that the staff feel trained and supported, are able to adapt to the new system and continue to perform their work effectively.

## Organisation change

It is often the case that there is a need for job roles to be redefined when a new system and revised business processes are introduced. This job redefinition is required in order to reflect any changed responsibilities or the need to perform different tasks. Sometimes, there are new ways of working that cause extensive changes to job roles and these cause organisational structure changes, such as the merger of teams. For example, if some of the administrative work is automated, clerical tasks are reduced which will result in job roles that are revised significantly or even removed. If teams are merged, this will require changes to the management structure and the nature of the new job roles may result in a different management style. For example, if the users are to be given additional information so that they are able to make more decisions, the style may have to become more facilitative rather than directive. Similarly, any new jobs, and their corresponding responsibilities, will need to be defined. The communications between teams, departments or individuals may also change. In such situations, the organisation will need to adapt in many ways to accommodate the introduction of the new system.

## CONCLUSION

Analysing the business needs is a vital step if organisations are to understand the problems to be addressed and identify relevant solutions. Failing to carry out this work can lead to unnecessary investment in projects that ultimately do not deliver the required benefits to the organisation. The business analyst plays an important role in this pre-project stage, uncovering the root causes of problems, investigating what is needed to take things forward and evaluating the potential actions to be taken. In a time of change and economic uncertainty, it is important to ensure that investment funds are not wasted, project teams are focused on 'doing the right things' and we deliver successful IT systems and business changes.

## REFERENCES

Drucker, P. (2001) *The essential Drucker*. Harper Business, New York.

Paul, D., Yeates, D. and Cadle, J. (2014) *Business analysis* (3rd edition). BCS, Swindon.

Various authors (2009) *A guide to the business analysis body of knowledge® (BABOK® Guide) Version 2*. IIBA, Toronto.

## FURTHER READING

Cadle, J., Paul, D. and Turner, P. (2014) *Business analysis techniques: 99 essential tools for success* (2nd edition). BCS, Swindon.

Checkland, P. (1993) *Systems thinking, systems practice*. John Wiley, Chichester.

Skidmore, S. and Eva, M. (2004) *Introducing systems development*. Palgrave Macmillan, Basingstoke.

# 4 MAKING A BUSINESS CASE

## James Cadle

## CONTENTS OF THIS CHAPTER

This chapter covers the following topics:

- the purpose of a business case;
- the business case and the development lifecycle;
- checking feasibility;
- elements of a business case;
- identifying, evaluating and selecting options;
- principles of cost–benefit analysis;
- principles of risk and impact analysis;
- investment appraisal techniques;
- references and further reading.

## THE PURPOSE OF A BUSINESS CASE

As Chapter 3 demonstrated, an IT system is not – or should not be – developed for its own sake but because an organisation has a business need that can be met through it. The organisation may wish to lower its operating costs, or improve the customer's experience or it may need to comply with new legal or regulatory demands. Even with a project which seems, at first sight, mainly technical in nature, for example replacing an obsolete system with a more modern one, there is usually a business driver behind it, in this case to enable the organisation to continue functioning. A business case is an analysis of the justification for undertaking the project and it should be a major governing document throughout the project lifecycle.

## THE BUSINESS CASE AND THE DEVELOPMENT LIFECYCLE

Figure 4.1 shows the typical lifecycle of an IT project, with a number of 'gateways' at which the business case should be reviewed.

## Figure 4.1  The business case in the lifecycle of an IT project

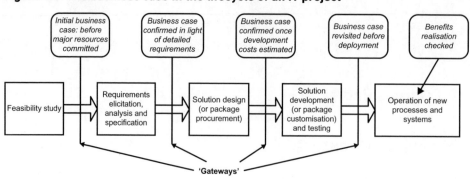

A business case is usually first prepared after a feasibility study of the proposed IT project. This is designed to establish the outline costs and benefits expected from the project and it supports a decision on whether, on the face of it, the project is worthwhile. Usually, the project is authorised in principle but, specifically, the team is allowed to move on to more detailed analysis and specification of the requirements.

Assuming that the project seems worthwhile, the requirements are now captured and analysed and a detailed specification of requirements is produced. The business case should be revisited to check that the costs of the project – of which the team should now have a better idea – are still justified by the expected benefits, about which there should also be more information.

With the requirements fully defined, the project team now has two basic choices available to it (see Chapter 1) – either a solution is to be developed (in-house or using third-party suppliers) or a commercial off-the-shelf (COTS) package is to be procured. If the solution is to be developed, system designers now work out how it is to be created using the hardware and software available. As a result of this stage, there should now be a much better idea of the costs of completing the development and, hence, there is a need to revisit the business case again.

In the next stage, either the IT system is built, or it is purchased and, as necessary, customised to meet the users' requirements. This stage also includes the sequence of tests (see Chapter 11) that are conducted to determine if the system has been built properly and is fit for purpose. The last thing to do is to put the system into live operation, but a further gateway has been shown here because – and especially if the development has taken a long time – we need to check that the business circumstances have not changed and assure ourselves that the system is still needed.

The final use of the business case occurs after the project has been completed. The project sponsor should initiate a benefits review to find out whether the hoped-for benefits have in fact been realised. There are two reasons for this. First, if some of the benefits have not been achieved, they may still be retrievable and the review should identify what further actions are needed to achieve them. Second, over time, the organisation gets better at deciding which benefits are, and which are not, achievable and so gets better at selecting which projects have the greatest chance of success.

The main lesson to take from Figure 4.1, however, is that the business case is not a do-it-and-forget-it document, created at the outset of the project and then never revisited. In fact, as the figure shows, the business case should be a governing document throughout the lifecycle of the project. In addition, if there is a significant change in the business environment – for example, a company is the subject of a takeover, or there is a change of government – the business case should be checked to ensure that the project is still viable in the changed circumstances the organisation now finds itself in.

## FEASIBILITY CHECKING

As the name suggests, the point of carrying out a feasibility study is to assess whether the proposed systems development project is achievable given the business, technological and financial constraints within which it is to be undertaken. Even if the project seems justified at the feasibility stage, however, the circumstances of the organisation will change over time and so feasibility must be reassessed at each gateway or if some significant external or internal situation develops – a change in business strategy or a downturn in the economy for example.

Figure 4.2 highlights some of the business, technological and financial issues to be considered as part of the feasibility checking.

**Figure 4.2  Aspects of feasibility**

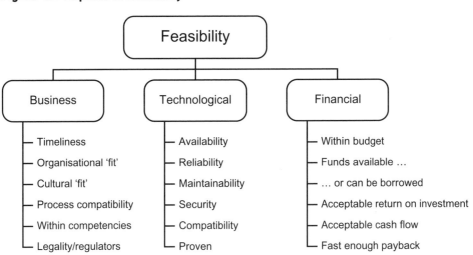

Incidentally, just because a problem is identified during feasibility checking, it does not automatically follow that the project should not go ahead. For example, if it were concluded that the organisation lacked the project management expertise to execute the project (an issue of competencies), this could be dealt with by hiring a top-grade project manager from the contract marketplace or using consultants to manage the project. However, both courses of action would raise the cost of the project and/or introduce additional risk and so must be taken into account in the impact and risk assessment (see later).

## ELEMENTS OF A BUSINESS CASE

Organisations vary widely in the way they like business cases to be presented. In some, huge documents of many hundreds of pages are required, whereas, in one major company, business cases had to be distilled into two sides of A4 paper (on the basis that senior managers do not have enough time to study anything larger). Whatever the format of the business case, however, the following list of contents is reasonably typical and the most of the sections are described in more detail later in this chapter.

**Introduction** — This should set the scene and explain what the business case is about.

**Management summary** — Aimed at senior management, this should summarise the nature of the problem, the options considered and the recommended course of action (with justification). In an ideal world, three paragraphs should suffice here (bearing in mind that senior managers are busy people) but, at any rate, the summary should make a persuasive case for the course of action recommended.

**Background** — If necessary, this should set out the business background to the proposed initiative and describe the problem that is to be solved or the opportunity to be seized.

**Options** — All the options considered should be described briefly, including what would happen if no action is taken, and the preferred option should be described in more detail.

**Benefits** — The benefits of the proposed initiative – both tangible and intangible (see later) – are described here.

**Costs** — Here, the short-term and longer-term costs of undertaking the project are described.

**Impacts** — Impacts are other things that senior management need to consider in reaching their decision on the project.

**Risks** — The possible risks of undertaking the project, together with actions to deal with those risks.

**Investment appraisal** — This contrasts the financial costs and benefits over time and assesses when, and by how much, the project pays for itself.

| Conclusions and recommendations | Usually, the writers of the business case sum up the document and make recommendations to senior management, although sometimes no recommendation is made and managers are left to make their own decisions based on the evidence provided. |
|---|---|
| Appendices | To avoid making the body of the business case too large, detailed information – for example, technical details of the proposed solution – is often put in an appendix, where it is available for consultation if required. |

## IDENTIFYING, EVALUATING AND SELECTING OPTIONS

There are usually alternative courses of action that should be considered in a business case, including that of doing nothing at all. (In fact, the discussion of the 'do nothing' option can be very important in some technical projects where non-technical managers need to be made aware that they cannot continue with their existing arrangements, perhaps because a package or operating system is no longer supportable.)

The process for options selection is illustrated in Figure 4.3.

**Figure 4.3  Option selection**

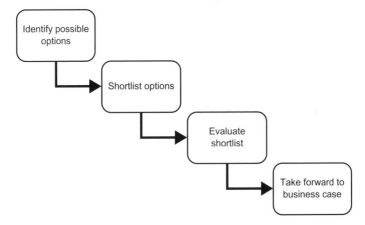

In a little more detail, the stages in option selection are:

| Identify possible options | All of the possibilities should be considered, including not doing anything at all. Sometimes, that might be a viable option and, in other cases, the reasons why it is not a good idea need to be explored. In principle, nothing should be excluded at this stage although, in practice, the range of practical options may be limited and thinking about 'off-the-wall' possibilities may prove to be a waste of time and effort. |
|---|---|

| | |
|---|---|
| **Shortlist options** | The initial 'long list' of options should now be whittled down to three or four realistic possibilities including, as usual, that of doing nothing. The reason for this is that presenting more than a handful of options makes the business case hard to understand and confuses the important issues that require decisions. |
| **Evaluate shortlist** | The three or four realistic options should now be evaluated using the criteria of the feasibility assessment (see Figure 4.2). Ideally, only 'ball-park' costs and benefits should be assessed for the options that are not to be recommended, with a detailed treatment reserved for the preferred option. However, in some organisations, it is required to perform a thorough analysis of all the options for management's consideration. |
| **Take forward to business case** | The assessed options, with more detail developed for the preferred one, are now taken into the business case. |

## COST–BENEFIT ANALYSIS

For the senior managers who will make a decision on the business case, this is probably one of its most important sections (apart from the investment appraisal discussed later). What, they will ask, are we going to pay to carry out this initiative and what benefits can we expect in return?

In fact, both costs and benefits are of one or either of the following natures:

| | |
|---|---|
| **Tangible** | These are provable in advance, usually in financial terms: for example, the savings from de-commissioning an old system or reducing headcount in the organisation. |
| **Intangible** | These either cannot be proved in advance, because there is insufficient data to do so, or they are genuinely 'soft' benefits, which are inherently hard to assess: for example, 'improved staff morale'. |

Note that the issue with tangible versus intangible costs and benefits is not whether they can be measured as such, but whether they are reasonably provable in advance. For example, increased sales resulting from a new web-based shopping channel may or may not be tangible depending on whether or not there is credible market research data available.

In addition, there is a timing issue associated with both costs and benefits. They are either:

| | |
|---|---|
| **Immediate** | These costs or benefits are incurred, or enjoyed, at the start of the project. |
| **Longer-term** | These costs or benefits become apparent later, sometimes over quite a long timescale. |

The reality on many projects is that immediate, tangible costs – for example, of developing and implementing the new system – are stacked up against a mixture of immediate and longer-term, tangible and intangible benefits.

The four categories of costs and benefits are summarised in Figure 4.4.

**Figure 4.4 Categories of costs and benefits**

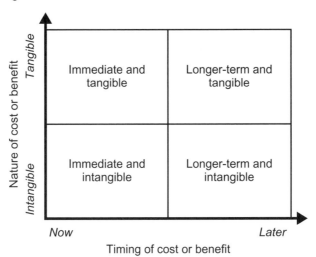

Although not exhaustive, the following are some of the costs and benefits that might arise in a typical IT development project:

Notice that, in these lists, costs tend to be tangible whereas benefits are often a mixture of the tangible and intangible. In some organisations, managers are reluctant to make a decision unless the balance of costs and benefits is clear – in other words, the tangible benefits must obviously outweigh the tangible costs. However, in reality, an intangible benefit – for example a more modern image for the organisation or better staff morale – may in the end prove to be more valuable than anything that can be easily proven in advance.

## RISK ANALYSIS

No IT project is without risk and some are very risky indeed. If senior managers are to make an informed decision on a proposed investment, they need to be appraised of the principal risks and, more importantly, what can be done about them.

In practical terms, a full risk appraisal is often impossible at the business case stage, not least because the project has only been scoped and planned in outline. But the principal

### TANGIBLE COSTS

- development staff time;
- user staff costs;
- purchase of hardware;
- purchase of operating system;
- purchase of packaged software;
- infrastructure;
- relocation;
- staff training and re-training;
- redundancy costs;
- ongoing hardware maintenance;
- ongoing software support.

### INTANGIBLE COSTS

- disruption during; implementation;
- short-term loss of productivity;
- recruitment of new staff.

### TANGIBLE BENEFITS

- staff savings;
- reduced effort;
- improved speed of working;
- faster response to customers;
- reduced accommodation costs;
- reduced inventory.

### INTANGIBLE BENEFITS

- increased job satisfaction;
- improved customer satisfaction;
- better management information;
- greater organisational flexibility;
- more creative problem-solving time;
- improved presentation or market image;
- better communications;
- improved staff morale.

risks should be identified and discussed in the business case. There are actually two types of risk that the decision-makers are interested in:

**Project risks**    These are things that might delay or otherwise adversely affect the IT project itself, for example difficulties in pinning down the requirements or problems with the delivery of hardware.

**Business risks**    These are the knock-on effects on the business, for example of reputational damage caused by a botched switch to a new system.

In practice, of course, the two types of risk tend to shade into each other; for example, a lack of skill within the project team leading to a botched implementation.

Once the principal risks have been identified, they need to be assessed and the following should be documented about each one:

**Description**

A description of the situation or circumstances that might give rise to the risk. For example, in a commercial, off-the-shelf procurement 'The risk is that the wrong package is selected for the organisation's needs'.

**Impact**

A description of what would be the impact if the risk occurred. For example 'Choosing the wrong package would mean that the organisation was unable to carry out some of its existing functions effectively and/or additional cost and delay would be expended in customising the package to meet the organisation's real requirements'. Notice how, in this case, a single risk cause could give rise to more than one impact.

**Scale of impact**

An assessment of how badly the risk would affect the organisation if it occurred. Sometimes, mathematical scales are used here but, often, a simple scale of small, moderate or large (or even catastrophic, if appropriate) will suffice. If there is more than one possible impact associated with a risk, consideration should be given to documenting them separately. For example, the organisation being unable to carry out its functions effectively might be a large impact, but the need for additional customisation might only be moderate.

**Probability of occurrence**

The other side of the risk coin is how likely it is that this risk will occur. Again, a simple scale of high, medium or low is often enough. In our example, we might consider it of only medium likelihood that the risk will occur.

**Avoidance actions**

These are aimed at reducing the probability of occurrence. In our example, an obvious countermeasure is to make sure that a complete set of requirements is compiled before looking at possible packages and ensuring that a structured procurement process is followed.

**Mitigation actions**

These are aimed at reducing the scale of impact if the risk occurs and they are needed because (1) sometimes avoidance actions are not available and (2) in other situations they do not work. In our example, one mitigation action might be to ensure that sufficient contingency in time and money is available for additional customisation, should that be required. Another might be to get the package vendors to underwrite their solution so that they bear the costs if the package needs a lot of adaptation. This is actually a specific form of mitigation called 'transference', whereby the impact of the risk falls on someone else (insurance is another example of the same idea).

**Owner**           Finally, we need to document who would be responsible for managing the risk, and taking the required actions to avoid or mitigate it.

Armed with this information about the principal risks, senior management is now in the best position to make a good decision on whether to proceed with the investment or not.

## IMPACT ANALYSIS

Impacts may incur costs, or incur risks, and so be discussed under those headings. But what we really mean here is things that the senior managers need to think about in making their decisions. For example, to make effective use of a new system, different people may be required in the organisation and that might entail adopting a different approach to recruitment. Or, if people are expected to exhibit new behaviours (perhaps because a lot of 'back room' work has been automated, thus freeing people for more customer-facing roles), different training and incentives may be required. Another impact that can be difficult for managers to take on board is if they themselves are going to have to adopt a different style of management; coaching and supporting instead of directing, for instance.

The point is that managers need to be made aware of these impacts so that they can consider how best to take them on board to make the project a success.

## INVESTMENT APPRAISAL TECHNIQUES

Having identified where costs and benefits will arise from a proposed IT project, the last – but in many ways most important – thing to do is to put these together in the form of an investment appraisal. Essentially, what senior management want to know is how long it will take to recover the investment in the project (if, indeed, they can in purely financial terms).

Preparing investment appraisals is, of course, the speciality of management accountants but others involved in IT projects – business analysts, developers, project managers – should at least have an understanding of the principles involved, and these are covered here.

The simplest way of presenting the investment appraisal is as a **payback** or **break-even** calculation, and an example is shown in Table 4.1.

Table 4.1 shows a typical IT project, where £250,000 is to be spent on new hardware and software in the initial year of the project (which accountants refer to as 'Year 0'), with a further £50,000 being spent each year on hardware maintenance and software support. The benefits expected to flow from this are savings of £60,000 per year in staff costs and increased sales estimated at £80,000 per year.

We can see from Table 4.1 that payback/break-even occurs in Year 4, when the cumulative benefits finally exceed the cumulative costs.

**Table 4.1 Example of a payback calculation**

| | Year 0 | Year 1 | Year 2 | Year 3 | Year 4 |
|---|---|---|---|---|---|
| Cumulative cash flow for project brought forward | | −300,000 | −210,000 | −120,000 | −30,000 |
| Hardware purchase | −150,000 | | | | |
| Software purchase | −100,000 | | | | |
| Hardware maintenance | −25,000 | −25,000 | −25,000 | −25,000 | −25,000 |
| Software support | −25,000 | −25,000 | −25,000 | −25,000 | −25,000 |
| Total costs for year | −300,000 | −50,000 | −50,000 | −50,000 | −50,000 |
| Staff savings | | 60,000 | 60,000 | 60,000 | 60,000 |
| Increased sales | | 80,000 | 80,000 | 80,000 | 80,000 |
| Total benefits for year | Nil | 140,000 | 140,000 | 140,000 | 140,000 |
| Cash flow for year (benefits less costs) | −300,000 | +90,000 | +90,000 | +90,000 | +90,000 |
| Cumulative cash flow for project carried forward | −300,000 | −210,000 | −210,000 | −30,000 | +60,000 |

The virtue of a payback calculation is that it is relatively straightforward and easily understood by non-accountants. However, from an accountant's perspective it suffers from a major deficiency, which is that it does not take into account what is referred to as the 'time value for money'.

The principle here is that, over time, an organisation has to pay for the money it uses. If its main source of finance is bank loans, it has to pay interest on them or, if it is funded by shares (equity) the investors expect to receive dividends on their investments. The cost of meeting this interest or these dividends must be added to the face value of any money used in a project. For example, if I borrow £100 for one year at ten per cent interest, I need to find £110 in a year's time to pay back the loan. Or, to put it another way, if I received £100 in a year's time, it is only worth £100/1.1 or £90.91 at today's value of money.

A method that takes into account the time value of money is called **discounted cash flow** (DCF) and this method applied to our example IT project is illustrated in Table 4.2.

In Table 4.2, we have worked out how much money flows in or out as a result of our project in each year and we have shown these as the 'net cash flow'. We now adjust these cash flows by a discount factor based on the chosen interest rate, in this case

**Table 4.2  Example of a discounted cash flow or net present value calculation**

|  | Benefits less costs | New cash flow | Discount factor at 10% interest | Discounted cash flow or present value |
|---|---|---|---|---|
| Year 0 | (0 – 300,000) | −300,000 | 1.000 | −300,000 |
| Year 1 | (140,000 – 50,000) | +90,000 | 0.909 | +81,810 |
| Year 2 | (140,000 – 50,000) | +90,000 | 0.826 | +74,340 |
| Year 3 | (140,000 – 50,000) | +90,000 | 0.751 | +67,590 |
| Year 4 | (140,000 – 50,000) | +90,000 | 0.683 | +61,470 |
| Net present value of project |  |  |  | −14,790 |

ten per cent again. (The factors can be found in textbooks on management accounting or are built-in as functions in spreadsheets such as Microsoft® Excel.) The net cash flow of - £300,000 in Year 0 is given its full value as it represents money spent today. But the apparent + £90,000 in Year 1 has been adjusted to be worth only + £81,810 and this is referred to its discounted cash flow or present value. The + £90,000 received in Year 2 is worth even less, + £74,340 and so on until the end of the evaluation period in Year 4. If we now add up all these present values we get a **net present value** (NPV) for the project of − £14,790.

So, whereas the payback calculation suggests that our project would pay back by £60,000 at the end of Year 4, using DCF/NPV to take into account the time value of money shows that it does not pay for itself over that period.

There is a third method used to present an investment appraisal and this is to work out the **internal rate of return** (IRR) of the project. The IRR is the interest rate that would have to be used in a DCF/NPV calculation to end up with a net present value of zero at the end of the assessment period and, unfortunately, there is no formula to work it out! One can either set up a spreadsheet and try various rates by trial and error until the correct one is arrived at, or Excel has a very handy algorithm built in that can work it out for us (again, using approximation). In the case of our example project, it turns out to be about 7.71 per cent and, in effect, provides a simulation of the return on investment from the project. This can then be compared with other projects that are competing for the same funding. So if, for example, two other projects offered IRRs respectively of five per cent and six per cent, this project would be a better investment. In addition, whatever the IRR turns out to be, it should be greater than the cost of capital used in the project – in other words than the interest or dividends the organisation expects to pay out.

To summarise, then, there are three commonly-used ways of presenting an investment appraisal:

| | |
|---|---|
| **Payback or break-even** | Simple and straightforward and, in times of low interest rates, provides a good assessment of the proposed project. But, it does not take account of the 'time value of money'. |
| **Discounted cash flow or net present value** | Takes account of the time value of money and adjusts future cash flows to factor in the cost of the capital used to finance the project. However, working out the correct discount rate to use is tricky and involves some subjective judgements on the part of management accountants, particularly for a long-timescale project. |
| **Internal rate of return** | Gives a single headline number that represents the return on investment and should be compared with the organisation's cost of capital. But it does not take account of the sheer size of a project. |

## FURTHER READING

Blackstaff, M. (2012) *Finance for IT decision makers: a practical handbook* (3rd edition). BCS, Swindon.

Gambles, I. (2009) *Making the business case.* Gower, London.

Ward, J. and Daniel, E. (2006) *Benefits management: delivering value from IS and IT investments.* Wiley, Chichester.

# 5  REQUIREMENTS ENGINEERING

**James Cadle**

## CONTENTS OF THIS CHAPTER

This chapter covers the following topics:

- a definition of requirements engineering;
- the requirements engineering framework;
- roles in requirements engineering;
- requirements elicitation;
- requirements analysis;
- requirements validation;
- requirements documentation;
- requirements management;
- requirements engineering and Agile development;
- requirements engineering and off-the-shelf solutions.

## REQUIREMENTS ENGINEERING DEFINED

The term 'requirements engineering' is a relatively new one and has come to prominence in the last 20 years or so. Aspects of what we now call requirements engineering – for example requirements specification – have been a feature of solution development since people have been working with computers but, in the past, these aspects were rather fragmented and, to a large degree, dependent on the skill and approach of those people responsible for defining the requirements.

Over time, however, it has been recognised that, particularly where teams of people are working together to define requirements, there needs to be a standardised approach and a set of recognised techniques that everyone can use. So, requirements engineering involves three key elements:

- a framework that people can follow and which can be replicated from project to project;
- a set of techniques that can be used at each stage within the framework;
- standards that define, for example, what we mean by 'good' requirements.

In the rest of this chapter, we shall explore each of these elements of requirements engineering.

Nowadays, the responsibility for requirements engineering rests primarily with business analysts (see Chapter 3 for more detail on this role). However, a variety of people need to contribute to requirements engineering if it is to be successful and the different business and project roles are explored later in this chapter.

## A FRAMEWORK FOR REQUIREMENTS ENGINEERING

Figure 5.1 shows the elements of the requirements engineering process.

**Figure 5.1  A framework for requirements engineering**

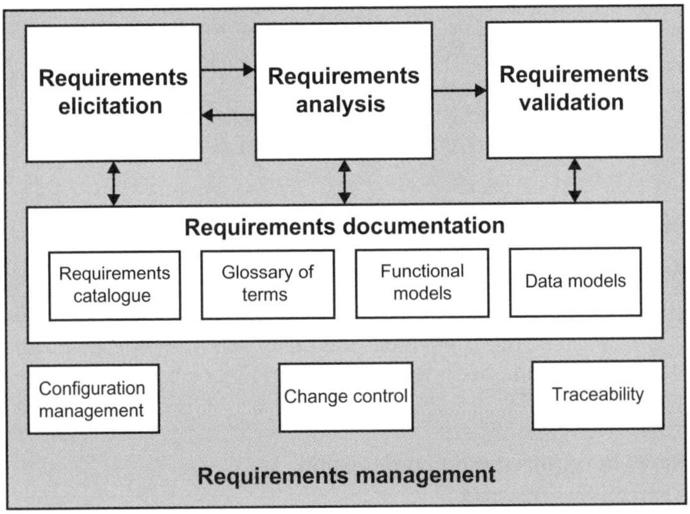

As Figure 5.1 suggests, there are three sequential stages of the requirements process and two supporting sets of activities. The sequential stages are:

| | |
|---|---|
| **Requirements elicitation** | The first stage of requirements engineering is to discover what the requirements are and the best term for this process of discovery is elicitation. As we shall see later, there are many techniques that can be employed at this stage, depending on the circumstances of the individual project. |
| **Requirements analysis** | The 'raw' requirements are now examined methodically to see if they meet the standards of 'good' requirements and further elicitation work is often required to ensure that they meet these criteria. |
| **Requirements validation** | Here, the requirements are reviewed and signed off before being used for the next stage of the development process, whether that is to build or buy a solution. |

61

The two supporting sets of activities are:

| | |
|---|---|
| **Requirements documentation** | During the three stages of the requirements process, the documentation of the requirements is gradually assembled and checked. The textual requirements catalogue can be supplemented and reinforced by using models to represent the functionality of the proposed information system and the data to be stored. In addition, a glossary of terms is usually helpful to remove the ambiguities that are inherent in any specification of requirements. |
| **Requirements management** | Finally, an overarching process is needed to manage the set of requirements as they emerge. Configuration management (version control) is needed to make sure that the correct versions of the various documents are being worked on; change control is needed to make sure that 'scope creep' does not occur; and it is important to be able to trace requirements back to their source and, if relevant, forward to their resolution. |

In total, then, the framework shown in Figure 5.1 provides a structure and a mechanism to manage and control the requirements engineering work.

## ROLES IN REQUIREMENTS ENGINEERING

As we have already mentioned, for requirements engineering to succeed – in the sense of providing a set of robust requirements to support solution development or procurement – a number of parties need to be involved in the process. The main roles involved in requirements engineering are shown in Figure 5.2

**Figure 5.2 Roles in requirements engineering**

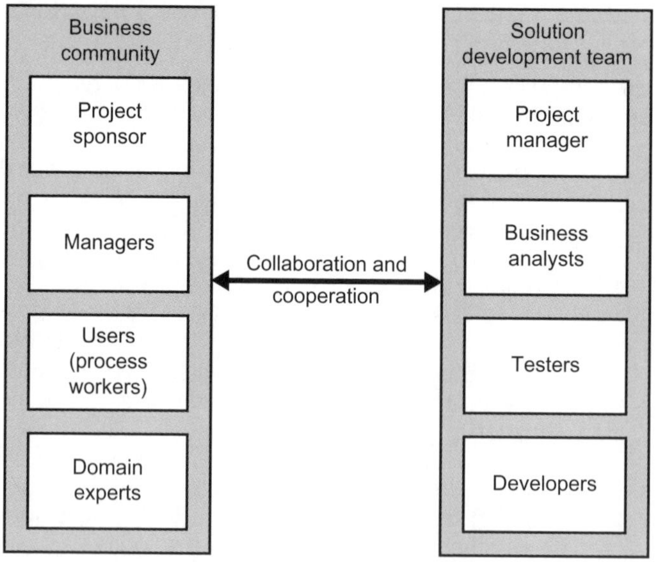

As can be seen, the 'actors' in requirements engineering fall into two broad groups – the business community and the solution development team. The roles in the business community are:

**Project sponsor**
This role – also known as the senior responsible owner or officer – is the person who 'owns' the project as a piece of business and is (or should be) accountable to the organisation for the delivery of its business benefits. The sponsor makes the final decision on key aspects of the project, for example on its scope and on whether individual requirements are in or out of the delivered solution.

**Managers**
In addition to the sponsor, other managers have inputs to the requirements process, perhaps as the 'owners' of individual requirements (see 'requirements documentation' later in this chapter). Managers will, of course, also have views about the project and needs, for example for information that must be documented as requirements.

**Users (process workers)**
The people who work with the existing systems and processes (if these exist) and who will have to use the new solution are a key source of information in requirements engineering. Their interest and commitment must be engaged throughout the process and their expectations of the proposed solution must be managed carefully if disappointment with the finished results is to be avoided.

**Domain experts**
One difficulty business analysts face when eliciting requirements from users is that the latter's thinking is often constrained by their experience in the organisation; this is especially the case when they have worked there for a long time and find it hard to conceive of different ways of doing things. To provide a broader – and perhaps more objective – perspective, domain experts can be consulted. These could be people within the organisation with a wider view (perhaps because they have previously worked in other, similar, organisations); or, sometimes, domain consultants can be engaged to give an alternative view.

Within the team that will develop the solution to the requirements, another four key roles can be identified:

**Project manager**
The project manager has overall charge of the development project and is therefore very focused on its key milestones and deliverables. The project manager also needs to keep control of the scope of the project although, as we shall see later under 'requirements management', the business analyst also has a role to play in that.

**Business analysts**
Business analysts are responsible for eliciting, documenting, analysing and managing the requirements.

**Testers**              As we shall see shortly, one of the key attributes of a good requirement is that it is testable. There is therefore a lot of benefit to be gained by involving testers in the earlier review of requirements (during analysis and validation) to ensure that these are, ultimately, testable.

**Developers**           Finally, the developers of the proposed system need to have good, clear requirements from which to work, so it is useful to consult them during the requirements engineering work. Also, if an Agile approach is to be taken to development (see later in this chapter), the developers will be responsible for fleshing out much of the detail of the requirements as they work with the users to create the solution.

Other actors may also be involved in the requirements engineering work. For example, if an organisation is subject to oversight by a regulator, representatives of that body will be able to assist in identifying the legal and regulatory requirements that must be satisfied. And, as we shall see later, a quality assurance or project office function may be responsible for checking the quality of the requirements during the validation stage.

## REQUIREMENTS ELICITATION

### Introduction to requirements elicitation

'Requirements elicitation' is a much better term for the first stage of the requirements process than 'requirements gathering', which is often used. The reason is that 'gathering' implies a rather passive role for the business analyst, and presents an image of them holding their hands out for people to give them requirements, whereas getting at the requirements is usually a much more arduous and proactive undertaking.

One of the reasons for difficulty in eliciting requirements relates to what is usually termed 'tacit' knowledge. This takes various forms but the two most common are:

- things that users think are so widely known – the common currency of their organisation – that they do not bother to mention them to the business analysts;
- things that users genuinely do not know that they know; things that have become so second-nature to them that they are not even aware of them anymore (like the ability a police officer develops to size up a developing situation and assess whether it is threatening or not).

As we shall see, some methods of requirements elicitation are better than others for ferreting out tacit knowledge, but none of these is fool-proof and business analysts must constantly be on the lookout for areas where tacit knowledge may be lurking unsuspected.

Elicitation techniques may be broadly classified as qualitative or quantitative. However, these categories are not definitive and some techniques straddle the boundaries between the two types.

## Primarily qualitative elicitation techniques

These include:

| | |
|---|---|
| **Interviews** | This is the oldest technique and is still widely used. Interviews are good for getting in-depth information from individual stakeholders and building relationships with them. They are also useful when there are sensitive 'political' issues that might not come out in a more open forum like a workshop. |
| **Workshops** | These have become, in the twenty-first century, the main elicitation technique, probably because they can take less time than interviews and are more collaborative (in both cases because all the key stakeholders are involved at the same time). However, a workshop will only succeed if it is well run and the keys to this include: |

- having a good facilitator, able to control the group and draw out the more reticent members;

- the presence of the right people, needing both good knowledge of the topics to be discussed and the authority to make decisions;

- a clear goal and a set of not over-ambitious objectives to be achieved.

| | |
|---|---|
| **Focus groups** | These are a special type of workshop, designed to elicit the views and opinions of the participants. The session is run by a moderator, who poses the questions and then encourages the participants to discuss among themselves the issues raised. In requirements engineering, focus groups are particularly useful when exploring non-functional requirements such as usability. |
| **Observation** | There is nothing like watching people perform a task to find out how they really do it, as opposed to what they tell us in interviews or workshops or what is defined in the organisation's procedures. Observation is very good for uncovering tacit knowledge. Business analysts need to be aware, though, that people sometimes change their approach when being observed and it is, at the least, a somewhat unnerving experience. When the workforce is unionised, it is important to observe any protocols agreed with the unions before starting observation. |
| **Shadowing** | This is a form of observation where the business analyst would follow a worker around to note what they do, and how they do it. The cautions mentioned under observation apply here too. |
| **Scenarios** | Probably used within the context of an interview, workshop, or focus group, this technique poses a scenario and asks how people would deal with the situation. For example 'What |

happens if a customer phones to cancel an order after the delivery van has left?' Scenarios encourage people to think about situations which they consider very unlikely, but which could cause difficulties in a system if they do occur.

**Prototyping**

Other engineering disciplines have always used prototypes, for example car designers and architects. Frequently, users do not know what they want until their imagination is sparked by being shown a prototype. They may like what they see or dislike it but, either way, they are further forward in being able to articulate their needs to the business analysts. In most other fields, prototypes are 'throwaway'; in other words, once the users have commented on them, they are set aside and the final product is designed. In IT, however, sometimes the prototypes are 'evolutionary'; in other words, they are enhanced to become the final product. This being the case, the management of prototyping in IT poses some particular challenges in that the users' expectations must be managed carefully to ensure that they do not expect immediate delivery at the conclusion of the prototyping exercise.

In fact, prototyping can be used in a number of ways in an IT project:

- to stimulate users' thinking about what they want;
- to check the business analysts' understanding of the users' requirements;
- to explore some non-functional requirements (see later), although this usually requires some form of working prototype to have been constructed.

## Primarily quantitative elicitation techniques

These include:

**Questionnaires and surveys**

Sometimes, because they are geographically widely dispersed, it is difficult or impossible to meet all of the stakeholders. In other cases, the business analysts want to know if what they have been told by a small group of stakeholders is representative of the wider stakeholder population. In both cases, a questionnaire can prove invaluable; either a traditional paper-based one or, increasingly, one conducted online. There are some specific issues that need to be considered when using questionnaires:

- Response rates are typically low, so how representative of the population at large are those who do respond?
- Completion is encouraged if the questionnaire is not too long and does not require too much research by the respondents.
- Questions must be carefully constructed to make sure that people can actually answer them in an unambiguous manner.

**Document analysis**  This involves taking a source document, or perhaps a screen on an existing computer system, and dissecting and recording the information it contains. Things to consider include:

- What is the purpose of the document?
- Who completes the document, and when?
- Who has access to the document and why?
- What information is contained in the document?
- How long is the information retained?

These, and other, questions give useful insights into the data requirements of a new system and also provide input to building data models (discussed later under 'Requirements documentation').

**Record searching**  Trawling through files of records can reveal useful quantitative data, for example: How many invoices are produced in a month? Is there a peak at any time during the month? Coupled with document analysis, this technique provides useful volumetric information that can be input into, for example, database design.

**Special-purpose records**  Sometimes, it is useful to know how people spend their time, so that the solution improvement effort can be directed to the most significant tasks. One way of finding out is to ask people to complete a simple form whereby they record each time they perform a certain transaction, like setting up a new customer account or raising an invoice. Obviously, the information gained this way must be treated with some caution, as most likely the people filling in the forms are busy and may forget or, less commonly, may inflate the figures to make a point.

**Activity sampling**  A more accurate way of finding out how time is spent is for the business analysts to perform some form of activity sampling exercise. Here, they take a turn around the office at pre-defined but ideally irregular intervals and note down what each person is doing at that time. Some things to consider about activity sampling are:

- A large enough time period must be chosen to get a reliable result and managers should be consulted to make sure that the period of the study is a reasonably typical one.
- Identifying what office workers are doing (especially when they are staring at computer screens) is actually rather more difficult than when surveying manual workers.
- As with any form of observation, activity sampling is unnerving.

## BUSINESS ANALYSIS TECHNIQUES

More detailed descriptions of all of the above techniques can be found in the book *Business analysis techniques* (see 'Further reading', later in this chapter).

### Types of requirement

Business analysts are looking for various types of requirement. Various classification schemes have been proposed for requirements and the following are quite widely used:

| | |
|---|---|
| **Functional requirements** | These define **what** a proposed solution is expected to do, in other words its functionality. An example might be 'The system shall identify when an invoice is overdue for payment and alert the financial controller.' |
| **Non-functional requirements** | These define how the solution should operate or, according to Suzanne Robertson (see References) 'the product's qualities'. An example might be 'the result of a query must be displayed within two seconds of the user hitting the enter key'. |
| **General requirements** | These are high-level, overarching requirements of a business policy nature. So, for instance, the need to comply with data protection legislation would be a general requirement, as might be a company policy not to trade in certain products. |
| **Technical requirements** | Finally, these are high-level, overarching requirements of a technical policy nature, for example, for a solution to operate on a certain platform or to be developed using a particular programming environment. |

There are connections between these types of requirement. For example, a functional requirement to display a customer's account balance would be associated with non-functional requirements concerning access rights, speed of response and so forth. Or, the general requirement to comply with data protection legislation would be expanded into more detailed functional and non-functional requirements, for example, to disclose to customers the information that is held about them.

The IIBA® (International Institute of Business Analysis) in its *Business Analysis Body of Knowledge*® (Version 2.0) offers a rather different system for classifying requirements. It proposes four main categories of requirement:

| | |
|---|---|
| **Business requirements** | These are, like the general requirements previously described, high-level statements of the goals, objectives and needs of the organisation as whole (as distinct from those of individual stakeholders). Such requirements provide context and a general direction for a solution development project. |
| **Stakeholder requirements** | These are statements of the needs of individual stakeholders, or groups of stakeholders. They tend to be at a higher level of abstraction from the solution requirements. |

| | |
|---|---|
| **Solution requirements** | These are more detailed and describe what the solution is required to do and how it is to operate. Solution requirements are sub-divided into functional and non-functional requirements, as previously described. |
| **Transition requirements** | These describe what is required to make a transition from the existing processes and systems to the proposed new ones. These features and facilities so described will not be needed again once the new systems are in operation. |

Each solution development project team needs to develop a system of classification for requirements – probably based on one or both of the schemes described above – and to use that system consistently in the documentation it produces.

## REQUIREMENTS ANALYSIS

Once the requirements have been elicited, the next stage of the requirements engineering process is to analyse them, to ensure that they are 'good' requirements, suitable to support the development or procurement of a solution. Inevitably, the analysis work will reveal further questions that must be asked and so lead to more elicitation work.

### Characteristics of good requirements

So what, then, is a 'good' requirement? It is one that satisfies the following criteria:

| | |
|---|---|
| **Categorised** | Each requirement needs to be categorised as discussed in the earlier section on 'types of requirement'. This makes it easier to group requirements for review. |
| **Relevant** | The question here is, is the requirement within the scope of the project? If it is (or appears to be) outside the scope, the project sponsor must be consulted to see if they want to broaden the scope to include it. If so, then the proper change control process, discussed later under 'requirements management', should be employed. |
| **Prioritised** | This important topic is discussed separately in the next section of this chapter. |
| **Achievable** | If it is clear that the requirement cannot be met – perhaps because it is technically impossible or too expensive – then the expectations of whoever raised it need to be managed downwards and, ultimately, the requirement needs to be removed from the requirements document. |
| **Understandable and unambiguous** | Requirements are useless unless they can be understood, in the same way, by the different stakeholders who are interested in them. Do the users, for example, have the same understanding of what a 'customer' is as the solution developers? Adjectives |

and adverbs always have the potential to introduce ambiguity and so should be removed and replaced with something more definitive; for example, 'a fast response time' is ambiguous, 'a response time of not more than two seconds after hitting the ENTER key' is not.

**Testable**

Making sure that a requirement is understandable and unambiguous goes a long way to making sure that it is testable. Special efforts need to be made to ensure that concepts such as 'ease of use' can be specified in such a way as to make them testable; for example, by defining how long it should take a typical user to master a feature, and with what training and support.

**Requirement not solution**

It is easy to wrongly document solutions as requirements. For instance, 'the field sales force shall be provided with laptop computers' would be better expressed as 'a means is needed for the field sales force to check product information and record orders when on the move', which would open up other solutions such as the use of tablet computers or smartphones.

**Consistent**

Requirements, especially very wordy ones, can be internally inconsistent. In addition, requirements can conflict with each other. For example, 'the system must be totally secure' is inconsistent with 'the system must be readily accessible to anyone'. Unless the inconsistencies are removed, the solution providers will later find that they cannot meet one requirement without not meeting the other one.

**Owned**

Someone needs to own each requirement. Ultimately, of course, the project sponsor owns them all but, as very senior managers, they are unlikely to be close enough to the detail to know whether a requirement is correct or not. So, the owner of a requirement is likely to be someone in the management tier who can make decisions about the relevance and content of that requirement.

**Unique and atomic**

We must ensure that each requirement is singular and doesn't cover several requirements.

**Traceable**

We need to know where a requirement came from, so that more detail on it can be sought if necessary. In the end, too, we need to know what happened to the requirement; was it met in the delivered solution or perhaps set aside as too expensive?

**Concise**

Insofar as this is compatible with meeting the quality criteria already described, it is desirable to make requirements as brief as possible, as this makes them easier to understand and review.

**Complete**
For a requirement to be useful, it must be a complete statement of what is required and not necessitate extensive reference to other documentation.

**Correct**
In one respect, meeting all the other criteria listed here means that a requirement is likely to be correct. However, a requirement could still be excellent in a technical sense and yet plain wrong in the sense of wrongly defining what the organisation needs. This is explored in more detail in the 'requirements validation' section later in this chapter.

**Conformant**
Finally, if the organisation has a set of standards as to how requirements should be documented and phrased, these should be followed. This is also explored in the section of this chapter on 'requirements validation'.

Clearly, this is a long list of quality criteria but requirements that do not meet them are almost certain to cause problems later in the solution development lifecycle.

## Prioritisation of requirements

We have already alluded to the fact that requirements need to be prioritised. This is because there is almost never enough time, money or resources to meet all of the requirements identified by the users and hard decisions need to be taken about which ones to meet and which can be set aside.

Various prioritisation schemes are used within organisations. For example, they may be classified as 'mandatory', 'desirable' and 'nice to have' or just 'high', 'medium' or 'low'. However, the prioritisation scheme that seems to have become dominant is MoSCoW. Before describing it, it is worth pointing out that its origins lie in the field of Iterative, evolutionary or Agile development, discussed in Chapter 2 of this book. MoSCoW has been used successfully with other, more linear, lifecycles but in that case it needs some modification. So, the 'standard' MoSCoW approach has four priorities of requirement:

**Must have**
These are fundamental requirements that, if they are not satisfied, would render any solution unacceptable or useless. For example, the main point of an inventory management system is to record items taken into and out of a storage facility so, without the ability to do that, any system would be of no value. Thus, 'Must have' features are mandatory and must be present from the first day of the system's implementation.

**Should have**
These requirements are also mandatory but, unlike the 'Must haves', they do not necessarily have to be met on day one. For example, with our inventory management system, it is obviously necessary to support activities such as an annual stock check. However, if that stock check takes place at the end of October each year, and the system is implemented in March, there are

a few months before the feature will be needed. With 'Should haves', either implementation can be delayed, or the users can continue to use their old system or a manual workaround may be acceptable for a short time.

**Could have**  These are the 'nice to haves' in the MoSCoW scheme. The basic test is, if they can be implemented easily alongside the 'Musts' or 'Shoulds', they will be but otherwise can be left out of the solution.

**Want to have (but not now)**  It is with these requirements that the Agile origin of MoSCoW becomes most apparent. On the assumption that there will be later iterations of the solution, requirements that are so classified are effectively 'parked' and will be reconsidered when deciding the scope of a later iteration. Then – perhaps because the business environment has now changed – they may become 'Musts' for that iteration.

If MoSCoW is to be employed in a linear, Waterfall lifecycle (see Chapter 2), and there is only going to be one phase of development and implementation, then the Musts and Shoulds are effectively merged into one, mandatory, category. The Coulds and Wants will then have to be classified as either 'desirable' or 'nice to have'.

The prioritisation of requirements often involves extensive negotiations between the business analysts and the various stakeholders who may well have differing views about what is important. Ultimately, if the business analysts cannot broker agreement among the stakeholders, the final priority will have to be decided by the project sponsor.

## REQUIREMENTS VALIDATION

The last sequential stage of the requirements engineering process is requirements validation. In fact, in the terminology of quality, there are two issues that need to be addressed at this stage:

**Verification**  This is concerned with making sure that the product has been made correctly; in other words, that it conforms to any standards for such products. In the context of requirements engineering, this means that the requirements have been documented using the right templates, have conformed to any syntactical rules or standards and comply with any house styles and such like. In short, 'have we done this right?'

**Validation**  This is concerned with making sure that the product meets the users' expressed needs. In requirements engineering, this means that the set of requirements is a complete and correct summary of the users' needs. In short, 'have we done the right thing?'

This distinction is useful because it helps us to understand what is meant by 'requirements validation' and also indicates who should be involved in the process. Requirements validation means, in effect, a final review of the requirements before they are signed off by the project sponsor and are passed forward as the basis for building, or procuring, a solution. As to who should be involved in this review:

**Verification**      Since we are concerned here with requirements meeting the standards set for them, this aspect of the review could be undertaken by business analysts – but, for obvious reasons, a different team of BAs from the ones who compiled the requirements. Alternatively, if the organisation has a quality assurance group or a project support office, people from those functions could undertake the review. Finally, if they have not been involved in the work before, this is a good point to seek the opinion of testers as to whether the requirements are, in fact, testable.

**Validation**       It is the responsibility of the users (process workers), their managers and, ultimately, the project sponsor to satisfy themselves that the set of requirements does fully and correctly encapsulate their needs. If the set of requirements is very large, it may be advisable to partition it so that individual stakeholders are only required to review the parts that are most relevant to them, although this does risk no-one being able to see the overall picture.

As to how to perform the review, two main possibilities suggest themselves. One is to send out the requirements document (see next section), possibly partitioned, and ask the reviewers to send back their comments. Alternatively, a workshop, or series of workshops, could be staged at which the requirements are examined systematically. If the previous analysis work has been performed thoroughly, one hopes that no major issues will be raised at this stage but that possibility cannot be entirely ignored, especially if some aspects of tacit knowledge now come to light.

## REQUIREMENTS DOCUMENTATION

This element of the requirements engineering process is concerned with making sure that a complete and consistent set of documentation is produced to capture the requirements.

Unfortunately, there is no agreement among the IT community as to what the final document to be produced is called; the terms 'requirements specification', 'statement of requirements', 'user requirements specification' and even 'functional specification', as well as many others, are encountered. So here, we shall just use the generic term 'requirements document' and its typical contents are shown in Figure 5.3.

**Figure 5.3 Contents of a requirements document**

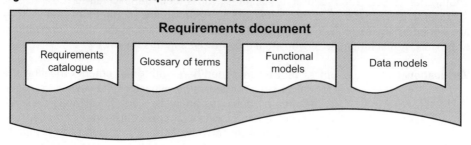

We shall now briefly consider the main sections of the requirements document and then look in more detail at the requirements catalogue. Functional models and data models are discussed in more detail in Chapter 7, 'System modelling techniques'.

| | |
|---|---|
| **Requirements catalogue** | As the name implies, this is a repository of all the requirements, usually in a textual format, although things like decision tables may be used to explain complex business rules. |
| **Glossary of terms** | Providing a glossary of terms goes a long way to removing ambiguity from the requirements document. If, for example, there are multiple definitions of what 'customer' means within an organisation, the glossary makes clear what it means in the context of this document and this project. |
| **Functional models** | The functionality of a system is often more easily understood by looking at models, so these can be provided to supplement the functional requirements. In the past, data flow diagrams were used for this purpose but, today, use case diagrams (see Chapter 7) have become the norm. |
| **Data models** | Similarly, it is necessary to capture the business rules that underpin the storage, use and deletion of data and this can be achieved by using an entity relationship diagram or (see Chapter 7 again) a class model. |

## The requirements catalogue

As we have seen, this major document is a repository of all the requirements. Typically, we would have an entry for each requirement, containing:

| | |
|---|---|
| **ID** | A unique identifier for the requirement, to facilitate identification and traceability. |
| **Title** | A one-line title, enabling the requirement to be found quickly in an index or summary of requirements. |

| | |
|---|---|
| **Version/status** | The current version of the requirement and its status (for example, draft, reviewed, signed-off, baselined). |
| **Business area/domain** | This is useful, because it enables the requirements to be linked to the business areas, whose managers need to approve them. |
| **Source** | Where the requirement came from. This could be an individual or perhaps a source document, such as an organisational policy statement. |
| **Owner** | The individual – usually a more senior manager – who will be asked to sign-off the requirement and satisfy themselves when it has been met. |
| **Stakeholders** | Other than the source and the owner, people who have an interest in the requirement and who ought, perhaps, to be consulted about it. |
| **Requirement type** | See the discussion earlier in this chapter. |
| **Description** | A more detailed statement and definition of the requirement. |
| **Priority** | Any priority assigned here (see the earlier discussion in this chapter) is provisional until the project sponsor has finally agreed it. |
| **Associated non-functional requirements** | If this is a functional requirement, any non-functional issues associated with it. |
| **Acceptance or fit criteria** | The basis on which the requirement will be accepted by its owner should be specified. This is **not** the same as an acceptance test specification, but should indicate the principles on which acceptance will be based. |
| **Rationale/justification** | Why the source considered the requirement important or perhaps a statement like 'legally required under data protection legislation'. This information is useful in prioritising the requirements. |
| **Related documents** | A cross-reference to documents where further information can be obtained; for example, to notes of an interview. |
| **Related requirements** | Cross-references to other requirements that need to be considered in parallel with this one. |
| **Resolution** | This eventually records what happened to the requirement. It could, for example, record how the requirement was met in the delivered solution or, perhaps, note when it was set aside by the project sponsor. |

## User stories

An additional, or different, way of documenting requirements, much used in Agile development projects, is as 'user stories'. These are small pieces of functionality that are to be developed in collaborative sessions between the users and software developers. As the name suggests, they take the form of a 'story' told from the point of view of a particular stakeholder and an example of one is shown in Figure 5.4.

**Figure 5.4  Example of a user story from an inventory management system**

> ### Story ID: 079
>
> As a warehouse manager, I want to be able to enquire on the quantity and location of any item held. This should be possible by part number or by using the name of the part and it would be good if only an approximate name could be used in case I cannot remember the full name.
>
> Priority:  Must
> Estimate:  3 days
>
> Note: Do we need to cater for multi-lingual matching here or will English be sufficient?
>
> Confirmations
> Before displaying details of an item, the system should ask the user to verify that the correct part has been identified.

## REQUIREMENTS MANAGEMENT

Requirements management refers to the set of processes and procedures through which the set of requirements is managed throughout the project. Three main aspects of requirements management need to be considered:

| | |
|---|---|
| **Configuration management (version control)** | It is vital to know the current status of a requirement, which is the latest version and how all the requirements and other documentation (for example, class models) fit together. The process of controlling these things is known as configuration management or sometimes just as version control. The importance of this lies in the fact that, otherwise, superseded versions of documents can be taken forward and people waste time working on outdated versions. |
| **Change control** | A process is also needed to document proposed changes to the requirements, their estimated impact on the scope, cost and timescale of the project and what decisions are made about these changes. |

**Traceability**

Finally, as shown in Figure 5.5, it is important to be able to trace requirements back to their source and forward to their resolution. Once a system goes live, too, those maintaining it need to be able to trace why certain features have been implemented as they have, before they make any changes or upgrades.

**Figure 5.5 Traceability**

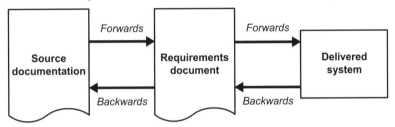

All three elements of requirements management can be handled using manual approaches – spreadsheets, logs and so forth. Traceability, for instance, can be achieved using a simple matrix that shows the links between the different pieces of documentation. However, on anything but a very small project, the use of some sort of support tool makes requirements management a lot easier and more certain. Such tools are discussed in Chapter 14, 'Solution development tools'.

## REQUIREMENTS ENGINEERING AND AGILE DEVELOPMENT

Agile approaches to software development are discussed in Chapters 2 ('Lifecycle types and their rationales') and 6 ('Programming and development approaches'). If an Agile approach is adopted, this requires adjustment to the requirements engineering approach.

In Agile software development, the requirements are scoped out at a high level in the early phases of solution development and detailed fully only during the iteration or 'sprint', where they will be delivered. This is known as 'just in time' development. In other words, the requirements are only detailed at the point in which they are developed. The premise for this is that Agile software development expects requirements to change and so builds this into the process. If the requirements are fully detailed early in the process, they may change as the solution evolves and the project is left with the additional effort of managing these changing requirements. In Agile, this is seen as unnecessary bureaucracy.

To combat this, Agile software development concentrates on producing a list of requirement titles – to compile the product backlog in a Scrum project for example – and enough detail so that the users and developers can work together (with the business analysts providing support and keeping an eye on the project's scope) to flesh out the detail only when it is needed and is going to be developed. Detail at the level of user stories (discussed earlier) is appropriate for this type of development.

So elicitation of requirements is still required, but not to the same level of detail in the early stages as with linear approaches.

## REQUIREMENTS ENGINEERING AND OFF-THE-SHELF SOLUTIONS

Where the project sponsor has expressed a preference for an off-the-shelf solution to the business need, this also necessitates some changes to the requirements process. This time, all the elements of the requirements engineering framework are required, but the business analysts must take special care to make sure that the requirements document **what** the users want the system to do and do not unduly constrain **how** it is to work. Inevitably, when a package is used, some compromise will be required between what the users would ideally like and what can practically be delivered within the limitations of the packages available. If the users insist too much on the system working in a particular way, extensive customisation of the package may be required, which would negate the main benefits (faster speed of implementation and lower cost) offered by an off-the-shelf solution.

## REFERENCES

Cadle, J., Paul, D. and Turner, P. (2014) *Business analysis techniques: 99 essential tools for success* (2nd edition). BCS, Swindon.

International Institute of Business Analysis (2009) *A Guide to the business analysis body of knowledge*® (BABOK® Guide) (Version 2.0). IIBA®, Toronto.

Robertson, S. and Robertson, J. (2012) *Mastering the requirements process: Getting Requirements Right* (3rd edition). Addison Wesley, London.

## FURTHER READING

Kotonya, G. and Sommerville, I. (1998) *Requirements engineering: processes and techniques*. John Wiley and Sons, Chichester.

# 6 PROGRAMMING AND DEVELOPMENT APPROACHES

## Peter Thompson

**CONTENTS OF THIS CHAPTER**

This chapter covers the following topics:

- approaches to development introduced;
- build or buy – bespoke development versus commercial, off-the-shelf (COTS);
- component-based development;
- development methodologies;
- software engineering paradigms;
- the influence of technological advances;
- references and further reading.

**APPROACHES TO DEVELOPMENT**

Using the term 'systems development' today seems somewhat limiting because, in practice, very few systems are actually developed from the ground up. Perhaps a better term would be 'systems assembly' (akin to car assembly, as distinct from car manufacture), or maybe even 'solution development'. The issue here is that the term 'development' suggests creating something from scratch whereas, in practice, development teams are often merely assembling a series of ready-made components to form a solution to meet a particular set of requirements.

In fact, even this definition is not as clear-cut as it may suggest, because it may involve the development of bespoke elements that act as the glue to bind the ready-made components together. Figure 6.1 summarises some of the key elements that make up a particular information system solution. We shall explore each of these as we progress through this chapter.

To provide a reasonably thorough coverage of development approaches in the twenty-first century, it is necessary to consider aspects of methodology, technology, software engineering, procurement and management.

**Figure 6.1  Development approaches: schematic overview**

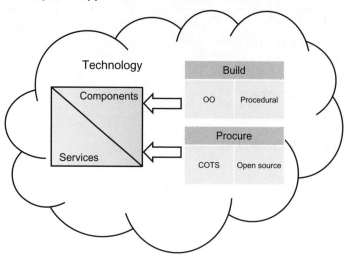

**Methodology**

Methodologies define repeatable processes. A systems development methodology also defines a set of deliverables to be produced at various stages of the process, the roles and responsibilities of people who participate in the process and, often, the techniques that can be used at various stages of the process.

**Technology**

The approach taken to developing a computer system cannot be completely divorced from the technology used within the solution. Some approaches are only possible as a result of specific enabling technologies; for instance cloud-based solutions.

**Software engineering**

A useful definition of software engineering is:

'the application of a systematic, disciplined, quantifiable approach to the development, operation, and maintenance of software.'
(IEEE *Standard Glossary of Software Engineering Terminology*, IEEE std 610.12 – 1990).

Since the inception of the concept of software engineering, a number of software engineering paradigms[1] have emerged, most notably the object-oriented paradigm, covered in more detail in Chapter 8.

---

[1]  Paradigm: a world view underlying the theories and methodology of a particular scientific subject.

**Procurement**    In the context of systems development, procurement refers to the process of evaluation, selection, negotiation and purchase of a software solution or set of services that make up the solution, or a part of it.

**Management**    Management incorporates the planning, monitoring and controlling of an activity or process. A key element of management is also governance, which, in the context of IT has been defined as:

> 'the theory that enables an organisation's principal decision makers to make better decisions around IT and, at the same time, provides guidance for IT managers who are tasked with IT operations and the design, development and implementation of IT solutions.'
> (*Governance of IT: An executive guide to ISO/IEC 38500*).

## BUILD OR BUY?

For many systems development projects, perhaps the most fundamental decision to make early on in the project is whether to procure a ready-made solution or to build a bespoke (tailor-made) solution. Some organisations have policies that state that they will always procure an off-the-shelf solution unless one cannot be found. So it seems that the old saying 'don't re-invent the wheel' is firmly in the minds of the decision makers when choosing whether to build or buy.

Realistically however, the decision to build or buy is dependent on the nature of the project being undertaken and, therefore, the type of system being sought. Hence, the decision on which approach to take will often not be made until the system requirements have been defined and agreed. Furthermore, a particular solution to a business need may be delivered through a combination of bespoke-developed and ready-made components, which we shall consider later in this chapter.

### Bespoke

At one time, in the not-too-distant past, bespoke systems development was the only option available to organisations wishing to adopt computer technology. If an organisation wanted to automate part (or all) of a business process, to make the process more efficient and reduce costs, then they would need to define a set of requirements and commission a developer to build the system. Many organisations had dedicated teams of systems developers who existed to build bespoke solutions to meet the precise computing needs of their organisations.

In more recent times, it seems that only the largest and most wealthy of organisations have the luxury of dedicated in-house development teams, and even those organisations often outsource the development work to a third-party organisation.

With the bespoke development approach, a 'tailor-made' solution is designed and developed to precisely meet a set of agreed requirements. Acceptance of the final solution is dependent on the solution exactly meeting these agreed requirements.

A number of methodologies have been established to formalise the approach to building bespoke systems. We shall consider these later in this chapter.

## Ready-made

Partly due to economies of scale, and partly due to a desire to minimise costs and time to benefits realisation, more and more organisations seek ready-made solutions to meet their computing needs. There are some very compelling arguments in favour of procuring a ready-made solution, but there are also potential risks and downsides.

There are two broad approaches to procuring a ready-made solution: purchase a commercial off-the-shelf (COTS) solution or obtain an open source solution. We shall consider each of these approaches in turn.

### COTS

In the context of computer systems, COTS software products are ready-made software packages that are purchased, leased or licensed, off-the-shelf, by an acquirer who had no influence on its features and other qualities.

According to ISO/IEC 25051, COTS products...

> 'include but are not limited to text processors, spreadsheets, database control software, graphics packages, software for technical, scientific or real-time embedded functions such as real-time operating systems or local area networks for aviation/communication, automated teller machines, money conversion, human resource management software, sales management, and web software such as generators of web sites/pages.'

The ISO definition embraces generalised software (such as spreadsheets and text processors) as well as software for specific application areas (human resource management, finance, supply chain management, and so on). However, for the purpose of this chapter, we shall focus on the latter group.

The procurement and implementation of a COTS solution has many advantages, such as speed of system delivery and cost. However, there are disadvantages, such as the lack of ownership of the software. Before pursuing this approach, it is important to consider both the pros and cons. A recognition of the disadvantages of this approach helps identify risks that need to be addressed throughout the solution development process. The key advantages and disadvantages of the COTS approach are identified in Figure 6.2.

**Figure 6.2  Advantages and disadvantages of the COTS approach**

| Advantages | Disadvantages |
|---|---|
| Cost | Not 100% fit to requirements |
| Time | Ownership issues |
| Quality | Financial stability of the vendor |
| Documentation & training | Lack of competitive advantage |
| Maintenance & enhancement | Limited legal redress |
| Try before you buy | Changing nature of requirements |

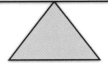

Advantages                                                      Disadvantages

*Advantages*

**Cost**
The procurement of a COTS solution is usually cheaper than developing a bespoke alternative. The reason for this is that significant development costs (detailed design, coding, unit testing and preparation of documentation) have effectively been spread across a large customer base by the vendor and are recouped through ongoing licence fees. Cost is usually an important factor in deciding to pursue the COTS approach. However, some purchasers do not take into account the ongoing costs associated with this approach, such as year-on-year licence renewal fees.

**Time**
By time, we mean the elapsed time between signing contracts and 'live' operational use of the new solution, although, from a business perspective, this could also be viewed as time to benefits realisation. Again, this is due to the fact that a significant part of the development activities (identified above) are avoided. These parts of the development lifecycle are very time-consuming and during this period requirements may change, so complicating the process even further. However, additional activities need to be factored into the project plan, including configuration of the new solution and integration with existing systems. Furthermore, as a consequence of the fact that a COTS solution will never realise one hundred per cent of the solution requirements (see disadvantages below), the adoption of a COTS solution also necessitates the development of manual process workarounds or even bespoke 'add-ons' to plug the gap.

**Quality**
Generally speaking, the quality of a COTS solution is very high. COTS vendors cannot afford to release a poor quality product, as this may lead to significant support and maintenance costs that cannot be recouped. Even worse, a poor quality product may have a damaging effect on the vendor's reputation, leading

to loss of future sales. Another factor leading to the high quality of a product is that it is likely to have been tried and tested by a large number of users within a range of different customer organisations.

**Documentation and training**

All products are supplied with some level of support and documentation, and this is no different with software products. With COTS software products, the documents (such as user manuals and online help systems) are usually of high quality because they represent an important part of the selling process; prospective customers may ask to review the quality of the supporting documentation as part of the evaluation of competing products. In contrast, the documentation supporting bespoke systems is not available until very late in the lifecycle, and even then there may be insufficient resources available to do the task of documentation justice.

Similarly with training, economies of scale allow the software vendors to produce and provide high quality training courses, supported by professional trainers. Furthermore, prospective purchasers can attend a training course prior to buying the product and evaluate the suitability of the training available.

**Maintenance and enhancement**

Software products are usually supported by a formal maintenance agreement that provides:

- access to telephone and/or email support, where experts can provide guidance and resolve common user problems;
- periodic upgrades to the software that correct known faults and also include new functionality defined and agreed with the user community.

The cost of support and enhancements is again spread across a number of users and so can be offered relatively economically to each individual customer. The availability of upgrades as part of the 'package' is particularly significant to customers of accounts and payroll packages, as these upgrades are essential to maintain compliance with legislative changes made by government.

**Try before you buy**

The ability to evaluate the software product before purchasing it (using a trial version or a more formal evaluation using the target hardware and software environment) is a major advantage over the bespoke approach, where it is not possible to evaluate the complete product until almost the end of the project. Such product evaluations can also be supplemented by visits to actual users (called reference sites), where the operation of the package can be observed and user comments and experiences documented.

It must be recognised, however, that the ability to 'try before you buy' places the onus on the user to ensure that the product will support their requirements, and not the supplier to warrant this.

*Disadvantages*
**Not 100% fit to requirements**

As a result of COTS solutions being ready-made, it is impossible for the vendor to be able to predict the requirements of all potential customers. Consequently, a COTS solution will never support all of the specific requirements for a given customer. Hence, when pursuing the COTS approach, the customer's definition of quality must be 'fitness for purpose' rather than 'one hundred per cent fit to requirements', and, in practice, this means that the customer must identify the gap between their requirements and the COTS product and determine how best to address it. This may be achieved in a number of ways:

- put in place manual workarounds for the areas of functionality not addressed by the product;
- build bespoke 'add-on' components/programs that interface with the product to provide the missing functionality;
- tailor the product to incorporate the missing functionality;
- change the way that the customer's business process works to reflect the functionality provided by the product.

All of these involve compromise, which is a key element of the COTS approach, when compared to a bespoke development, which can fit one hundred per cent of the requirements.

Although common, tailoring the product is perhaps the most risky approach, because this often means that the resultant product no longer provides the benefits of the COTS approach, nor those of the bespoke approach. This is especially the case when the vendor no longer provides support and maintenance for the modified product in the same way as it does for its standard ('vanilla') product, and hence, ongoing support and maintenance costs increase significantly. Furthermore, tailoring of the 'vanilla' product can lead to disagreements over the ownership of the modifications made.

**Ownership issues**

With a bespoke system, if the system is developed by an in-house development team, then the ownership of the software clearly resides with the customer organisation. Even when the customer commissions a third party to build the software on their behalf, the ownership generally resides with the customer and not the third-party developer.

With a COTS product, the ownership of the software usually remains with the vendor, and customers are **licensed to use** the product under the terms of a licence agreement, which, generally does not grant them any rights of access to the product source code. This ownership issue has a number of implications:

- The vendor, not the customer, decides the future of the package, both in terms of any future development work (and hence, new product features).

- The vendor may decide to withdraw support from earlier versions of the product, which may force customers into unnecessary (for them) and potentially expensive upgrades.

- The vendor may completely change the basis of the licence, leading to significant, unforeseen cost increases for customers.

- The vendor may decide to sell their product to a third party, which may unnerve or inconvenience customers, possibly causing them to make plans to move their systems to a rival product.

These ownership issues represent risks to the customer, who must consider the impacts of these risks and look at possible avoidance and mitigation (impact reduction) actions before procuring the COTS solution.

**Financial stability of the vendor**

The financial stability of the vendor is another key risk of the COTS approach, and is closely related to the issue of ownership. If the vendor ceases to trade, typically as a result of financial instability, then the customer is left without the ongoing support and maintenance that the vendor provides. This is further complicated by the fact that the customer does not have access to the product source code, which would enable them to support and maintain the product in-house (if the customer has an in-house development team) or find an alternative vendor willing to take on the support and maintenance. A common approach to mitigating this risk is to enact an escrow[2] agreement during the procurement of the COTS product.

**Lack of competitive advantage**

A COTS product can never truly be used to provide the customer organisation with a competitive advantage over other organisations in the same marketplace, because these competitors can also buy the same product. Consequently,

---

[2] An escrow agreement is between three organisations: the customer, the vendor and a third party (often the National Computing Centre), who holds a copy of the source code for the product. The agreement grants permission to the third party to make available the source code to the customer in the event that the vendor ceases trading.

COTS solutions are generally used for automating the non-niche business processes, such as HR, payroll, finance, supply-chain management, and so on.

**Limited legal redress**   With a COTS product, the ability to resolve issues relating to the failure of the product to fulfil the customer's requirements is limited, because the product is essentially 'bought as seen', and the onus is on the customer to confirm that the product meets their requirements before purchase. Furthermore, the license agreement is defined in favour of the vendor, and there is usually a clause that states that the package may not support the functional requirements of the customer – and it is the customer's responsibility to ensure that it does. There is also a limit in terms of the vendor's liability, which is explicitly defined within the license agreement.

**Changing nature of requirements**   The selection of a COTS product is obviously based on the customer's requirements **at that point in time**, which will have been defined by the relevant stakeholders **at that time**. However, stakeholders change and so do system requirements, and there is no guarantee that the COTS product will change in accordance with the customer's changing requirements.

### *Open source*

An alternative to the COTS approach, that promises to provide a 'best of both worlds' option, is open source software. With this option, the customer obtains a ready-made solution but also gains access to the source code to enable in-house or third-party developers to tailor the solution to meet the precise needs of the customer. Furthermore, open source software is available at zero cost to the customer. It is, however, still subject to the terms of a license agreement, but this agreement is much more flexible than its commercial (COTS) equivalents.

The principles behind the open source movement are:

- The end-product (and source materials) are available to the public at no cost.

- Independent developers can gain access to the product's source code to maintain and support the application within their own organisation.

- The source code is made available under a software license that meets the Open Source Definition or similar criteria.[3]

- Anyone with the necessary skills and tools can change, improve and redistribute the software free of license fees.

- Open source software is typically developed and maintained collaboratively in the public domain, rather than being a product that is developed by a single software house.

---

[3] One popular set of open source licenses are those approved by the Open Source Initiative (OSI) based on their Open Source Definition (OSD), although other initiatives also exist.

The open source option clearly offers a number of benefits: zero license costs (although this doesn't mean a zero cost solution) and the provision of a ready-made solution that can also be tailored and maintained as necessary to suit the customer organisation.

However, open source solutions still carry risks for the customer. For example, the customer takes full responsibility for ensuring that the solution meets their needs, and for having the available resources for the ongoing support and maintenance of the solution. Some open source products are maintained and supported through public collaboration and, thus, bug fixes and enhancements are also made available to the customer free of charge. However, because public collaboration is a voluntary activity, there can be a question mark over the quality of these products and the availability of support and ongoing maintenance, unless the customer has their own in-house resources who can undertake this work.

Furthermore, if the customer modifies the software, then they are in a similar position to a COTS solution that has been tailored and the 'vanilla' product is then enhanced; the open source solution could be enhanced and if the customer wants to take advantage of the recent enhancements, they may be forced to make their own modifications again!

As the open source software marketplace is maturing, a number of commercial organisations have been established to provide tailoring, support and maintenance activities based around the open source product. This can mitigate the risks associated with the public collaborative development of the solution, whilst maintaining the benefits of a ready- (or near ready-) made solution with zero license costs.

The advent of open source software has also encouraged large software corporations, such as Microsoft™, to offer what they call 'shared source' software. Microsoft's Shared Source Initiative was launched in May 2001 and includes a spectrum of technologies and licenses. Most of its source code offerings are available for download after eligibility criteria are met. The licenses associated with the offerings range from being closed-source (allowing only viewing of the code for reference), to allowing it to be modified and redistributed for both commercial and non-commercial purposes.

## COMPONENT-BASED DEVELOPMENT

Earlier, we explored bespoke and ready-made as two separate approaches to developing and delivering an information system solution to meet a particular business need. However, in practice, modern information systems comprise a series of separate, but integrated, building blocks referred to as components.

A useful working definition of a software component is as follows:

> A component is something that can be deployed as a black box. It has an external specification, which is independent of its internal mechanisms.

With component-based development, software applications are assembled from components from a variety of sources; the components themselves may be written in several different programming languages and run on several different platforms.

What is common to most definitions of a software component is the notion that a component has an inside and an outside, and there is a relationship between the two. The inside of a software component is a discrete piece of software satisfying certain properties. It is a device, artefact or asset that can be managed to achieve reuse. The outside of a software component is an interface that exposes a set of services (that the component provides) to other components.

Components can exist independently of each other but can also be assembled together to build new solutions; they provide services to other components and use services provided by other components, as shown in the UML component diagram in Figure 6.3.

**Figure 6.3 Integrated components forming a Sales order processing solution**

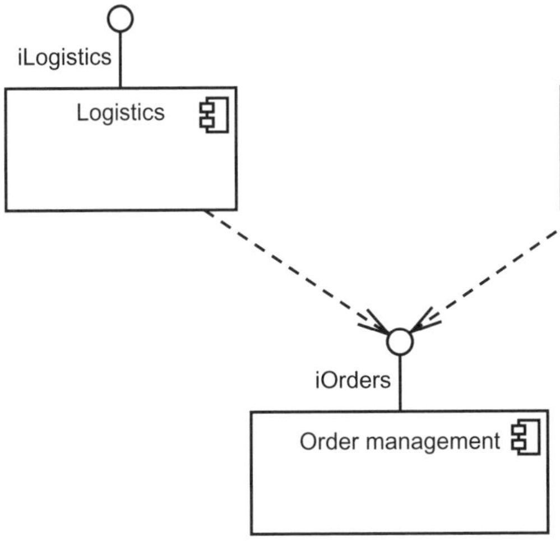

Figure 6.3 shows three independent components: **Logistics, Accounts** and **OrderManagement**. The **Logistics** component exposes an interface called **iLogistics**, that can be used by other components to consume the services that it provides. Similarly, the **Accounts** component exposes an interface called **iAccounts** and the **OrderManagement** component exposes an interface called **iOrders**. Furthermore, Figure 6.3 shows that the **Logistics** and **Accounts** components are both using services provided by the **OrderManagement** component, by virtue of the fact that they have dependences on the **iOrders** interface (shown as dashed arrows).

Figure 6.4 shows the definition of the **iOrders** interface using UML class diagram notation.

**Figure 6.4 Definition of the *iOrders* interface**

| «interface» iOrders |
|---|
| +   getOrderDetails(orderNo) :xml<br>+   checkOrderStatus(orderNo)  :char<br>+   pickOrder(orderNo, pickDate) :void<br>+   despatchOrder(orderNo, despatchDate) :void<br>+   confirmDelivery(orderNo, deliveryDate) :void<br>+   cancelOrder(orderNo, dateCancelled) :boolean |

The interface in Figure 6.4 shows the discrete services (such as **getOrderDetails**) that can be invoked by other components, along with a detailed definition of the message format that must be used to invoke each service and any return values provided by the **OrderManagement** component. If we consider the example of **getOrderDetails**, we can see that any component invoking that service must provide the order number to uniquely identify the order that they require the details for, and, in turn, the **OrderManagement** component will return an XML data structure containing the required details.

Components exist at different levels of granularity. Some are defined at a very low level and are seen as a basis for extensive reuse across a wide range of systems development projects (for example, software houses establish an extensive internal inventory of documented and tested components that developers use to create their applications from), whilst others are complete encapsulated applications in their own right that can be integrated with other application-level components to form a much broader scope solution.

As granularity increases, it is likely that components will be purchased externally and implemented into the application software. External purchase of components requires a clear understanding of the service that the component provides and the interface it requires. Small, low-level components may also be purchased and these find their way into many applications. Furthermore, some components are 'open source' and may be modified to suit local circumstances, whilst others are closed and the program code inside the component is not accessible or visible to the systems developer. In fact, entire COTS products could be treated as components within the context of a broader, multi-application solution.

Figure 6.5 shows a UML deployment diagram that highlights how a series of discrete components can be assembled to form a solution.

**Figure 6.5  UML deployment diagram showing a component-based solution**

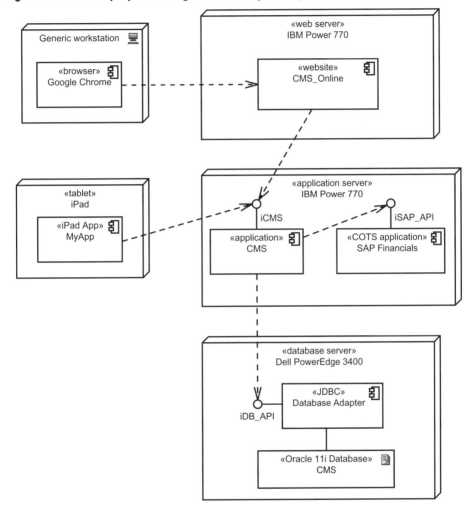

In Figure 6.5 the three-dimensional cubes represent Nodes in UML, which equate to devices within the solution infrastructure. UML stereotypes are used to further clarify the roles of each device (<<tablet>>, <<web server>>, <<application server>>, <<database server>>) and also the different types of component or technology used (<<browser>>, <<iPad App>>, <<website>>, <<application>>, <<COTS application>>, <<Oracle 11i Database>>, <<JDBC>>).

A more detailed explanation of component-based system design is provided in Chapter 8.

## DEVELOPMENT METHODOLOGIES

A software (or system) development methodology (SDM) is a framework that is used to structure, plan, and control the process of developing an information system. The idea of software development methodology frameworks first emerged in the 1960s.

While some methodologies prescribe specific software development tools, such as Integrated Development Environments (IDEs) or Computer Aided Software Engineering (CASE) tools, the main idea behind the SDM is to pursue the development of information systems in a structured and methodical way from inception of the idea to delivery of the final system, within the context of the framework being applied.

The framework within which systems development takes place is determined by the systems development lifecycle (SDLC) model used. In Chapter 2, we introduced four basic models:

- Waterfall
- 'V' model
- Incremental
- Iterative

However, systems development projects also comprise a number of other elements, as shown in Figure 6.6.

**Figure 6.6 Elements of a systems development methodology**

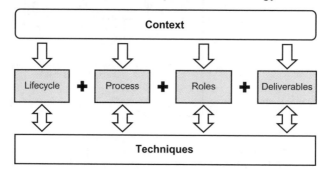

Context          The approach taken to systems development has to be context sensitive, and the context in this case is the business and project environment within which the development takes place, which includes (amongst others):

- the business strategy and drivers for undertaking the development;
- the key stakeholders involved;

- the organisational culture;
- existing hardware and software constraints;
- architectural standards and principles;
- the legislative and regulatory framework that the organisation must operate within;
- resource and skills availability;
- time and budget constraints.

The context influences the other key elements: lifecycle, process, roles and deliverables.

**Lifecycle**

The lifecycle model provides a framework (in terms of a series of either linear or Iterative stages) within which the activities are conducted in order to deliver the required outcome.

**Process**

The process provides a definition/description of the flow of work that must take place in terms of a series of activities, and who undertakes each activity. In this sense, processes provide a more detailed breakdown of what should happen during each stage of the lifecycle. For example, during the analysis stage of the Waterfall and 'V' model SDLCs, requirements engineering defines a process for eliciting, analysing and validating a set of good quality requirements.

Note: The term 'system development process' is sometimes used more loosely to refer to a methodology that encompasses all of the elements in Figure 6.6.

**Roles**

The roles define a set of responsibilities that need to be assigned to individuals or groups of individuals in order for systems development to be successfully completed. Generic roles related to systems development are discussed in Chapters 1 and 5 but some systems development methods define their own specific roles.

**Deliverables**

The deliverables from a systems development project comprise a series of artefacts that are produced during various activities that take place within systems development processes. Some artefacts are merely enablers of the process – such as a meeting report following a fact-finding interview – whilst others form the basis of project governance, whereby their approval and sign-off are required before progress can move on to the next stage – such as a requirements document signed-off by the project sponsor.

**Techniques**     A technique is essentially a way of completing a task; for instance, the MoSCoW prioritisation technique discussed in Chapter 5 provides a way of completing the prioritisation of requirements. Or it can be a systematic method to obtain information; for instance, prototyping provides a method to obtain feedback regarding the functionality and usability aspects of a system design. The variety of techniques deployed within systems development is therefore diverse.

Lifecycles, roles, deliverables and techniques are all covered elsewhere in this book, so we shall focus here on the process aspect of a systems development approach.

Systems development processes broadly fall in to one of two categories: 'defined' or 'empirical'. We shall now compare each of these types of processes in turn.

## Defined processes

A defined process is one that is based upon the defined process control and management model. This model is extensively used in manufacturing industries; it has been adopted for use with software development, which is thus treated as a manufacturing discipline, where the product is software.

The premise behind a defined process is that each piece of work can be completely understood and that, given a well-defined set of inputs, the same outputs are generated every time. Management and control arise from the predictability of defined processes, and, since the processes are defined, they can be grouped together and expected to continue to operate predictably and repeatably. Hence, when applied to systems development, approaches based on defined processes work on the premise that it is possible and desirable to define a set of simple, repeatable development processes, with associated techniques, in order to ensure a predictable outcome from systems development projects. The approach (or methodology) revolves around a knowledge base of processes and techniques, and the dependencies between elements in the knowledge base form defined project templates, each tailored to meet the needs of specific types of project (such as online transaction processing, batch processing, web development, and so on). In theory, processes defined with sufficient accuracy, granularity and precision can ensure predictability of outcome.

A typical defined approach to systems development is explained succinctly by Ken Schwaber:

> 'A project manager starts a project by selecting and customising the appropriate project template. The template consists of those processes appropriate for the work that is planned. He or she then estimates the work and assigns the work to team members. The resultant project plan shows all the work to be done, who is to do each piece of work, what the dependencies are, and the process instructions for converting the inputs to the outputs... Having a project plan like this gives the project manager a reassuring sense of being in control. He or she feels that they understand the work that is required to successfully complete the project. Everyone will do what the methodology and project plan says, and the project will be successfully completed.'
>
> (Schwaber and Beedle 2001)

Systems development approaches based upon defined processes are often criticised because they lead to increased levels of documentation and bureaucracy. In inexperienced or ill-informed hands, the use of such methods can lead to the adoption of a 'cookbook' approach, whereby the various steps and activities of the method are followed blindly without considering the reasons why they should be carried out, often with disastrous consequences.

A number of so-called defined (also referred to as procedural) systems development methodologies and frameworks have sprung up over the years and the more common of these are listed in Table 6.1, along with some of their defining features.

**Table 6.1  Common defined (procedural) methodologies and frameworks**

| Methodology/ framework | Category/defining features |
|---|---|
| **SSADM (Structured Systems Analysis and Design Method)** | Document-led approach to the analysis and design of information systems, based around the Waterfall SDLC. Produced for the Central Computer and Telecommunications Agency (now Office of Government Commerce), a UK government office concerned with the use of technology in government, from 1980 onwards. Builds on SSM, Structured Analysis, Structured Design, Yourdon and JSP (see below). See also 'Structured Methods' below. |
| **Structured Analysis** | Devised by Tom DeMarco. See 'Structured Methods' below. |
| **Structured Design** | Devised by Larry Constantine, Ed Yourdon and Wayne Stevens. See 'Structured Methods' below. |
| **Yourdon Structured Method** | Devised by Ed Yourdon. See 'Structured Methods' below. |
| **Information Engineering** | Devised by James Martin. See 'Structured Methods' below. |
| **Structured Analysis and Design Technique (SADT)** | Devised by Douglas T. Ross. See 'Structured Methods' below. |
| **SSM (Soft Systems Methodology)** | Devised by Peter Checkland and his colleagues at Lancaster University, this, approach is not specific to developing computer systems, but provides a framework within which problematic business situations can be resolved by computer systems. It should be noted that the resolution of the problem does not necessarily need to involve technology. |

*(Continued)*

**Table 6.1 (Continued)**

| Methodology/ framework | Category/defining features |
| --- | --- |
| **Structured Programming** | Devised by Edsger Dijkstra. See 'Structured methods' below. Also covered later under software engineering paradigms. |
| **Jackson Structured Programming (JSP)** | Devised by Michael A. Jackson. See also 'Structured Programming' and 'Structured Methods'. |
| **IDEF0** | Based on SADT (see above). |
| **Structured Methods** | Structured methods refers to a collection of analysis, design, and programming techniques that were developed in response to the problems facing the software world from the 1960s to the 1980s: <br><br> • there was little guidance on 'good' design and programming techniques; <br><br> • there were no standard techniques for documenting requirements and designs; <br><br> • systems were getting larger and more complex; <br><br> • information system development was becoming harder and harder to do. <br><br> So, as a way to help manage large and complex software, a number of so-called 'structured methods' emerged, including those identified above. These techniques were characterised by their use of diagrams to aid communication between users and developers and to impose more discipline around the work of analysts and designers. |
| **Unified Process** | Flexible process for systems development (can also be used in an iterative and incremental way) based around UML. Originally devised by Rational Software Corp. (now part of IBM) as Rational Unified Process. |

## Empirical processes

The problem with applying defined processes to the discipline of systems development is that defined processes are based on the premise that the product being built is always the same and, hence, the process is predictable and repeatable. However, systems development does not meet these criteria. In fact, systems development more closely resembles research and development of new products, which is more of an empirical process. Hence, the recent trend towards 'Agile' development, which is based upon an empirical process model.

One of the first major approaches to systems development that used a more empirical approach was Rapid Application Development (RAD). The term Rapid Application Development (RAD) was first used during the mid 1970s to describe a software development process developed by the New York Telephone Company's Systems Development Center. The approach, which involved iterative development and the construction of prototypes, became more widely adopted with the publication of James Martin's book of the same name in 1991.

More recently, the term 'RAD' has been used somewhat less and the alternative 'Agile' has gained currency. Agile development was established when 17 independent thinkers about software development met at The Lodge at Snowbird ski resort in the Wasatch mountains of Utah on 11–13 February 2001. The result of this gathering was the creation of a Manifesto for Agile development, discussed in Chapter 2 but repeated here:

> We are uncovering better ways of developing
> software by doing it and helping others do it.
> Through this work we have come to value:
>
> **Individuals and interactions** over **processes and tools**
> **Working software** over **comprehensive documentation**
> **Customer collaboration** over **contract negotiation**
> **Responding to change** over **following a plan**
>
> That is, while there is value in the items on
> the right, we value the items on the left more.

The group named themselves the 'Agile Alliance' and included representatives from Extreme Programming (Kent Beck), Scrum (Ken Schwaber), DSDM (Arie van Bennekum), Adaptive Software Development (Jim Highsmith), Crystal Clear (Alistair Cockburn), Feature-Driven Development, Pragmatic Programming (Andrew Hunt), and others sympathetic to the need for an alternative to documentation-driven, heavyweight software development processes.

In addition to the manifesto, the group formulated a set of 12 underlying principles, as follows:

- Our highest priority is to satisfy the customer through early and continuous delivery of valuable software.
- Welcome changing requirements, even late in development. Agile processes harness change for the customer's competitive advantage.

- Deliver working software frequently, from a couple of weeks to a couple of months, with a preference to the shorter timescale.

- Business people and developers must work together daily throughout the project.

- Build projects around motivated individuals. Give them the environment and support they need, and trust them to get the job done.

- The most efficient and effective method of conveying information to and within a development team is face-to-face conversation.

- Working software is the primary measure of progress.

- Agile processes promote sustainable development. The sponsors, developers and users should be able to maintain a constant pace indefinitely.

- Continuous attention to technical excellence and good design enhances agility.

- Simplicity – the art of maximising the amount of work not done – is essential.

- The best architectures, requirements, and designs emerge from self-organising teams.

- At regular intervals, the team reflects on how to become more effective, then tunes and adjusts its behaviour accordingly.

Agile systems development is an evolutionary approach based around an iterative SDLC with rapid, incremental delivery (whereby each release of production-ready software builds upon the functionality delivered in the previous release).

Agile approaches also demonstrate the following characteristics:

**Exploratory**            Requirements evolve in parallel with the solution.

**Collaborative**          System users, analysts, designers, developers and testers work together to define, build and review evolutionary prototypes, which evolve into production-ready software.

**Focus on working software**          The approach is based on an understanding that documentation is important when it adds value to the quality of the software, but more emphasis should be given to the development and refinement of working software, which is more accessible to the end user.

**Flexible**               The project team focuses on the business need at all times, which may change as the project progresses.

Several discrete Agile development methodologies and frameworks have evolved in recent years (although some were in existence before the Agile Manifesto was devised, and have since been absorbed into the general category of Agile approaches). The most common are listed and summarised in Table 6.2.

**Table 6.2 Common Agile methodologies and frameworks**

| Methodology/ framework | Category/defining features |
| --- | --- |
| Extreme programming (XP) | Exploratory/empirical; iterative; frequent, incremental delivery; pair programming; test-first development. |
| DSDM | Exploratory/empirical; iterative; frequent, incremental delivery. Fully formed methodology including role, technique and deliverable definitions. |
| Scrum | Exploratory/empirical; iterative; frequent, incremental delivery; lightweight framework. No definition of how to conduct the work required within an iteration (Sprint). |
| Adaptive software development | Evolved from Rapid Application Development work by Jim Highsmith and Sam Bayer. Exploratory/empirical (based on continuous adaptation of the process to the work at hand); iterative (series of speculate, elaborate and learn cycles); frequent, incremental delivery; feature-based. |
| Crystal clear | Exploratory/empirical; iterative; frequent, incremental delivery; lightweight framework; focuses on people not processes or artefacts; reflective improvement; encourages osmotic communication[4] with small teams (6–8) of co-located developers. |
| Lean systems development | Exploratory/empirical; iterative; frequent, incremental delivery; based on Toyota manufacturing principles. |
| Test-driven development | Approach to development where developers write test cases before commencing coding and, using short development cycles and automated testing tools, iteratively write and refactor code until it passes the test cases. Related to test-first concept within XP but is also used in its own right. |
| Feature-driven development | Iterative; frequent, incremental delivery; model-driven. Based around the concept of a feature (a client-valued unit of functionality), similarly to Scrum, but with its own five-stage process, whereas Scrum has no process associated with how a feature (product backlog item) is to be developed. |
| Kanban | Based on Toyota manufacturing principles, Kanban is a method for managing knowledge work with an emphasis on just in time delivery, while not overloading the team members. Often combined with other approaches, such as Scrum. |

*(Continued)*

---

[4] Osmotic communication: gradual or unconscious assimilation of ideas and knowledge achieved by a group of individuals working in close proximity.

**Table 6.2 (Continued)**

| Methodology/ framework | Category/defining features |
|---|---|
| Agile unified process | Exploratory/empirical; iterative; frequent, incremental delivery. Agile adaption of Unified Process. |

## SOFTWARE ENGINEERING PARADIGMS

A number of different paradigms (world views underlying the theories and methodology of software engineering and programming) have evolved since the early 1960s, each proposing a radically different approach to building software. We shall focus on the three most prevalent paradigms that underpin modern software development.

### Structured programming

Structured programming (SP) emerged in the 1960s from work by Boehm and Jacopini and a famous letter, 'Go to statement considered harmful', from Edsger Dijkstra in 1968. The principles behind structured programming were reinforced by the 'structured program theorem', and the emergence of languages such as ALGOL, which provided the necessary control structures to practically implement the concept.

SP is aimed at improving the clarity and quality of a computer program, whilst simultaneously reducing the amount of time needed to develop it. This is achieved by making use of three basic programming constructs: **sequence** (block structures and subroutines), **selection** (conditional execution of statements using keywords such as `if..then..else..endif`, `switch`, or `case`), and **iteration** (repetition of a group of statements using keywords such as `while`, `repeat`, `for` or `do..until`), in contrast to using simple tests and jumps such as the `goto` statement, which could lead to 'spaghetti code' which is both difficult to follow and to maintain. Additionally, there are recommended best practices such as ensuring that each construct has only one entry and one exit point.

Michael A. Jackson devised a variation to the original SP called **Jackson Structured Programming** (JSP), that became widely adopted by mainframe development teams for the design of COBOL programs, although it is by no means limited to this environment. JSP used structure charts with specific notation for sequence, selection and iteration constructs, and one of the key rules was that no two types of construct could be mixed at the same level.

The basic principles behind SP are still applied during systems design in the form of modular design and its associated principles of coupling and cohesion, which is covered in more detail in Chapter 8.

## Object-oriented development

Object-oriented development (OOD) is a programming paradigm based around the concept of an object and the fact that objects can collaborate directly with each other in order to realise required system functionality.

In software terms, an object is a discrete package of functions and procedures (operations), all relating to a particular real-world concept such as an order, or a physical entity such as a car. In addition to a set of operations that they can perform (behaviour), objects also have a set of properties (data items or attributes) associated with them.

Objects are classified by classes, which define the attributes and operations that a particular type of object will possess. Classes are often modelled using a class diagram, which shows the class definitions and the relationships between them.

In OOD, objects represent business entities (such as customer, order and product) as well as artefacts that make up the built system (such as windows, forms, controls and reports), and when designing and writing program code, there is less focus on discrete programs performing functions defined in a functional specification but, instead, classes are built individually and the operations of certain classes invoke the operations of other classes that provide services to them. Objects can only access other objects by sending messages to them, which, in turn, invoke one of their operations – a concept known as **encapsulation**, which is explained further in Chapter 8. Isolating objects in this way makes software easier to manage, more robust and reusable.

There is a correlation between OOD and component-based development (discussed earlier). Components interact with each other via interfaces, which expose services to other components and, similarly, objects interact with each other by sending messages that invoke their publicly visible operations.

Although it is possible to build systems in an object-oriented way using non-OO programming languages (such as COBOL, C, ALGOL, Pascal, RPG and PL1), OO programming languages (such as C++, Java, Perl, PHP, Visual Basic.NET, Visual C#.NET and Smalltalk) automatically enforce the OO principles of encapsulation, abstraction, inheritance and polymorphism, which would otherwise have to be explicitly coded by the developer.

Object-oriented systems design is covered in more detail in Chapter 8.

## Service-oriented development

The principle behind service-oriented approaches to systems development is similar to OOD in that services collaborate with each other to realise the required functionality. However, service-oriented development (SOD) does not rely on the use of objects in the same way that OOD does. In fact a service is a more abstract concept than an object in that it can effectively be implemented using any technology. Consequently, SOD is said to be 'technology agnostic'. However, in practice, the physical implementation of SOD relies on the use of certain technologies, including XML web services, HTTP (Hyper Text Transport Protocol) and SOAP (Simple Object Access Protocol), amongst others. Detailed coverage of these technologies is outside the scope of this book.

The concept behind SOD is very simple: required services are matched to available services. Required services are identified through the decomposition of high-level business processes and use cases, and available services are discovered in some form of services catalogue and invoked across a network via a services directory. Available services are invoked by the passing of messages.

If we take the example of an ecommerce website, a required service may be to take payment from the customer to confirm an order. The invoker of the service (the website) does not need to know how the service provider (in this example, a payment processing service such as PayPal) provides the service but only the nature of the service required and details of the message formats. Consequently, the consumer of the service is completely ignorant of the technologies used to implement the service, and also even where the service provider resides geographically or within the IT infrastructure.

## THE INFLUENCE OF TECHNOLOGICAL ADVANCES

Advances in technology provide opportunities for software developers that enable them to deliver significant business benefits. Sometimes these benefits manifest themselves in cheaper and quicker solution development, whilst others are more far-reaching and can actually revolutionise the provision of IT solutions for the entire IT industry. Two such technological advances are considered here.

### Cloud-based

A useful definition of cloud computing is provided courtesy of the National Institute of Standards and Technology:

> 'a model for enabling convenient, on-demand network access to a shared pool of configurable computing resources [...] that can be rapidly provisioned and released with minimal management effort or service provider interaction.'

Cloud computing consists of three separate types of service:

- **Software as a service (SaaS)** – the provision of applications in the cloud.
- **Platform as a service (PaaS)** – the provision of services that enable the customer to deploy applications in the cloud using tools provided by the supplier.
- **Infrastructure as a service (IaaS)** – the provision of computing power, storage and network capacity that enable the customer to run software (including operating systems and applications) in the cloud.

These three services together are referred to as the cloud computing stack and, with each of them, the services are hosted remotely and accessed over a network (usually the internet) through the customer's web browser, rather than being installed locally on a customer's computer.

#### On demand software

The cloud-based approach to application delivery provides flexibility to the customer, who can access the application from any computer connected to the internet (whether desktop PC or mobile device); it provides a multitude of IT services rather than being limited to using only locally-installed software and being dependent on the storage capacity of the customer's local computer network. For organisations large and small, this offers a scalable IT resource without the complexity of managing the IT infrastructure and application upgrades typical with more traditional applications.

On demand software is effectively a subset of SOD. The premise here is that software is licensed as a service on demand. The service consumer pays for the service as and when it is used rather than via a more traditional licensing arrangement.

SaaS vendors (also known as Application Service Providers (ASPs)) typically host and manage the application themselves, and their customers access the application remotely via the web. This approach to the provision of software applications provides a number of benefits:

- The solution is usually scalable as the number of users can grow with the demand for the service, without the need for the consumer to invest in additional hardware or software infrastructure.

- Lower licensing costs (typically) as the user only pays for the service that they use, as opposed to buying separate licenses for all devices that may be required to access the application.

- Low maintenance costs, as activities such as feature updating are managed from central locations rather than at each customer's site. This means that all customers gain access to the latest software version, without the need to upgrade individual client workstations, by downloading patches and installing upgrades.

- Customers access applications remotely via the web, independent of the hardware location and, hence, are not restricted to using the application from a particular workstation or geographical location.

Other benefits are similar to those associated with COTS solutions, covered earlier in this Chapter.

Perhaps one of the most widespread implementations of on demand software via SaaS is Microsoft's Office 365 offering, which has revolutionised the way organisations deploy and use generic office and team collaboration applications.

## Model Driven Architecture (MDA)

Model Driven Architecture refers to an approach to the production of executable software directly from a set of design models, without the intervention of a human programmer.

Producing program code directly from a set of design models has long been an objective for systems development tools vendors but, until recently, the supporting technology was either not up to the job or was prohibitively expensive. Furthermore, a lack of industry-wide standards led to proprietary tools that could not be interchanged and, hence, represented a huge investment and major risk for development teams.

103

With the adoption of UML as an open modelling standard by the Object Management Group (OMG) in 1997, tools vendors could focus on building MDA tools around UML. In fact, since the release of version 2.0 of UML, the OMG has focused its efforts on enhancements aimed at the use of UML with MDA tools, to enable much more precise model definitions to be produced.

Apart from the obvious benefits of reduced cost and increased speed of development, a major advantage of this approach, from the perspective of the development team, is that the model and the physical system it represents are kept synchronised. This is particularly significant when it comes to system maintenance, as a common problem encountered at that stage is out-of-date documentation. An additional benefit is that the MDA tools can potentially be used by systems analysts, who may already be producing the required models using a similar tool.

The way MDA works is summarised in Figure 6.7 below.

**Figure 6.7  The MDA process**

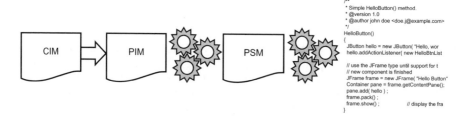

With MDA, software is produced by a specialist software tool through a series of automated transformations. Hence, in practice, MDA tools are also UML modelling tools.

The start point is an abstract computer-independent model (CIM). This is essentially a conceptual model of a business domain that captures the key requirements of a new computer system. The CIM is then used as a basis for developing a platform-independent model (PIM). The PIM is based on the main analysis models expressed using UML notation and represents the business functionality and behaviour without the constraints of technology. The PIM is then converted into a platform-specific model (PSM), which takes into account the software and hardware environment that the solution is to be implemented in. Finally, the PSM is used to generate the actual executable program code.

## REFERENCES

Boehm, C. and Jacopini, G. (1966) 'Flow diagrams, turing machines and languages with only two formation rules'. *Comm. ACM*, 9, 5, 366–371.

Holt, A. L. (2013) *Governance of IT: an executive guide to ISO/IEC 38500*. BCS, Swindon.

IEEE (1990–2002) *Standard glossary of software engineering terminology, IEEE std 610.12-1990*. IEEE Computer Society, Washington, USA.

ISO/IEC 25051:2014 (2014) *Software engineering – Systems and software Quality Requirements and Evaluation (SQuaRE) – Requirements for quality of Ready to Use Software Product (RUSP) and instructions for testing*. ISO/IEC, Geneva.

Schwaber, K. and Beedle, M. (2001) *Agile software development with Scrum*. Pearson Education, London.

The Agile Alliance (2001) 'Agile Manifesto'. The Agile Alliance. www.Agilemanifesto.org (accessed on 4 June 2014).

## FURTHER READING

Anderson, D. A. (2010) *Kanban*. Blue Hole Press, Seattle, WA.

Arlow, J. and Neustadt, I. (2004) *Enterprise patterns and MDA: building better software with archetype patterns and UML*. Pearson Education, Boston, MA.

Arlow, J. and Neustadt, I. (2005) *UML 2 and the unified process: practical object-oriented analysis and design*. Addison-Wesley, Boston, MA.

Avison, D. and Fitzgerald, G. (2006) *Information systems development: methodologies, techniques and tools* (4th edition). McGraw-Hill, Maidenhead.

BCS (2012) *Cloud computing: moving IT out of the office*. BCS, Swindon.

Beck, K. (2002) *Test driven development*. Addison-Wesley, Boston, MA.

Beck, K. and Andres, C. (2004) *Extreme programming explained: embrace change* (2nd edition). Addison-Wesley, Boston, MA.

Burgess, R. S. (1990) *Structured program design using Jackson structured programming*. Nelson Thornes Ltd, Cheltenham.

Cadle, J. and Yeates, D. (2007) *Project management for information systems* (5th edition). Prentice Hall, Harlow.

Checkland, P. and Scholes. J. (1999) *Soft systems methodology: a 30-year retrospection*. John Wiley and Sons, New York.

Cockburn, A. (2004) *Crystal clear: a human-powered methodology for small teams*. Addison-Wesley, Boston, MA.

DSDM (2012) *The DSDM Agile project framework*. DSDM Consortium, Ashford, Kent.

DeMarco, T. (1979) *Structured analysis and system specification*. Prentice-Hall, Harlow.

Erl, T. (2005) *Service-oriented architecture: concepts, technology, and design.* Pearson, Boston, MA.

Goodland, M. and Slater, C. (1995) *SSADM Version 4.* McGraw-Hill, Maidenhead.

Highsmith, J. A. III (2000) *Adaptive software development: a collaborative approach to managing complex systems.* Dorset House Publishing, New York.

Hollander, N. (2000) *A Guide to software package evaluation and selection: the R2isc method,* Amacom, USA.

Hughes, B. and Cotterell, M. (2009) *Software project management* (5th edition). McGraw-Hill, Maidenhead.

Jansen, W. and Grance, T. (2011) 'Guidelines on security and private in public cloud computing'. http://www.nist.gov/manuscript-publication-search.cfm?pub_id=909494 (accessed 15 June 2014).

Jordan, J. M. (2012) *Information, technology, and innovation: resources for growth in a connected world.* John Wiley and Sons, New York.

Linger, R. C. *et al.* (1979) *Structured programming: theory and practice.* Addison Wesley Longman Publishing Co., Boston, MA.

Martin, J. (1991) *Rapid application development.* MacMillan, New York.

Ogunnaike, B. and Harmon Ray, H. (1995) *Process dynamics, modeling, and control (topics in chemical engineering).* Oxford University Press, Oxford.

Palmer, S. R. (2002) *A practical guide to feature driven developmen.* Prentice-Hall, Harlow.

Poppendieck, M. and Poppendieck, T. (2003) *Lean software development: an Agile toolkit.* Addison-Wesley, Boston, MA.

Skidmore, S. and Eva, M. (2003) *Introducing systems development.* Palgrave Macmillan, Basingstoke.

Yourdon, E. and Constantine, L. L. (1979) *Structured design: fundamentals of a discipline of computer program and systems design.* Prentice-Hall, Harlow.

# 7   SYSTEM MODELLING TECHNIQUES

**Julian Cox**

## CONTENTS OF THIS CHAPTER

This chapter covers the following topics:

- what is modelling?
- rationale for modelling;
- the need for multiple models and views;
- commonly used modelling techniques;
- cross-referencing models and views;
- documentation and specification;
- references and further reading.

There are many modelling notations and frameworks in use and this chapter does not attempt to describe them in detail. It does, however, discuss some theoretical issues of modelling, with examples, that will allow readers to understand and assess alternative approaches with the aim of being able to select and apply models appropriate to the problem presented by the specific solution requirements.

## WHAT IS MODELLING?

A model is a representation of a subject. Typically that subject is a real-world object or system that either already exists or may exist in the future. There are also models of imagined subjects, for example a science fiction space craft being rendered in CGI for a film or to be flown by the player of a computer game; but these are not the concern of this book.

This chapter focuses on modelling systems, in particular business and IT systems that are employed by organisations to support their operating model. This loose definition of a system that focuses on more than just the IT allows for systems to exist within other systems at different levels of granularity and in different contexts.

In order to be able to describe any such system we need to understand that:

- A system has a boundary outside of which are external entities (people or other systems) that interact with the system in focus.

- Within this system are components (systems, people) that implement that system's behaviour.

- These interactions and internal system behaviours involve data being exchanged, transformed and stored.

- Any system exists within a broader context that needs to be understood and the system should be defined in terms of how it delivers functionality and services within this context, usually in the form of requirements.

Modelling is the act of producing appropriate models of these systems through the fundamental act of abstraction that allows all these issues to be examined, explored and refined prior to development of the system elements.

## Abstraction

In philosophical terminology, abstraction is the thought process wherein ideas are distanced from objects. In system modelling, abstraction is the process of removing anything unnecessary or irrelevant from a system model (or the view of that model) depending on its purpose.

Different system models tend to focus on specific facets[1] of the system, for example its functionality or implementation. A single model is therefore an incomplete abstraction of the real thing but a combination of models can between them provide a more complete description, providing they are consistent with each other.

'The model is not the reality, but the best models are the ones that stick very close to reality.' (Booch, *et al.*, 2005)

## 'All models are wrong'

Any model, as an incomplete abstraction, is therefore imperfect. As George Box, a renowned twentieth-century industrial statistician put it:

> Remember that all models are wrong; the practical question is – how wrong do they have to be to not be useful?

> (Box and Draper, 1987)

Usefulness is the key, although intangible, measure of the value of any model. Usefulness can be increased by abstracting out details irrelevant to the facet being focused on, providing that what remains in that model is effective in communicating or describing that facet to the appropriate level. What is appropriate and effective usually depends on the nature of the intended audience. A representation that works effectively for a

---

[1] The author has chosen to use the term 'facet' over the terms 'aspect', 'view' and 'perspective' in this generic context, as they all have specific meanings in this chapter and elsewhere, for example 'Aspect-Oriented Development'.

technical developer is unlikely to be equally useful for a business stakeholder and vice versa.

Probably the best known form of abstraction in system modelling is creating a Logical model of a physical system where anything to do with the 'how' (technology), 'who' (specific people or organisational units) or 'where' (location), is removed leaving a Logical model that focusses on the 'what?', 'when?', logical 'who?' and encourages consideration of the most important 'why'.

Creating a Logical model of something physical is known as idealisation; just one of a number of forms of abstraction typically used in system modelling that are explained later in the chapter. Given these different forms, there are several words used to describe the opposite of abstraction such as:

- specification;
- specialisation;
- realisation;
- reification.

In modelling, we can work in both directions; typically we abstract to understand and analyse; whereas design activities take us back towards the finished specific, physical model.

## Structure over words

The alternative to modelling, visually or otherwise, is to attempt to explain these complex systems using textual descriptions. Modelling does not need to be visual, although as the saying goes 'a picture paints a thousand words'. System modelling typically involves a combination of visual representations (diagrams) and structured textual descriptions of:

- model elements; for example, tasks in a process model, classes or entities in a data model;
- links and dependencies between elements; for example, arrows that show the sequence of tasks or lines that represent some semantic dependency between classes or entities.

### Diagrams and models

A diagram by itself is not typically the whole model; it may have insufficient detail to provide the necessary information to its intended audience. Many modelling notations and languages treat diagrams as views onto the model, where the model is a structured set of model element objects (data) that each describe a single model element, link or dependency within that system.

The underlying element objects are represented visually in diagrams and, by using appropriate tools, can be manipulated through those diagrams. For example, adding a visual element to a diagram creates a new element object in the underlying model and when its name or other characteristic is specified on the diagram, that is captured in the element object. A single element object can then be represented in a number of diagrams and changing any of its characteristics in one diagram is captured in the underlying model element, so all diagram instances of that object are automatically updated. However, each diagram may show or hide different features to create a view suitable for a particular audience. This **multiple views of the same model** principle supports the fact that different audiences find value in different abstractions. The use of such tools is described in more detail in Chapter 14.

## As-Is and To-Be

When using modelling in any form of development process, it is critical that it is clear just what needs to be developed. Often there are existing elements to the solution, some of which may remain intact, others changed and some discarded or replaced. To help understand these differences, it is useful to produce at least two versions of each model; one representing the current system and another the proposed system. The world of system modelling often refers to the 'As-Is' and 'To-Be' models; architects tend to refer to 'Baseline' and 'Target' models.

In order to compare these two temporal versions ,it is essential that equivalent views of them conform to similar standards in terms of:

- notation used;
- levels of abstraction.

Consistent views are more easily compared to identify the differences between the models that represent the development needed (gap analysis).

## Views and viewpoints

Views and viewpoints are terms used in systems and software engineering and architecture. It is sensible to employ a framework that defines a coherent set of viewpoints that define views to be used in the description and construction of a system. Viewpoints are designed to meet the concerns of a particular group of stakeholders and support the 'multiple views of the same model' principle described above.

Using this terminology, a viewpoint can be considered a template for a view; each view (for example the As-Is and To-Be views) conforms to that viewpoint template.

## The U-curve process pattern

Many early development methods such as SSADM followed a process that combines the concepts of Logical/Physical and As-Is/To-Be in a basic matrix often referred to as the U-curve (see Figure 7.1).

The basic process reflected in Figure 7.1 is:

**Figure 7.1 The U curve**

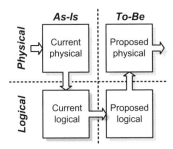

1. Document/model the current system (Physical As-Is).
2. Abstract out the physical details of the current system (Logical As-Is).
3. Incorporate the logical business requirements, including questioning the ongoing value of any existing elements and removing them if appropriate (Logical To-Be).
4. Specify and design the physical implementation details of the proposed system, which may involve a different technology set to the previous model (Physical To-Be).

In the early days of solution development, there was often little IT involved in the existing system, so jumping straight across from the Physical As-Is to the Physical To-Be risked potentially missing important new business requirements, while carrying forward redundant legacy features. This pattern is still applicable today, particularly when migrating solution components to new technologies. Ongoing maintenance activities may often skip across the physical level but doing so is not without risk.

## RATIONALE FOR MODELLING

Modelling is employed in many disciplines for many reasons, for example:

- Building architects commission three-dimensional models of new structures that allow the client to get an early vision of what the finished structure will look like.

- Engineers produce structural models that allow them to perform various calculations that validate the integrity of the structure.

- Economists produce dynamic models of the economy that allow them to run various scenarios in an attempt to predict likely outcomes.

- Formula One car designers produce scale models of body components that can be placed in wind tunnels to test their aerodynamics and to refine the shapes until the finished version is produced and used on the actual car.

One can relate each of these examples to how modelling can be employed within solution development with the ultimate aim of developing a solution which meets key stakeholder requirements; in other words a quality solution.

111

## What does modelling facilitate?

Modelling is more than simply producing a model in place of documentation to hand over as part of a process; when appropriate useful models are produced, they facilitate a range of development activities that assist the aim of developing a high-quality solution.

### Communication and understanding

At the most fundamental level, a model is not useful if it does not capture and communicate a level of understanding of the system. Such communication can occur during collaborative modelling activities, for example developing models during workshops; or through models as deliverable artefacts, for example at development stage handovers.

### Experimentation

Within modelling activities, the models can be experimented with, supporting exploration of alternative designs and different 'what-if?' scenarios – including risk assessment. The model can often act as an early prototype allowing stakeholders to review, challenge and consider. Misunderstandings and other defects revealed in the model should be corrected in the model and re-examined until correct.

### Validation

Hopefully, the outcome of the review and experimentation activities just discussed enable key stakeholders to confirm the quality of the understanding of requirements and suitability of solutions before considerable cost and effort is expended in further development.

### Gap analysis

The U-curve described earlier in this chapter, together with the concepts of consistent views based on defined viewpoints, provides an ideal basis to perform gap-analysis that compares the As-Is and To-Be models to reveal:

- new elements required in the system to meet requirements;
- existing elements that need to be changed or replaced to meet new requirements;
- existing elements that are no longer required;
- existing elements that will remain unchanged, but may need to be regressively tested to ensure they have not been compromised by changes to other linked or inter-dependant elements.

These 'gaps' can then support the planning of design, build, test and implementation activities; either as a single change or as a number of incremental changes.

## Limitations of modelling

As discussed earlier, but in a shorter form, 'all models are wrong, but some are useful' (Box and Draper, 1987). The key to the activities facilitated by modelling is that appropriate, useful models and views are discovered and employed. Every development project is unique, with different facets needing more attention than others compared to previous projects; so a rigid approach that 'locks down' what models and views the development team may or must produce can often be counter-productive.

Modelling will not, by itself, ensure a high-quality solution, but it can usually identify and remove a significant number of defects earlier in the project than its absence would.

## The value of modelling

Earlier in the chapter, we introduced the concept of 'usefulness' as a primary measure of the value of modelling. Producing models takes time and effort, incurring cost in the development process; clearly the value of modelling needs to offset this. How can this value be accrued?

### Value from the act of modelling

The very act of modelling, such as in the collaborative experimentation and validation activities mentioned above, can produce significant value. Barry Boehm and others have demonstrated that the costs of fixing defects increase through a project due to the amount of re-work required the later they are discovered, so fixing them in an early model can save time and effort later in the process.

Defects include incorrect model elements derived from misunderstandings and incorrect assumptions that are included in the model; defects also exist where model elements are missing. The structure of models and their visual, diagrammatic representations makes these missing elements more obvious to identify and rectify than from a structured list of requirements or specifications.

### Value of the delivered model

'A picture is worth a thousand words' is a phrase of indeterminate origin that we often use to explain how a single diagram, with the appropriate syntax and content, can explain a situation more accurately and succinctly than a large amount of descriptive text. It is not, however, just the visual representation of the model that we need to consider; it is also the structured nature of the whole underlying model that has value.

The formality of a structured model – and the benefit of standardised visual syntax being less prone to ambiguity – have led us towards a world where models can be interpreted by humans and development tools alike, with automation of model development increasingly possible.

An example of automated model generation is using a tool to analyse and reverse engineer those elements from the existing IT system. Forward engineering is also possible; Model Driven Architecture (MDA) employing and evolving Unified Modelling Language (UML) models has been in existence since 2001 when it was launched by the Object Management Group (OMG). The underlying process is to evolve from a computation-independent model (CIM) to a platform-independent model (PIM) to a platform-specific model (PSM) at which point little coding is left to perform. The MDA process mimics and automates what is often performed through a manual Model Driven Software Engineering process.

A significant risk of an automated model transformation approach to development is that most of the development effort may go into the tool-interpreted models at the cost of a lack of other stakeholder relevant views that allow them to analyse and validate the quality of those models.

## MULTIPLE MODELS AND VIEWS

Models and diagrammatic views of those models work best when they focus on a limited subset of the facets of a system. From the early days of IT, developers have recognised the need for a range of models and documentation that between them cover enough facets to be confident that nothing important has been overlooked. This issue is well summarised in this quotation:

> 'No single model is sufficient to cover all aspects of software development. We need multiple models to address different concerns. These models must be coordinated carefully to ensure that they are consistent and not too redundant.'
> (Kruchten, 2001)

### The three-view approach

The three-view approach is a framework focused on three particular views of a system, which has been used since the early days of data processing. It involves:

- **Functionality:** What the system does or is required to do, typically, to process data. This often incorporates the 'who?' – which people or systems need to interact with the system as external entities or perform this behaviour as internal agents. This could be described logically or physically and from an internal or external angle (see 'opaqueness' later in this chapter).

- **Static data:** The system is typically required to manage the input, manipulation, storage and output of data. At run-time, the system processes a number of dynamic data objects that are created, manipulated and eventually deleted from the system. Static data is an abstract representation of the types of data objects and their structures that can be defined during analysis and design. As well as structure, the static data view can capture the semantics of the data, such as the meaning of the data and any related integrity rules. There can be many representations of the static data employing all forms of abstraction discussed later in the chapter.

- **Events:** Systems are driven by events, in other words the triggers to which the system has to react, typically by processing data in some pre-determined manner. It is key that all these potential events are identified so that the functionality triggered by each event can be defined (see Figure 7.2).

Between these three views, questions such as 'who?', 'what?', 'how?', 'when?' and 'where?' can be addressed. This assumes that the underlying requirements represent the 'why?' Combinations of diagram types typically cover these three facets.

Figure 7.2 The three-view model of a system

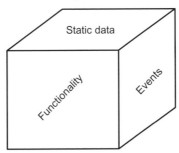

## PRE-UML MODELLING TECHNIQUES

At this point, it is worthwhile looking at the range of techniques available to system modellers and to provide tangible examples of how they can represent different views of systems.

In conventional or traditional modelling approaches (in this context, non-UML), there is a wide range of diagram types and modelling notations available, some defined in specific methods (such as SSADM), others as standards (for example iDEF); yet others are generically used in a variety of forms: The examples given here all relate to an imaginary bookseller, BookStack Mountain Ltd.

### Functionality

Examples of functional diagram types include:

- data flow diagram (DFD);
- flow chart (including variants such as swimlane diagrams);
- Jackson structure chart.

Figure 7.3 is an example of a DFD that shows how functionality, in the form of processes, handles inputs and outputs, shown as data flows. The endpoints of these data flows include external entities (users or other systems), data stores and processes. There should always be at least one process involved in each data flow at one end or the other.

### Static data

Examples of static data model notations include:

- entity relationship diagram (ERD), also known as a Logical data model;
- hierarchical tree diagram;
- bubble diagram.

## Figure 7.3 Data flow diagram

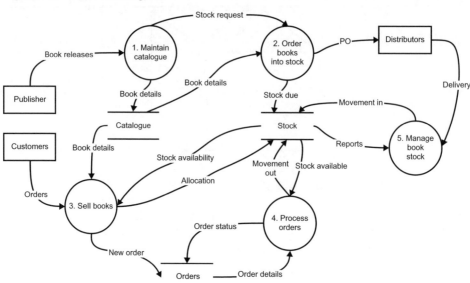

Although ERDs (see Figure 7.4) have been prominent for the last couple of decades, reflecting the prevalence of relational databases, other structure types remain relevant for modelling data held in other ways, such as hierarchical data held by some mainframes. With 'NO-SQL' database systems, in other words non-relational systems, becoming popular to support trends such as Big-Data, these alternative structures are becoming increasingly relevant again.

## Figure 7.4 Entity relationship diagram (Everest's 'crows foot' notation)

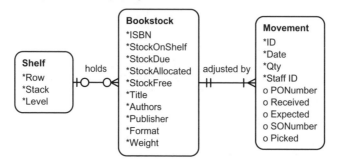

## Events

Examples of techniques used to model events include:

- Entity Life History (ELH), for example using Jackson structures;
- Statechart, for example those promoted by Harel pre-UML (see Figure 7.5).

### Figure 7.5  Statechart (Harel)

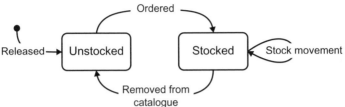

There are other diagram types that relate to multiple models such as an effect correspondence diagram (ECD), which provides a dynamic view of what data entities are traversed in response to an event (to be performed by a function).

## THE UNIFIED MODELLING LANGUAGE (UML)

The Unified Modelling Language has emerged as the predominant standard for model and diagram notation since its standardisation in 1997. UML is particularly effective in the twenty-first century, as it is based upon the 'multiple views of a single model' principle described earlier and it was designed to model modern object-oriented, component based, event-driven system architectures. It is purely a notation standard independent of any specific method technology or approach. UML 2.4 specifies 13 diagram types:

UML classifies the diagram types into either 'Behavioural' or 'Structural'; these diagram types can also be mapped to the three-view types. In Figure 7.6, italicised text shows an abstract grouping of diagram types rather than a diagram type itself.

### Figure 7.6  UML diagram types

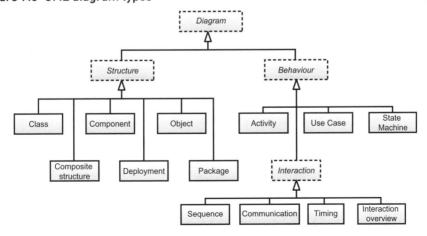

## Functionality

The following behavioural diagram types are each useful at different levels of abstraction:

- use case diagram;
- activity diagram;
- interaction diagrams:
  - sequence diagram
  - communication diagram
  - timing diagram
  - interaction overview diagram.

Figures 7.7 to 7.9 include a use case diagram that shows the functional scope of a system or application, an activity diagram representing the flow through the 'order book' use case and finally an extract from a sequence diagram that shows how that same use case can be realised by a series of internal interactions between components.

---

**Figure 7.7  BookStack Mountain stock management system – use case diagram**

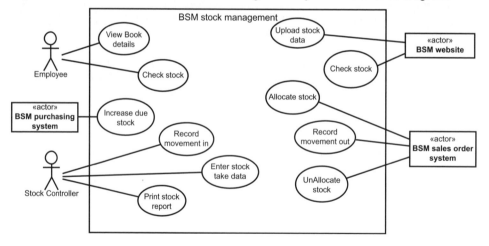

---

**Figure 7.8  Activity diagram for 'record movement' in use case**

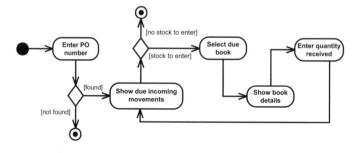

## Figure 7.9 Sequence diagram (incomplete)

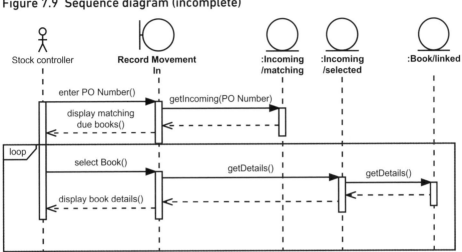

## Static data

The class diagram (see Figure 7.10) may be used to model static data, while abstracting out any behavioural facet to the class. Many data modellers are nervous of using UML for this purpose, as they regard it as being too object-oriented and concerned with developing executable code. The syntax can be adapted to do what any data modelling syntax can do. David C. Hay's book, *UML and data modeling: a reconciliation* (2011) is an excellent guide to doing this effectively.

## Figure 7.10 Class diagram used purely to model static data

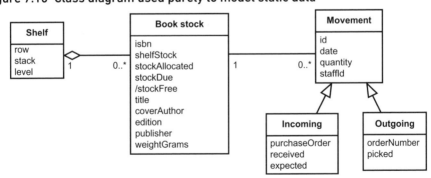

In Figure 7.10, the level of abstraction is such that this is modelling the business view of data and related semantics.

## Events

The State machine in UML is an evolution from Harel's Statechart mentioned earlier, and previously called state transition diagram in earlier versions of UML (see Figure 7.11).

**Figure 7.11  State machine for a BookStock instance**

## ABSTRACTION, LEVELLING AND SCOPE

At the beginning of this chapter, we described modelling as 'the act of producing appropriate models of these systems through the fundamental act of abstraction'. The consideration of various forms of abstraction were mentioned, so what are these forms of abstraction?

### Classification

This fundamental form of abstraction is a very natural device that we, as humans, employ all the time; it is fundamental to our thought processes wherein ideas are distanced from objects. You are currently reading this book, possibly by holding a physical copy of it or viewing an electronic version through another physical device. We must even consider that some readers are in fact listeners having the book read to them either by choice or necessity. We will revisit these physical issues later.

A 'book' is a relatively universal concept that we use to classify the idea of a collection of words and/or pictures, such as this specific object that you are currently interacting with. This is one of a number of such objects that you will interact with in your lifetime; there are many more books that you won't have time for or interest in. Once we have classified such a group of similar objects then we can begin to analyse what they mean as a concept.

A book means a collection of words and/or pictures assembled by an author (or collection of authors as in this instance), usually given a title, associated with a publisher and potentially allocated an ISBN number. A bookshop would know and use this information even if they didn't have any physical copies in stock.

Classification of, and defining the structure of, a class is the basic abstraction form that is performed during static data modelling. It is not only data that can be classified; for example, user or actor type and component type are elements of other models that we classify.

In entity relationship diagrams, these object types are referred to as 'entities', whereas in class diagrams (for example in UML) they are called 'classes'. These different model forms are described earlier in this chapter.

## Generalisation

Generalisation extends the classification abstraction form by recognising that we don't just group objects into a single class. Objects can be classified at various levels. For example we've identified that the 'book' class discussed above can come in many different formats; such as printed, electronic or audio book. The content and the author(s) remain the same but there may be different publishers and ISBN numbers for each format. Although the data has a similar structure in this instance, that we may not reflect in an entity relationship diagram, we may wish to identify these specialised types in a class diagram, as they are interacted with in different ways; in other words they exhibit different behaviour.

Figure 7.12 shows an entity relationship diagram and a class diagram for these book types. This class diagram has a different focus to the example in Figure 7.10, as it incorporates behaviour (operations) and so specialises out the formats as they have different ways of being 'read' or listened to; whereas the ERD is more concerned with how the data for these various formats can be stored in a single database table.

**Figure 7.12  Generalisation and specialisation in class diagram and Barker Ellis ERD form**

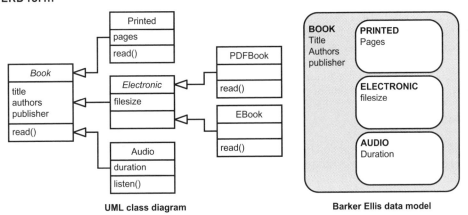

UML class diagram                                    Barker Ellis data model

Generalisation is therefore a means of simplifying a model by grouping a number of classes or entities together, based on their common characteristics. Specialisation is the opposite, where the differences are important and need to be modelled. The general type, or super-type, can describe the common structure and semantics and the specialised types focus on these specific differences. Multiple views of the model, for different stakeholders, may choose to show different levels of specialism.

## Composition

Composition is a form of abstraction that recognises that when a number of objects of various types are assembled together, they may form a new kind of object; some stakeholders may only be interested in this composite object, whereas others will need to see its component parts.

A bookshop system is unlikely to be interested in how this book is a composition of several chapters, each written by a particular author, but the editor's and publisher's systems will be. So, whereas the decomposition of a book down to chapters is worth modelling for certain systems, other systems are only interested in the composite 'book' (see Figure 7.13).

---

**Figure 7.13 Books composed of chapters (UML)**

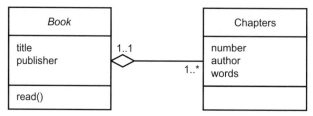

It is not only data modelling that uses composition; other model elements can also be composed into coarser-grained composite units. For example, in a use case model, a number of related use cases can be organised into a package that represents a broader set of functionality. In software architecture, functional classes can be combined into components, components assembled to form sub-systems and sub-systems assembled into a larger system. Examples of this can be found in Chapter 10. Similarly, a workforce will typically be organised into composite units such as departments or teams, which in turn can be combined into organisations.

## Idealisation

The last form of abstraction is idealisation, which was briefly discussed at the start of the chapter. There are various levels of model in addition to Logical and Physical already referred to:

- **Contextual model**: typically, an unstructured representation that helps to outline the scope and purpose of an element or system. It provides the background for the other levels. It should not be confused with a context diagram which is a black-box, composite view (see below for black-box).

- **Conceptual model**: a structured description and high-level detail about the element without regard to implementation, for example a business process or data structure. Conceptual models are often incomplete or not structurally robust. When analysing requirements, there are usually multiple Conceptual models presented by different stakeholders based upon their level of understanding or world view; these typically need to be resolved into a single consistent model. This level is extremely useful for modelling business semantics.

- **Logical model**: Logical models should be more complete and structurally robust while still ignoring implementation issues; this may be the single consistent model resolved from multiple Conceptual models. Logical models can be evolved or 'designed'. For example, a logical entity relationship diagram can be normalised to be consistent with the mathematically-based rules of relational database design. Functional components can be defined by the services they provide and how they can be assembled in a logical software architecture.

- **Physical model**: the Physical model considers implementation issues, such as technology-specific details, physical location details and so forth. For example a Logical data model (entity relationship diagram) can be converted into a platform-specific database schema. Functional components can be designed for the technology-specific issues such as the programming language and run-time platform. Usually these models should be described to a point where the solution can be built.

The order and descriptions of the idealisation levels just presented suggest how we can evolve models from an idealised state to a physical state. This can work the other way, by analysing a current physical system and deriving Logical or even Conceptual models from there; see the description of the U-curve process pattern earlier in this chapter.

## OPAQUENESS OF MODEL ELEMENTS

As was mentioned earlier, systems are often composed of other systems or components at various levels of granularity. Composition is the form of abstraction that we can use to represent these systems at each level. There are models where we need to show how a system is de-composed down to its component parts and other models where we are only interested in representing the composite, particularly when seeing how it is assembled with other composite elements to deliver a larger system.

### Black-box elements

The term 'black-box' is used in a number of disciplines to refer to a view of an element (system, component etc.) in a model where we are not concerned about its inner workings, but only concerned with it as a whole and its links and dependencies on other elements. Composition abstraction is key to this, hiding the detail of the next level down. This could be at any level of idealisation (Conceptual, Logical or Physical).

#### Context diagram

A context diagram is a good example of a black-box view of a whole system. Figure 7.14 is a context diagram for the BookStack Mountain Stock Management system.

In this context diagram, the system is an application represented by a boundary within which there are no details. We can, however, see how this application will need to interact with various external entities (actors), including users such as customers and staff together with other systems such as the accounts system and wholesalers. The nature and detail of these interactions is not defined, so at best this is a conceptual model.

**Figure 7.14 BookStack Mountain – context diagram**

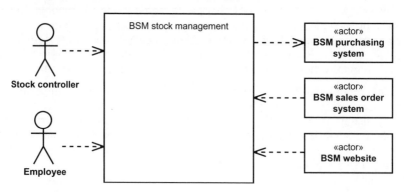

We can evolve this to a logical, black-box view if we begin to define the nature of these interactions as services this application will provide to some actors, and services this application will consume from others. The use case diagram presented earlier and repeated in Figure 7.15 is an example of this.

**Figure 7.15 BookStack Mountain – system use case diagram**

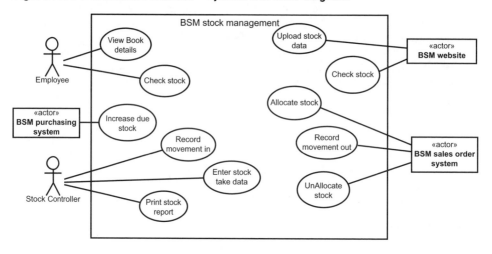

The term 'service' is deliberately chosen at this stage, not only as it suits a service-oriented approach to developing systems.

A functional component of a system can be described in this service-oriented, black-box fashion allowing the developers choices as to how that component is implemented. This is a key feature of architecture, as discussed in Chapter 10.

## White-box views

One stakeholder's black box is usually another's white box (where we are interested in its internal workings), whoever is responsible for implementing the functionality specified by the black-box view. This is effectively a decomposition of the functionality.

## Black- and white-box testing

Once a black-box element has been defined, tests can be prepared that will test this element independently of how it is implemented. It will pass this black-box test if it does everything it was specified to do and we do not need to examine or even understand its inner workings to perform this type of test.

White-box testing is usually performed by developers and testers to identify where defects are occurring. For example, if a black-box test on a component reveals issues, then white-box testing allows the relevant developer to view its inner workings to find out where the defect exists and hopefully fix it.

See Chapter 11 for more information on the difference between black- and white-box testing.

## Service-oriented analysis and design models

The term 'service' effectively refers to a logical, black-box view of the functionality of a component or system where its interface in terms of functional calls and their inputs and outputs is defined, but not the internal implementation. This provides a means of defining the system or component's functional requirements; for example, a system use case description typically details the interaction between the actor and a system from the actor's external perspective without detailing how the system will perform the interaction; so it is effectively a black-box description of what the service is. See more about service-oriented architecture in Chapter 10.

## LEVELS OF MODELS AND MODEL ELEMENTS

Throughout this chapter, the concept of layers or levels of models keeps appearing, representing different forms of abstraction (idealisation, composition and generalisation). There are many ways of levelling and layering based upon the forms of abstraction. A common approach with functional models is decomposition of high-level behaviour into more detailed behaviour through levels of complexity.

As a general rule of thumb, diagrams as views of models work best if they attempt to represent a shallow set of model elements; mixing too many levels in one diagram tends to make it confusing to understand. A hierarchy of separate, stepped diagrams is preferred.

## Business process levels

A good example of functional decomposition is Business Process Modelling. Starting from the top, an organisation's value chain can be presented as a process model, where each element is a high-level business process. Each of those business processes can in turn be decomposed to processes or sub-processes until we reach task level, and tasks can in turn be decomposed to steps. There are many alternative opinions as to how many levels are required; that tends to depend on the complexity of the organisation's processes!

## Functional decomposition

IT systems can be decomposed into similar levels and, at each level, a set of functional units (processes or tasks) can be identified. There is a point at which decomposing the functionality in one diagram form becomes less useful and a different diagram form is more appropriate. An example of this would be to consider each process on the data flow diagram in Figure 7.3 and produce a more detailed data flow diagram for each. When these have reached a certain level, then either a flow chart or a Jackson structure would be more appropriate to model the detail.

## Cockburn use case levels

Use cases are an important concept in UML, although their invention and use by Ivar Jacobson pre-dates UML considerably and they are still frequently used in non-UML approaches as a means of modelling requirements.

One important thing to note is that UML only specifies how to draw a use case diagram; it does not specify what use cases represent or how they should be documented. There are many applied uses of use cases in organisations and they can be shaped to whatever people desire them to be; and there often lies a problem of inconsistency and confusion as to what a use case is describing.

The definition we will employ for a use case is:

A description of a required interaction between an actor (user or other system) and the system in focus which is of value to the actor as it helps them achieve a goal. It incorporates multiple scenarios, each telling a whole story, some of which describe the actor succeeding in their goal while others show them failing, usually by not meeting rule based conditions.

But what do we mean by 'system' and what are these actor goals?

In his book, *Writing Effective Use Cases* (Cockburn, 2001), Alistair Cockburn provides two scales by which to classify different types of use case. He also provides a generic template for use case descriptions, from which thousands of organisation-specific templates have been created and within which these scales are used to define the type of use case being described.

The two scales Cockburn provides are:

- Design Scope;
- Goal Level.

Cockburn employs icons in the book to represent these which he has made available to the public domain under the Creative Commons license and are available at his website http://alistair.cockburn.us. These icons are used in the next few pages.

### Design scope

This defines what type of system the boundary, if drawn, represents. This also, by implication, defines the type of actor and the nature of their interaction with that system. A couple of the scopes have black- and white-box versions. Cockburn distinguishes between:

- Organisation: effectively a business system which includes all its manual and IT functionality. A business actor is a person (or system) outside that organisation, who interacts with that organisation in the manner described in the use case description.

    - 🏠 Black-box: the internal business functions, IT systems, departments and organisation staff are not specified in the description.

    - ⌂ White-box: the internal elements are referred to in the description.

- System: effectively an IT system or application. A system actor is typically a user or a distinctly separate IT system or application, which interacts with that system in the manner described in the use case description.

    - 📦 Black-box: the internal components, sub-systems and system architecture are not revealed or discussed in the description.

    - 📦 White-box: the internal architecture is revealed, to a degree, in the description.

- ▭ Component: the system is one of the architectural elements revealed in the white-box, system use case. Its actors will be other components within that architecture.

If we relate these to our forms of abstraction, we can see aspects of idealisation where black box is conceptual or logical, and white box is logical or physical depending on how specific the descriptions are.

### Goal level

Across these different system scopes, actors have different goals. These goals should not be to use part of a system, but to what end are they using the system as a means. For example, a system use case called 'Record new order on the system' does not represent the real-world goal that an actor would want to achieve; their goal is to 'Create new order' and the system will aid them in achieving this. So 'Create new order' is the better name as the first example is too focused on the system itself.

Across these system scopes, different actor types can have goals at different levels, which Cockburn refers to as:

- ⋆ Summary Goal (kite-level): typically equivalent to an end-to-end business process goal, which will take place over an extended period (typically hours, weeks or even months) and involve a number of people and systems to perform distinct activities, each of which can be described at the next level.

- ⋙ User Goal (sea-level): equivalent to a task, performed by a single person or application, in one place at one time (seconds or minutes at worst). This goal is a complete, meaningful objective akin to a transaction.

- ⋈ Sub-goal (fish level): not a meaningful goal in its own right, so only decomposed if it is a significant interaction to be reused within several user-goal use cases.

Use cases at sea level and above are typically focusing on requirements and the 'why?'; whereas below sea-level they begin to describe the 'how?'

Cockburn also defines a higher level, ☁ 'very high level' or cloud level, but this is too strategic a level to be useful to model with use cases. Relating this to other concepts, this level is equivalent to the complete business process value chain, where strategic goals are measured with key performance indicators and critical success factors.

There is also at least one lower level, ⋐ 'too low' or clam/sea-bed level. Some have even alluded to lower levels such as worm-level. This is where we may find lines of executable code! These levels are certainly too low to model with use cases.

Cockburn's *Writing effective use cases* (2001) provides many examples of use cases of various types and suggests employing a variety of use cases in any project.

## Functional model map

### *A grid to classify functional modelling elements*

This author has successfully utilised the scales defined by Cockburn, and described above, to define a framework for classifying functional models including use cases. Alternative equivalent scales can be utilised if they are a better fit to how the organisation currently models or intends to in the future.

The functional model map (FMM) is used to select which model types a team should employ at which levels in order to provide a mappable, traceable route from high-level business requirements to low-level technical design. Figure 7.16 presents the basic grid these levels (including those defined but not used by Cockburn). The black-/white-box sub-columns can be removed if desired.

## Figure 7.16 The Functional model map and development activities

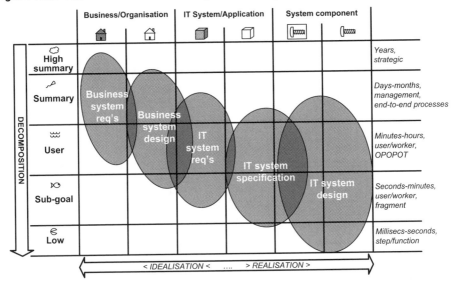

The general trend in most solution development processes is to start with high-level business objectives and to end up with a delivered solution, including – but not exclusively – IT. In the functional model map, this means plotting a route from top left to bottom right.

Models and techniques to explore those requirements and to define changes to business processes are explored down the business system column levels (Cockburn's organisation).

Some of these changes to the business model will involve the use of IT systems, which is where the system black-box column is useful to define the requirements of IT, in the form of applications and application services, to support the business.

As one moves into the system, white-box column and the component columns, then IT system specification, system architecture and design become the focus.

It is not the aim that every cell of this grid is populated with a functional model or technique. Rather, the aim is to identify and employ a set of techniques that will allow the team to map a route from business requirements and models to detailed design without any large leaps.

One could employ use cases of various types to traverse the grid; the following grid shows the use of use case types referred to as business use cases (BUCs), system use cases (SUCs) and design use cases (DUCs) (see Figure 7.17).

**Figure 7.17 Functional model map, populated with typical use case types**

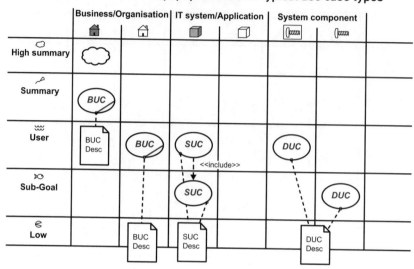

There are, as already discussed, other functional models that can be employed to populate the model. In Figure 7.18, the business use cases have been replaced with business processes, decomposing from the value-chain (cloud-level) down to business tasks (sea-level). In the system columns, system use cases remain the ideal choice. Detailed technical design with use case descriptions is possible but not recommended. There are many alternatives, such as activity diagrams, but interaction diagrams (usually sequence diagrams) are especially useful to capture the detail of sub-systems, components or classes interacting with each other via service or function calls to perform logical or physical design.

**Figure 7.18 Functional model map, populated with diagram types selected for a specific project**

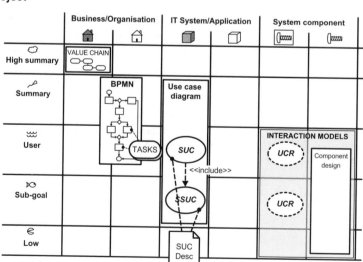

At sea-level, interaction diagrams that model the steps of a system use case are often referred to as 'use case realisations'. In the Unified Process, these are represented by dotted ellipses to reflect this link. The participants in this interaction are the top-level architectural sub-systems and components that will be reflected in software architecture (covered in Chapter 10). Below this level, the internal mechanisms of each component can be designed (black boxes in black boxes) until functions/methods and source code-level are reached.

### The pivotal role for system use cases

What this framework reveals all too clearly is how, without the system column(s), we are left with a gap in understanding between business and IT. Business models are designed to be understood by business stakeholders, but usually lack sufficient detail for the developers to understand the businesses requirements of the IT system as components of their solution. Similarly the technical models with all the logical and physical IT design elements are too detailed to reveal to the business stakeholders what the IT solution will do for them.

System use cases, even lightweight versions, bridge this gap when employed correctly; that is their role and there are few, if any, alternative modelling techniques that perform this task as well as they do. They tend to find a place at the heart of this framework.

## CROSS-REFERENCING MODELS, FACETS, PERSPECTIVES AND TRACEABILITY

Producing a number of models is all well and good, but in order to be effective they need to be consistent with each other in terms of:

- validating that model elements can be traced back to underlying business requirements;
- cross-referencing elements in one view or model to related elements in other models where there is some dependency; for example, certain events can be mapped to use cases, which in turn are mapped to the static data they manipulate;
- ensuring different views are modelling consistent system scopes;
- checking that models and views conform to the same semantics; i.e. calculations and conditions in Physical models correctly implement business rules defined in Conceptual and Logical models.

Maintaining and checking these cross-references and mappings is essential to ensure quality:

- Traceability from business requirements to deliverables via intervening models can reveal the following:
  - which requirements have been met or not;
  - how to plan incremental delivery based on requirement priority;

- which deliverables, and intervening models, are effected by a proposed requirements change request; the first dimension of impact analysis.
- Links between models and views can reveal:
  - structural inconsistencies due to misinterpreted requirements and poor assumptions;
  - consequential impact from changes to elements in one model or view on which other elements have some dependency; the second dimension of impact analysis.

Maintaining cross-references and mappings requires effort and is where true modelling tools (rather than just diagramming tools) earn their keep.

## Matrices

A common way to maintain and view these dependencies is in the form of matrices, where the set of one element type is reflected in the rows and a set of related element types is reflected in the columns. Each cell can be annotated to indicate some relationship between the row and column element in a manner suitable to the relationship type.

Examples of such matrices include:

- Mapping functional business requirements to system use case: this reveals which requirements have and, more importantly, have not been incorporated into the system functional model.
- Mapping entities in a Conceptual data model to those in the Logical data model or on to physical database tables: at the first level, this is done to ensure that all the data entities have been incorporated; then to indicate where the data semantics (meaning and rules) need to be checked for consistency.
- Mapping external entities of a system (actors) to the services they require from the system: this can be done as a matrix, but a commonly used graphical alternative is a use case diagram.
- Mapping events to the functional elements that are triggered.
- Mapping functional elements to static data elements at any level of idealisation: a commonly used example of this is referred to as the CRUD matrix (see below).
- Mapping events to the data elements that are likely to be effected can also be shown in a CRUD matrix.

These last three reflect the triangular dependency between the main three views: events, functionality and static data.

### *CRUD matrix*

The name of this matrix reflects the annotations that are made in the cells, where for every function or event mapped to a static data type whether an instance of that data type is:

- Created: a new entity instance or object is created in the system usually capturing some input.

- Read: an existing entity instance or object has its data read, either for internal processing purposes or to produce output.
- Updated: an existing entity instance or object has its data changed based upon some input or to reflect a change of status.
- Deleted: an entity instance or object is removed from the system, deleting the data contained.

The actual elements on each axis depends on the nature of the models. Commonly, this is one of the following:

- functions or processes mapped to entities in an entity relationship diagram;
- use cases mapped to classes representing data (see Figure 7.19 for an example);
- business trigger events mapped to either entities or classes depending on which notation is used.

**Figure 7.19  CRUD matrix – mapping use cases to classes**

| CLASSES / USE CASES | UC1: View book details | UC2: Check stock | UC3: Increase due stock | UC4: Record movement in | UC5: Enter stocktake data | UC6: Print stock report | UC7: Upload stock data | UC8: Allocate stock | UC9: Record movement out | UC10: Unallocate stock |
|---|---|---|---|---|---|---|---|---|---|---|
| Shelf | R | | | | U | R | | | | |
| Bookstock | R | R | U | U | U | R | R | U | U | U |
| Incoming movement | | | C | U | | R | | | | |
| Outgoing movement | | | | | | R | | C | U | U |

A cursory analysis of Figure 7.19 reveals that the use case model is probably missing use cases that delete any of the class instances and a use case to create shelf instances.

## Functional model map

The functional model map, described earlier, provides a route showing where paths traverse models across two dimensions of abstraction. Vertical paths indicate where composition/decomposition needs to be managed and horizontal paths where idealisation/realisation is being performed. Figure 7.20 shows where these paths can be combined to provide traceability from high-level business objectives through the models previously chosen in Figure 7.18 to low-level technical design artefacts.

**Figure 7.20 Functional model map, overlaid with traceability paths from requirements to code**

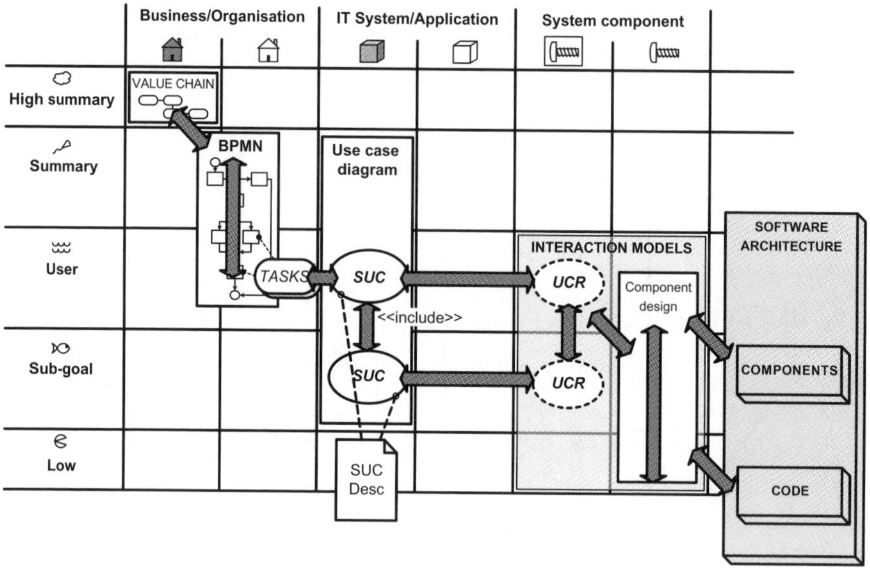

## DOCUMENTATION AND SPECIFICATION WITH MODELS

Models are representations of systems, and a picture may well paint a thousand words. There are, however, circumstances when models have to be combined with other artefacts and words to create documentation. Different development lifecycles tend towards different styles of documentation; these exist along a continuum from Waterfall lifecycles to Agile approaches through various incremental processes.

### Waterfall lifecycle documentation

A Waterfall or linear development lifecycle typically progresses on the basis of producing a series of documents as products of each stage that can be thoroughly reviewed and signed off before acting as input to subsequent stages:

1.  business case and feasibility study;
2.  requirements document;

3.  system specification document;
4.  system design document;
5.  test documentation;
6.  implemented system documentation:
    a.  operations manual
    b.  user documentation
    c.  training materials.

Note the distinction between the requirements document and a system specification. These are different documents to different levels of abstraction, especially idealisation, although many combine them to either the detriment of the requirements or the specification.

There will also exist a set of related management documentation, such as project plans.

## Agile documentation

There are some who believe that an Agile approach requires no documentation; beware of such snake-oil sellers. An Agile approach certainly does not require all the documents listed above in that form, but there usually needs to be:

- a business case defining scope and providing the project justification with which to control the project;
- evidence of testing and quality control;
- documentation for the released product (ops manual, user documentation and training materials).

An issue within Agile approaches is determining what documentation is maintained about the requirements, specification and design activities. The Agile Manifesto (discussed in Chapters 2 and 6) states that the authors have come to value 'Working software over comprehensive documentation', but that still means that some is required. Requirements may typically be in the form of user stories written on cards (Cohn, 2004) or on sticky notes on a kanban board.

One of the Agile Manifesto's 12 principles is 'The most efficient and effective method of conveying information to and within a development team is face-to-face conversation.' The act of modelling on whiteboards and within suitable tools as an activity is wholly consistent with this, so as much of the documentation as possible should take the form of these models.

Earlier in this chapter, we indicated that the value of modelling can be accrued from both the act of modelling and the finished model as a deliverable. Take a picture of the whiteboard after the conversation and store it for future reference at least!

## Incremental approaches

There are many Incremental processes with different patterns; these distinguish themselves from 'pure' Agile approaches in that they tend towards developing a certain level of requirements and architecture design up front.

These approaches are different from 'Big Analysis Up Front' approaches that can lead to 'analysis paralysis' (the inability to move out of analysis as things keep changing) or 'Big Design Up Front' that tends to inhibit re-factoring the architecture at a later stage when issues arise.

In these approaches, high-level requirements and logical design decisions are reached in an initial phase, then a series of Incremental stages perform detailed analysis and design of that part of the system before developing, testing and potentially delivering the increment to the end user. In this situation, the requirements, specification, design and test documentation will not be complete until the end of the project. An example of this is the 4 + 1 architecture approach of the Unified Process.

### Unified Process

The Unified Process is a development process evolved as a generic version of the original Rational Unified Process (RUP). RUP was originally developed alongside UML, which provided the modelling notation while RUP described the process.

The Unified Process 4 + 1 view model of architecture (Kruchten, 1995) considers five views of a system that start empty but 'fill up' at different rates through the project; all will be full when the project is completed (see Figure 7.21).

**Figure 7.21  Unified Process 4 + 1 architecture**

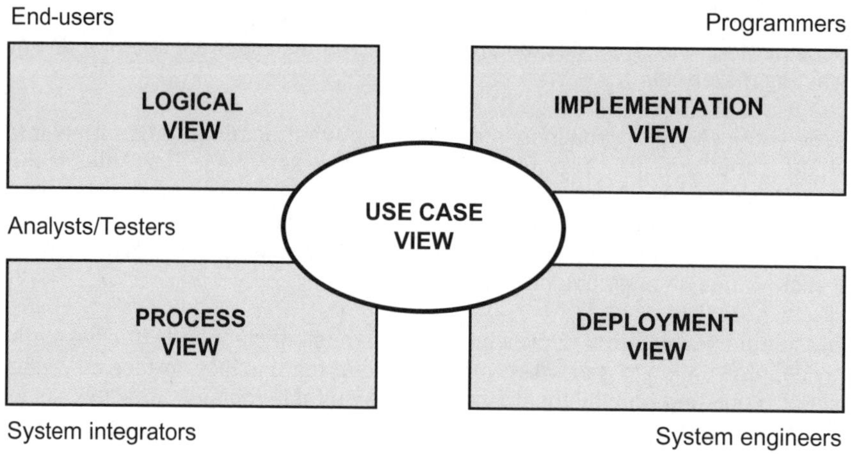

The 4 + 1 views are:

- Logical view: the functional requirements of the system.
- Implementation view: the organisation of static software modules, data files, components and so forth that implement the system.
- Process view: the behaviour of the system at run-time.

- Deployment view: how executable and other run-time components are deployed onto platforms on a network.
- Use case view: the means of chunking the system into bite-size deliverables that can drive the planning of the iterations (stages) and all the activities therein. This is the + 1 in the model.

## CONCLUSION

With so many alternative lifecycles, methods, frameworks and notations – or whatever pick-and-mix of these you adopt as an approach to developing business solutions incorporating IT – modelling is likely to be a key activity. This chapter, indeed this whole book, would be unable to describe all of the alternative models and diagrams that the twenty-first-century development team have on offer; it does, however, aim to provide readers with the ability to understand why there are so many choices and enable them to understand the value of selecting a set of appropriate models for any given project.

A significant factor in these choices will be practical ones such as:

- what modelling skills team members possess;
- what tools, whether pen and paper, diagramming software or modelling software are available to the team;
- what standards are adopted within the organisation or even industry.

Even if the selection is mandated, most of the techniques mentioned can be used in a number of contexts, so the team needs to determine what each diagram or model should mean in terms of:

- What is its purpose and at what part of a process?
- Who is its audience and what are their concerns?
- What level of abstraction(s) are therefore suitable?

Most important of all, before spending time and effort modelling each artefact:

- Is it or will it be useful?

## REFERENCES

AgileManifesto.org (2001) *Manifesto for Agile Software Development*. www.agilemanifesto.org (accessed 4 June 2014).

Booch, G., Rumbaugh, J. and Jacobson, I. (2005) *The unified modeling language user guide* (2nd edition). Addison Wesley, Upper Saddle River, NJ.

Box, G. E. and Draper, N. R. (1987) *Empirical model-building and response surfaces*. Wiley, Upper Saddle River, NJ.

CCTA (2000a) *Behaviour and process modelling.* TSO, Norwich.

CCTA (2000b) *Data modelling.* TSO, Norwich.

CCTA (2000c) *Database and physical process design.* TSO, Norwich.

CCTA (2000d) *SSADM foundation.* TSO, Norwich.

Cockburn, A. (2001) *Writing effective use cases.* Addison-Wesley, Boston, MA.

Cohn, M. (2004) *User stories applied: for Agile software development.* Addison-Wesley, Boston, MA.

Date, C. J. (2000) *An introduction to database systems* (7th edition). Addison-Wesley, Boston, MA.

Hay, D. C. (2011) *UML & data modeling: a reconciliation.* Technics Publications, Westfield, NJ.

Jacobson, I. (1992) *Object oriented software engineering.* Addison-Wesley, Boston, MA.

Kruchten, P. (1995) 'The 4+1 view of architecture'. *IEEE Software,* November 12, 6, 45–50.

Kruchten, P. (2001) *The rational unified process, an introduction* (2nd edition). Addison-Wesley, Boston, MA.

Larman, C. (2005) *Applying UML and patterns* (3rd edition). Prentice Hall, Indianapolis, IN.

Martin, J. (1977) *Computer data-base organization.* Prentice Hall, Indianapolis, IN.

Podeswa, H. (2010) *UML for the IT business analyst.* Course Technology, Boston, MA.

Skidmore, S. and Eva, M. (2004) *Introducing systems development.* Palgrave MacMillan, Basingstoke.

# 8 SYSTEMS DESIGN – 1

## Peter Thompson

## CONTENTS OF THIS CHAPTER

This chapter covers the following topics:

- the objectives and constraints of systems design;
- systems design in the development lifecycle;
- the scope of design;
- input and output design, technologies and their application;
- the objectives and principles of process design.

## OBJECTIVE OF SYSTEMS DESIGN

The objective of systems design is to formulate a solution to realise the system requirements. These requirements will typically be categorised as functional or non-functional (as explained in Chapter 5). However, there are several additional objectives identified by the manufacturer (in this case, the system developers). Figure 8.1 summarises these objectives.

### Functional requirements

**Functionally correct** The design provides the functionality specified in functional system requirements, including data maintenance, transactional processes (such as raise invoice, despatch order, renew policy), generation of reports and other outputs.

### Non-functional requirements

**User-friendly** Delivers the functional requirements in a consistent, intuitive way to support the relative experience of the intended users.

**Reliable** Ensures that the system is robust and available at all times when needed. See also available.

## Figure 8.1 Objectives of systems design

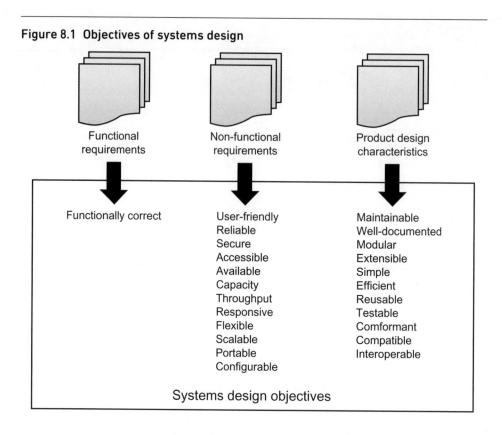

Functional requirements

Non-functional requirements

Product design characteristics

Functionally correct

User-friendly
Reliable
Secure
Accessible
Available
Capacity
Throughput
Responsive
Flexible
Scalable
Portable
Configurable

Maintainable
Well-documented
Modular
Extensible
Simple
Efficient
Reusable
Testable
Comformant
Compatible
Interoperable

Systems design objectives

| | |
|---|---|
| **Secure** | Provides adequate controls to restrict access to the system and its data, often for the sake of commercial sensitivity or to satisfy privacy legislation and similar regulations. |
| **Accessible** | Ensures that the system is accessible to all potential users regardless of the limitations of disability, their native language or other similar considerations. |
| **Available** | Ensures that the system is available when required to fulfil its purpose, often determined by business working hours. |
| **Capacity** | Supports transaction and other data volumes as necessary to provide continuous operation into the foreseeable future. |
| **Throughput** | Similar to capacity but relates to data/transactional volumes within a specific timeframe, such as the ability to capture 1,000 orders per hour or to support 100,000 simultaneous accesses to a specific internet site. |
| **Responsive** | Ensures that the system provides a response to a particular request within a pre-determined timeframe. |

| | |
|---|---|
| **Flexible** | Provides the ability to adapt to changing business situations. This is a difficult objective to achieve, and is impossible to guarantee. The objectives of scalability, portability and configurability essentially break this objective down into more specific, testable system features. |
| **Scalable** | Provides the ability to up- or down-scale the number of transactions and/or users, to support changing business requirements. |
| **Portable** | Provides the ability to 'port' the design to different technology platforms and devices. |
| **Configurable** | Provides the ability to change the system's behaviour by setting configuration options or defining system parameters. |

## Product design characteristics

| | |
|---|---|
| **Maintainable** | This objective is essentially covered by the sub-objectives of simple, flexible and well-documented. |
| **Well-documented** | Provides documentation to enable the support and maintenance of the system once it passes into operational use. |
| **Modular** | This means that the design is based upon the principles of loose (or low) coupling and high cohesion. These concepts will be explored later in this chapter. |
| **Extensible** | This is synonymous with flexible. |
| **Simple** | The design is not unnecessarily complex. Some developers try to make their programs as complex as they can as a sort of intellectual challenge to other developers, leading to code that is difficult to maintain or error-prone. |
| **Efficient** | Makes efficient use of computing resources such as power, processor capacity, memory and storage. This is particularly important for software that will need to be running whilst other software is also sharing the same computing resources. |
| **Re-usable** | The design makes use of existing functionality, where available. This may take the form of generic functions, components or web services provided by third-party providers, or even standardised functions, components and services developed in-house. |
| **Testable** | Enables system testers to develop test cases and scripts directly from the design deliverables (artefacts), for example, the use of system models such as use cases, class diagrams and state machine diagrams (introduced in Chapter 7) that incorporate business rules and constraints. |

**Conformant**    The design adheres to standards such as modelling notation and industry-wide, user-interface standards as well as complying with architectural principles and policies, such as modularity and simplicity.

**Compatible**    Uses a standard data file or message format that can be shared with another system. For example, many independent software products provide the ability to read and/or generate files that can be used by Microsoft Office™ applications.

**Interoperable**    This literally means the ability to work (operate) with other systems. In practice this may refer to the ability for a system to share data with another system (through the use of a common database, or a data file that is exported by one system and imported into another) or through the consumption of services provided by another system.

In addition to these overarching objectives, individual design activities, such as input design, have their own objectives, which we shall look at in the relevant sections later in this chapter.

## CONSTRAINTS UPON SYSTEMS DESIGN

The system designer has a number of constraints placed upon their work. Some common constraints are shown in Figure 8.2.

**Figure 8.2 Constraints upon systems design**

| Project constraints | Technical constraints | Organisational constraints |
|---|---|---|
| Money (budget)<br>Timescale<br>Skills/resources | Hardware<br>Software<br>Legacy systems<br>Programming language<br>Standards | Politics<br>Stakeholders<br>Standards<br>Legislation<br>Cultural differences<br>Quality of requirements |

Constraints on Design

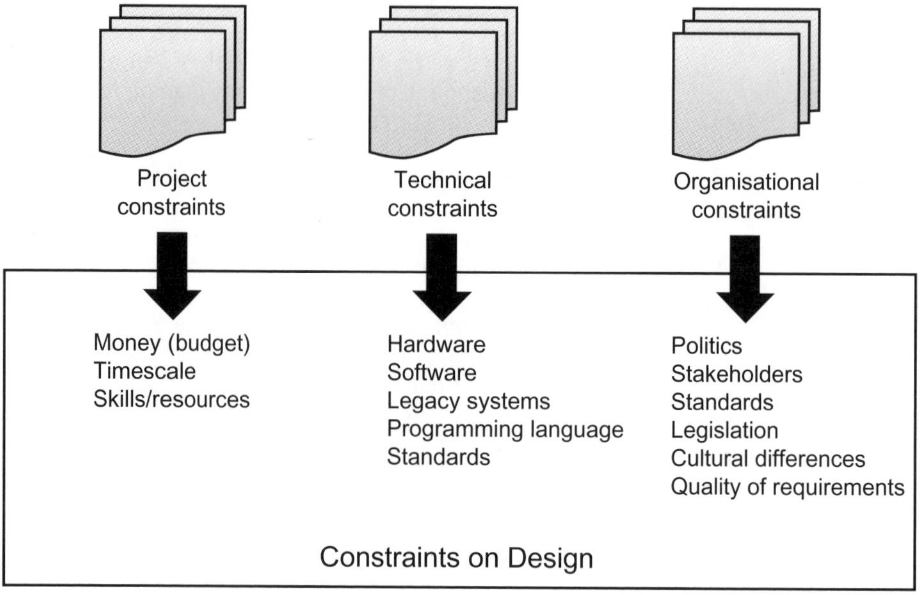

## Project constraints

These represent limitations imposed by project stakeholders and agreed during project initiation.

| | |
|---|---|
| **Money (budget)** | It is very rare for a project to proceed without a pre-defined budget. Systems development projects are no exception and this may restrict the scope of features that can be delivered. However, more specifically, the impact may be that the designer has to reduce not just the number of features that the project will deliver, but the way those features are delivered. This may also lead to trade-offs between design objectives. For example, reusability may be a desirable objective, but it is often more costly to build a software component in such a way that it could be reused in other projects. |
| **Timescale** | Generally imposes similar restrictions to budget as the two are intricately linked. |
| **Skills/resources** | Projects rarely have unlimited resources at their disposal, generally as a consequence of a fixed budget. Although resources are broader than just people, it is the people restrictions that have the most impact on the design stage of development, in terms of a lack of skills in a particular technology. A lack of access to the latest technology (in terms of hardware and software) may also be a constraining factor. These factors often steer the design of a system down the tried and tested path that an organisation is familiar with rather than attempting to break new ground. |

## Technical constraints

Similarly to project constraints, technical constraints are often identified during project initiation. However, unlike the project constraints, they tend to relate to more strategic issues often defined within enterprise-wide architectural policies, standards and principles that govern a range of or all projects.

| | |
|---|---|
| **Hardware and software** | We have already touched on this, but organisational standards may also dictate that only certain hardware or software may be used. This is especially true of organisations that have introduced enterprise architecture teams to define and govern the use of IT. |
| **Legacy systems** | If the system under development needs to interface to legacy systems (those perhaps built using old technologies that the organisation no longer uses for new systems development), then the system may need to use specific protocols that are perhaps no longer supported, or specific file formats that are no longer used for new developments. This may require proprietary development languages to develop interfaces with the legacy |

143

systems. One way to deal with these situations is to build a layer of software called a 'wrapper' that acts as an adapter, translating between old and new formats and protocols.

**Programming language**

Organisations often have enterprise-wide standards regarding the programming languages and development tools to be used during systems development. This may constrain the designer as not all languages provide the same features. Furthermore, the more traditional languages, such as COBOL, do not provide support for object-oriented design – discussed later.

**Standards**

Typical industry-wide technical standards that must be complied with when designing a new computer system include:

- **User-interface style guides** – such as those defined by Apple.

- **Data formats** – such as the use of open standards like XML.

- **Protocols** – such as SOAP (Simple Object Access Protocol) and REST (Representational State Transfer), used for passing messages in a service-oriented architecture.

- **Security** – such as ISO 27001 (the international standard describing best practice for an Information Security Management System), ISO/IEC 7498 (Open Systems Interconnect (OSI) security model), ISO/IEC 13335 (IT security management), ISO/IEC 27005 (Information technology – Security techniques – Information security risk management).

- **Application specific standards** – such as PCI DSS (Payment Card Industry Data Security Standard).

- **Modelling standards** – such as the use of the Unified Modeling Language (UML) notation when producing design models.

## Organisational constraints

The development organisation, or even the customer organisation if the developers are a third-party provider, often imposes constraints that must be adhered to by the designer. Some of these have been covered under technical standards, but other constraints include:

**Politics**

Sometimes, for seemingly unfathomable reasons, an organisation chooses to follow an inappropriate project approach or to use an unsuitable technology or software tool. This may be as a consequence of a new CIO (Chief Information Officer) or IT Manager wishing to make their mark or introduce technology, standards or processes that they are more familiar with, even though they may not be suitable within their new organisation.

**Stakeholders**

There are typically three key issues relating to stakeholders that constrain the designers ability to complete their work:

- **Availability** – perhaps the greatest constraining factor regarding stakeholders is their availability for providing clarification regarding their requirements. Even accepting that the requirements provided to the designer are of good quality, they often change during the development process;

- **Authority** – sometimes the ability to obtain authorisation for changes is restricted due to the stakeholders requesting them having insufficient authority;

- **Sign-off** – the ability of stakeholders to approve and sign-off the design before software construction commences is highly-questionable in many system development projects, mainly down to the use of esoteric notations and models during the design process. Consequently, design specifications are rarely approved and signed off by business stakeholders.

**Standards**

Every organisation tends to define its own standards, in addition to industry-wide standards adopted for achieving 'best practice'. Some typical examples of organisation specific standards include:

- **User-interface style guides** – prescribing consistent use of fonts and corporate colours, positioning of logos, use of standard terminology, for example;

- **Reporting standards** – similar to user-interface guidelines, but governing the look and feel, layout, sorting, filtering and totalling on reports generated by computer systems;

- **Module design guidelines** – some organisations define standards that must be met during process design regarding the coupling, cohesion and simplicity of system processes/modules/components. These standards also form the basis for static testing of programs once written.

**Legislation**

The most prevalent legislation affecting computer systems is data protection legislation, for example the UK Data Protection Act 1998 (DPA). However, each sector has its own legislation to contend with, which typically places restrictions on the designer, who needs to ensure compliance within the solution.

| | |
|---|---|
| **Cultural differences** | Often, systems need to work in different environments, in different countries, which have different ways of working and different languages or currencies. This may restrict the way a solution is designed or may require a particular approach that conflicts with design objectives such as simplicity and maintainability. |
| **Quality of requirements** | Perhaps the factor most commonly attributed to the failure (or success) of a systems development project, is the quality of requirements. Requirements engineering (the subject of Chapter 5) strives to produce high-quality requirements, but unfortunately it is still commonplace to see requirements that do not meet such stringent quality criteria. This leaves some system features open to interpretation, which, ultimately, requires more of the designer's time through seeking clarification, or worse, having to re-work the design later in the Systems Development Lifecycle (SDLC). |

## SYSTEMS DESIGN IN THE DEVELOPMENT LIFECYCLE

Systems design is a critical stage within systems development, but the extent of the design and approach taken varies considerably depending on the approach to development taken. For example, with defined approaches to development, the emphasis is on producing a complete design up-front (often referred to as 'big design up front') that comprehensively supports (realises) the entire set of requirements. Alternatively, with Agile approaches, the emphasis is on a 'divide and conquer' approach, whereby an agreed subset of system features is explored and built within a short development lifecycle, that repeats (iterates) a number of times until a complete set of functionality has been delivered.

Chapter 2 considered four fundamental systems development lifecycle (SDLC) models that provide the framework for systems development:

- Waterfall
- 'V' model
- Incremental
- Iterative

Within the first three, there is a dedicated stage or stages for design, whereas the Iterative model does not have a dedicated design stage.

### Waterfall

The position of design in the Waterfall lifecycle (Figure 8.3) is clearly defined and follows requirements engineering. Consequently, design commences only after a definitive set of requirements have been validated and signed-off by the project sponsor.

This approach has advantages and disadvantages. First, it means that a comprehensive design can be undertaken in one stage, providing a robust set of blueprints as a basis for programming. However, if any of the requirements change after design approval, this necessitates that the design be re-evaluated, modified and re-validated.

146

## Figure 8.3  The place of design in the Waterfall SDLC

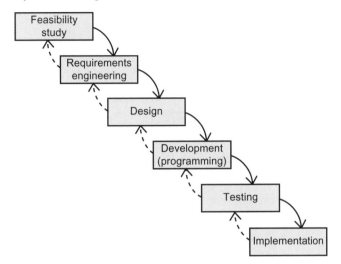

## 'V' model

The 'V' model is very similar when it comes to the approach to systems design. However, as a consequence of aligning the stages of specification to explicit test stages later in the lifecycle, design is split into high-level system design and individual unit or component design (also referred to as module design), as shown in Figure 8.4.

## Figure 8.4  The place of design in the 'V' model SDLC

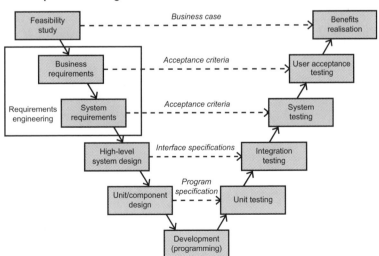

The high-level system design stage identifies (but does not define in detail) the components (modules or units) required to realise the requirements and the required interfaces between them. The unit/component design stage provides a detailed specification for each component identified in the high-level design to enable a systems developer to write the code. This is also referred to as a program specification.

The 'V' model, in addition to showing the discrete stages of design, also shows explicitly the outputs from the design stages (interface and program specifications) that drive the corresponding integration and unit testing stages.

## Incremental

Similarly to the 'V' model, the Incremental model (Figure 8.5) effectively splits design into both high-level and module design. The high-level design is performed 'up-front' to ensure a coherent solution that fits together robustly but the module design is deferred to the individual incremental development stages, where a subset of features is designed in detail, built, tested and deployed (implemented).

**Figure 8.5  The place of design in the Incremental SDLC**

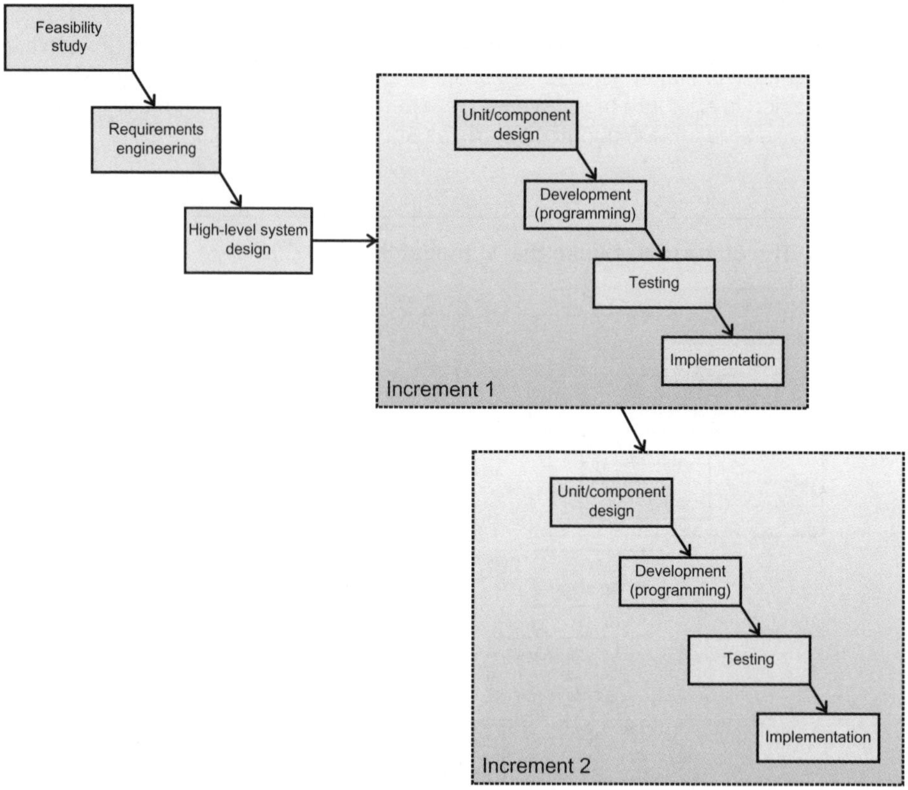

## Iterative

Design is an explicit step in the original Spiral lifecycle model (the original basis for modern iterative lifecycles) that takes place after an operational prototype is produced in the final iteration. More recent interpretations of the Iterative lifecycle do not explicitly show design as a stage or step, however, that is not to say that approaches based on the Iterative lifecycle do not recognise design as a key activity within systems development.

Figure 8.6 shows a typical Iterative SDLC used as a foundation for Agile systems development (introduced in Chapters 2 and 6). Agile approaches focus on developing and delivering working software without reliance on formal specifications produced early in the lifecycle. Key design decisions are still made, but they are reflected in the development of evolutionary prototypes rather than documented as a specification for developers to use. It is only at the end of an Iterative development cycle when a production-ready version is completed that the key design decisions are documented, to provide an important reference for ongoing support and maintenance.Consequently, the overall system design evolves throughout a series of Iterative development cycles, where each cycle explores and builds a new set of system features.

---

**Figure 8.6  The place of design in an Iterative SDLC**

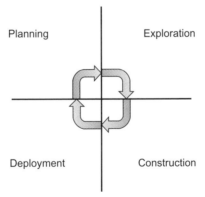

## THE SCOPE OF DESIGN

Although each systems development project is different, a good place to start considering the scope of design is to identify the key elements of a computer system, as shown in Figure 8.7, which has been reproduced by permission of Assist Knowledge Development Ltd.

**Figure 8.7 Key elements of a computer system**

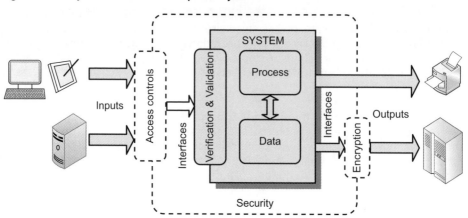

Figure 8.7 identifies four key elements: inputs, outputs, processes and data. However, it also includes system controls, such as verification, validation, security and encryption. Hence, the key activities of the designer's work can be summarised as:

- input and output design (often referred to as I/O design or external design);
- process design;
- data design;
- security and control design.

These design activities are typically driven by the products (or deliverables) of the analysis stage that precedes systems design, depending upon which SDLC approach is taken. These products of analysis generally include a requirements document (containing functional, non-functional, general and technical requirements) and supporting documents, including models of the functional and data requirements, such as a UML use case diagram with supporting use case descriptions (functional) and an analysis class diagram (data).

The next four subsections explore each of these activities in more detail.

**Input and output design**

Input requirements are defined during requirements engineering and specified in either a requirements catalogue, a functional specification, or both. Therefore, the start point for I/O design is the requirements catalogue and some form of functional specification, the latter generally comprising a function model with supporting descriptions. A de-facto standard these days is a use case diagram and associated use case descriptions (from UML); however, a data flow diagram (DFD) and associated elementary process descriptions are also commonly used. The functional specification

150

and requirements catalogue are often supplemented by prototypes of example screens and reports.

Figure 8.8 shows an example of a use case diagram for a sales order processing system. The inputs and outputs requiring design are clearly identified from the points where associations between actors and use cases cross the system boundary. Hence, we can identify the following potential inputs and outputs:

- order details;
- picking details;
- despatch details;
- delivery details;
- invoice details.

**Figure 8.8  Use case diagram for a sales order processing system**

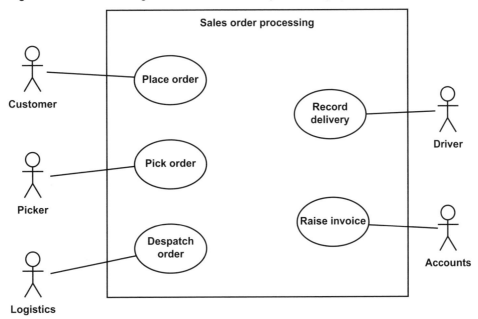

It is not possible to determine from the diagram alone whether each of these associations are actually inputs, outputs or two-way dialogues. This is where the supporting use case descriptions come in, to clarify the nature and content of the interaction between the user (the actor on the use case diagram) and the system being designed.

I/O design has two distinct areas that we refer to as macro design and micro design. At the macro level, the designer considers the overall mechanism for achieving the inputs and outputs, including the use of appropriate technologies. At the micro level, the designer focuses on the detailed design of the user interface, including content and layout of forms, reports and interface files.

### User interface design

To the end user, the user-interface (UI) **is** the system. They do not have visibility of the internal workings of the system; the way it stores and manipulates its data. Consequently, the design of the UI is arguably the most critical part of the work of the designer, except for batch processing systems, where the UI is minimal.

The purpose of the UI is to make the computer system **usable** by the end user, a quality often referred to as 'user-friendly'. Hence, the most critical aspect of a UI is its **usability** – adapting a computer system to the humans who use it. If a UI is difficult to learn or confusing/tedious to use, then the system will become an obstruction to the user rather than a helpful tool. In the case of web-based systems, this may even result in a customer deciding to visit a competitor's site to make their purchase!

Usability is subjective and can only be determined (and measured) with specific reference to the type of user, the task they are performing and the environment within which they are using the system. Some of these considerations will have been captured within explicit usability requirements during requirements engineering.

What constitutes 'user-friendly' is sometimes difficult to quantify, which is why designers often use prototypes (storyboards and wireframes), checklists and style guides to assist them when undertaking detailed UI design. A usability checklist includes:

- consistency (consistent look and feel, use of terminology, and so on);
- following the logical workflow;
- logical tab sequence;
- meaningful field descriptions and formats (for example, 'Enter order date (dd/mm/yyyy)');
- identification of mandatory values;
- default values;
- confirmation messages;
- clear error messages;
- progress indicators;
- facilities to undo/back out;
- context-sensitive help;
- alternative data entry mechanisms (such as keyboard shortcuts);
- limited entry options (such as drop-down lists and tick boxes);

- use of jargon-free language;

- simplicity (uncluttered screens, reports with only relevant information, and so on).

### User considerations

In addition to specific considerations for users with disabilities, the designer should also consider each user's level of IT expertise. An infrequent or inexperienced user may need a UI that guides them through a process step by step, whereas an experienced, frequent user may need shortcuts to enable them to achieve a task quickly.

With the advent of the internet, more uses of computers are via websites, where it is impossible for the developers to provide training to the users in the same way that they would with office-based systems. Hence, the challenge is to make the UI intuitive, whereby the user requires little or no guidance in terms of how to use it, and what guidance is provided is usually in the form of tool-tips or context-sensitive help to access a help-screen that provides explanation about the screen that they are currently using, or the feature that they have selected.

## Input design

The principal objective of input design is to specify how the system will collect data in its raw form (for example a paper-based form or a third-party system's database) and convert that data into an internal format (all computers use a binary code internally, which uses only the two binary digits 0 and 1) that the system can understand. In addition to ensuring that the functional requirements are met, the designer must also take into account a number of other considerations:

- **Efficiency** – to ensure that the input mechanism makes efficient use of resources, such as mains power, processor and memory usage.

- **Reliability** – to ensure that the input mechanism is available whenever it is needed.

- **Timing** – to minimise any delay during the data collection and translation process.

- **Accuracy** – to minimise the introduction of errors in the captured data.

- **Usability** – to ensure that the approach taken is easy for the user to perform and supports their level of ability.

- **Cost** – the cost should not outweigh the benefits derived from using a particular approach/mechanism.

To understand the decisions that the designer makes during input design, it is necessary to understand how the input process works. Figure 8.9, which has been reproduced by permission of Assist Knowledge Development Ltd, shows the various stages involved.

**Figure 8.9 Stages during data input**

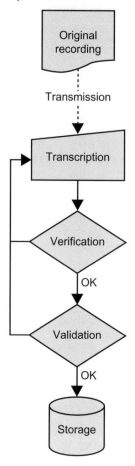

**Original recording**  Data is created or captured at its source. In the early days of computerisation this was achieved using a hand-written data capture form, although modern computer systems may capture data using a number of different mechanisms, as explored later in this chapter.

**Transmission**  The captured data is sent to some location, where it is converted into an internal format understandable by the system. Modern computer systems tend to achieve the transmission electronically.

**Transcription**  The captured data is converted (transcribed) into the internal format used by the computer system. Historically this would have been achieved by a data entry operator 'keying' the data using a keyboard, but, again, modern systems have a number of options available, discussed later.

**Verification**    Whilst the data transcription process is being performed, the transcribed data is checked to ensure that no errors are introduced, most commonly, that the data entry operator has mis-keyed some of the data. Such errors are referred to as **transcription errors**. Being a form of system control, verification is considered later in the section on controls and security.

**Validation**    The transcribed data is subjected to further checks to ensure that it complies with pre-defined data integrity principles and business rules defined by the business stakeholders. Again, validation is considered under the section on controls and security later.

**Storage**    The final stage is to store the data in a permanent or semi-permanent storage system for future use.

The designer needs to make decisions covering the above stages to ensure that the approach taken meets the objectives identified above, most notably to minimise delay and cost whilst maximising accuracy and usability. These guidelines should be borne in mind when deciding how to achieve these objectives:

1.  **Minimise the amount of data recorded.** The more data to be captured, the greater the effort required (cost and time) to collect, transmit and transcribe the data, and the higher the likelihood of error.

2.  **Minimise data transmission.** Each transmission of data incurs cost, has the potential to delay the input process and increases the chance of errors being introduced.

3.  **Minimise data transcription.** Transcribing data from one form into another increases the chance of error and incurs cost and delay.

4.  **Verify and validate to ensure accuracy.** Choose appropriate checks based upon the nature of the data involved and the data capture environment. This is discussed further later in the chapter.

5.  **Choose appropriate input technologies.** The chosen technology should support the needs of the intended user whilst being appropriate to the application (timing requirements, data volumes and so on) and target data capture environment, whilst providing value for money.

As the last point suggests, designers must be familiar with a wide range of technologies so as to select those appropriate to support the system requirements. Different technologies score differently in terms of the considerations we identified earlier (efficiency, reliability, timeliness, accuracy, usability and cost). Table 8.1 provides a list of the most common technologies and typical uses, but a detailed explanation of these technologies is outside the scope of this book.

Input devices can be classified as direct or indirect. Indirect input devices require a human user to interpret the source data and translate it into key presses or some other form of interaction with the system. Direct input devices enable capture and transcription into a computer-readable format without the need for a human user to undertake any translation, thus eliminating transcription errors almost completely.

A further consideration during input design is whether the input must be undertaken in real time (often referred to as 'online') or whether it can be batched up and processed at a later time (for instance, overnight). Key factors in deciding whether a batch input approach may be more practical are the volumes of data being captured/processed, the timing constraints of the application and the costs involved. Online data input is more desirable from a business perspective but it is sometimes difficult to justify the costs involved and hence batch input becomes a more practical solution.

**Table 8.1  Common input technologies**

| Technology/Device | Uses |
| --- | --- |
| **Keyboard** | Suitable for most input requirements. |
| **Touch screen (including smartphones and tablets)** | Similar to keyboard, but tailored more to novice users (such as patients arriving at doctors' surgeries) or applications that require high-volume, rapid entry (such as point-of-sale terminals in retail outlets). Portable devices are used extensively in logistics applications to record status updates for orders at various stages throughout the fulfilment cycle. |
| **Mouse** | Although fast becoming replaced by touch screens, used as an alternative or addition to keyboard entry to simplify the selection of information, to resize pictures, drag and drop, and so on. |
| **Scanning (bar codes, OCR, OMR, MICR)**<br>• **bar codes** | See subsections below.<br>Used extensively in retail to encode product information for fast, high-volume scanning at point-of-sale. Use of newer QR codes provides quick access to a wealth of information by extending accessibility to individuals with an appropriate app on their smartphone. |

*(Continued)*

**Table 8.1  (Continued)**

| Technology/Device | Uses |
| --- | --- |
| • OCR (Optical Character Recognition) | Used for large-volume form processing (such as order forms, application forms and questionnaires) where the range of possible inputs is varied. |
| • OMR (Optical Mark Recognition) | Similar to OCR but where the range of possible inputs is limited, such as UK Lottery tickets or multiple-choice examination answer sheets. |
| • MICR (Magnetic Ink Character Recognition) | Used mainly in the banking industry for processing cheques and transaction vouchers. |
| Voice recognition | Used to automate high-volume data entry, thus reducing costs and minimising delays, often in a service desk or order capture environment. |
| RFID (Radio Frequency IDentification) | Used for high-volume transactions where the amount of data to be captured is limited (for instance just a unique identifier). Data capture can be both active (such as a user swiping an Oyster card over a reader in a London Underground station) or passive (such as an engine passing a sensor on a car assembly line). |
| Swipe cards | Similar to the active uses of RFID. |

### *Input user-interfaces*

The detailed design of input interfaces depends upon the mechanism and technology the designer has selected to achieve a particular input. Consideration of all options is outside the scope of this book, but we consider here the most common options available to the designer when designing interfaces for use with standard desktop computers and laptops.

User interfaces are often referred to as 'dialogues', which can cover both input and output. UML use cases provide a useful start point for designing a dialogue because they define the required flow of input and output responses needed. The structure of the dialogue will control the interaction between the user and computer and determine how information is presented and received. Dialogues vary in this degree of control from user-initiated (where the user is in command) to computer-initiated (where the user simply responds to the requests of the system).

To be effective, a dialogue has to be functional and usable. Functionality is concerned with ensuring that all the required data has a mechanism for input and output. Usability means that the users of the system should be given a dialogue that is 'user-friendly', as described above.

The most common types of dialogue structure used in modern computer systems are explained below:

| | |
|---|---|
| **Menus** | Menus present a selection of the possible options for users to select from, typically by clicking on the option using a mouse or similar device. A distinction can be made between a drop-down menu, where the menu option appears in the menu bar of the application window and a pop-up menu, that appears when specifically invoked by the user, typically by right-clicking a specific element on the screen. The items displayed on a pop-up menu depend on where the pointer was located when the button was pressed. Menus may also have sub-menus (cascading menus). |
| **Form filling** | Input data is entered onto screens that resemble a form. Areas of the screen are protected from input and the cursor is placed at relevant points to indicate where and in what order the data is to be entered. |
| **Command language** | With menus and form-filling, the dialogue is initiated by the system. However, command language dialogues are user-initiated. The system waits for an instruction and the user initiates the dialogue by entering pre-defined commands or codes, known to the system, and the system then responds accordingly. |
| **Question and answer** | The system guides the user through the dialogue in the form of a series of questions to respond to. A variant of the Q and A dialogue was originally called a 'wizard' and this style of dialogue is now combined with form-filling on modern web-based systems. |

Selection of appropriate dialogues depends on a number of factors, not least the experience of the target user.

## Output design

The principal objective of output design is to define how data that is stored and/or manipulated by the system will be extracted and presented in a format that can be interpreted and used to meet certain functional requirements that would have been defined during requirements engineering. The recipient of outputs is either the system end user or another system. In addition to ensuring that the functional requirements are met, the designer must also take into account a number of other considerations, many of which are also common to input design:

- **Efficiency** – to ensure that the output makes efficient use of resources, such as mains power, processor and memory usage and consumables like paper and toner/ink.

- **Reliability and timing** – to ensure that the outputs are available when they are needed.

- **Accuracy** – to ensure that any data output from the system is correct and up to date.

- **Usability** – to ensure that the outputs are easy for the user to obtain and interpret.

- **Clarity** – (arguably a subset of usability) to ensure that the format and content of the output can be clearly understood by its intended recipient, ideally without separate instructions to clarify.

- **Relevance** – to ensure that the output provides only the data that is required to fulfil its purpose. Any data beyond this will detract from its purpose and compromise its effectiveness.

- **Quality** – the required quality of the output will often be determined by whether the output is intended for personal or public use, for internal use or distribution to external stakeholders, such as customers. There may also be regulatory or legal requirements governing the precise specification of certain outputs.

- **Cost** – the cost of generating the output in the chosen format and using the selected technology should not outweigh the benefits derived from the use of the output.

One of the key decisions that a designer must make when undertaking output design is the choice of technology to use and different technologies score differently in terms of the above considerations. Table 8.2 provides a summary of the most common output technologies and their potential uses.

**Table 8.2 Common output technologies**

| Technology/Device | Uses |
| --- | --- |
| **Monitor (CRT, LCD, LED, TFT, OLED, Plasma, UHD)** | Suitable for most output requirements. However, depending on the size and quality requirements, there are a number of different technologies available. For instance, plasma screens are suitable where large formats are required but OLED and UHD are used where high definition is required. |

*(Continued)*

**Table 8.2 (Continued)**

| Technology/Device | Uses |
| --- | --- |
| | Note: TFT is an older technology used in laptops and CRT has now been super-seded by LCD and LED screens due to their cumbersome nature. |
| **Touch screen (including smartphones and tablets)** | Similar to monitors but have the additional benefit of doubling up as an input device. |
| | See Table 8.1 for further details. |
| **Printer (laser, ink-jet, thermal, impact)** | Printers are used for permanent 'hard-copies' of output. Laser printers are good for high-volume printing as they have a high PPM (pages per minute) rating. Inkjet printers are lower-cost than lasers and are generally used where colour output is required. Some ink-jets are higher quality and are referred to as photo printers, as they produce high-quality photographs. Thermal printers are used for mobile applications and high-volume, small format outputs, such as till receipts and hand-held credit card machines. Impact printers (such as dot-matrix and drum printers) are all but extinct now, having been super-seded by laser and inkjet printers. However, some are still used where multi-part, carbon copy stationery is used. |
| **Plotters** | For specialist use with design applications such as CAD (Computer Aided Design), which require high-quality outputs, often in large formats, such as A2. |
| **Speakers and headphones** | Used for specialist audio applications or where voice recognition is used as an input mechanism; spoken inputs are converted into audio outputs for verification purposes (see subsection under system controls later). Headsets combine speakers with a microphone to act as both input and output device. |
| **SMS & MMS** | Used as immediate alerts (usually SMS rather than MMS) or reminders. |

*(Continued)*

**Table 8.2 (Continued)**

| Technology/Device | Uses |
|---|---|
| Email | Similar to SMS, but also used more for confirmatory messages that are less critical or to send documents as attachments. |
| Digital media (magnetic, solid-state, optical)<br>• Magnetic media (magnetic tape, magnetic disk)<br>• Solid-state media (SD cards, USB memory sticks)<br>• Optical media (CD, DVD, Blu-ray) | Other than with specialist applications in the film, television and music industries, use tends to be limited to backup systems and archiving historical data to permanent, 'hard-copy' for ad hoc reference. |
| XML | Mainly used for interfaces between disparate systems due to it being an open standard. There are a number of industry/application-specific XML schema standards defined to enable integration between compatible systems, such as HR-XML for HR systems, FpML/FIXML for financial products and financial information exchange and ONIX for book industry applications. |

When choosing appropriate output technologies, the designer must pay particular attention to the following:

• **The application itself.** For example, the production of payslips for a payroll bureau will impose quality, volumetric and timing constraints necessitating the deployment of high-quality printer technology. A simple, screen-based enquiry showing the status of an order to assist a despatch clerk with the scheduling of deliveries may only require a basic monitor, whereas the scoreboard at a major sporting stadium will require large-scale plasma technology to enable spectators to read from a significant distance.

• **Circumstances.** User and environmental constraints also influence the selection of the output device. Sight-impaired people will require special consideration and audio or touch devices may be needed. The location of the information requirement may demand output devices that have certain security features, are tolerant to dirt and dust or which are mobile and can be handheld.

- **Cost.** Budgets are usually a constraint on system development projects, so the designer must be careful to select technologies that are justified and deliver benefits that outweigh their cost. Whilst business stakeholders may want to use the latest, state-of-the-art devices, their cost is often difficult to justify, as they may not deliver any additional benefits over and above more established, cheaper devices.

### Output user-interfaces

The most common output interfaces are screen-based enquiries (including graphical dashboards), printed reports and documents (such as invoices or payslips), although reports and documents are increasingly being generated in electronic form, such as Adobe's Portable Document Format (PDF). Often the precise content, and even the layout, will be pre-defined within the system requirements documentation, frequently as prototypes. Sometimes the content and format may even be determined by legislation, such as key documents produced by payroll systems.

When considering reporting requirements, the designer needs to consider the most appropriate format to use, unless this has already been pre-empted in the requirements. The most common options are:

| | |
|---|---|
| **On demand** | These are usually produced to satisfy ad hoc queries about data stored in the system. Ad hoc reports are often executed on extracted data that perhaps reflect figures as at a point in time, such as end of previous day. |
| **Summary** | These only provide totals from a set of more detailed data records. Often produced at specific intervals such as end of day, month end, end of financial year. Again, most summary reports are produced from extracted data. |
| **Exception** | These reports highlight exceptional or extraordinary situations to prompt investigation or action. For example, a list of orders that have not been fulfilled at the end of the day, to prompt immediate action to deal with them as a priority at the start of the next day. |
| **Data dumps** | Often data is output as a file for use by a software-based reporting or analysis tool (such as a spreadsheet), for subsequent manipulation and analysis. |
| **Archive** | Some reports are produced when the appropriate data is no longer required on the system. For example the details of a dead person's medical records may be output on paper or microfiche[1] for research purposes. Similarly, reports of historical financial transactions may be required for company taxation purposes. |

---

[1] Microfiche is a sheet of microfilm, six by four inches, holding several hundred reduced images of document pages; read using a microfiche reader or microfilm reader.

Increasingly, organisations are looking for flexible reporting options, as it is not cost-effective to continually produce 'built-in' reports within their systems as new information requirements are identified. Consequently, a popular option available to the designer might be to recommend a dedicated reporting tool that can be used by business stakeholders to create their own reports as and when the need arises. These reporting tools often access data stored in a data warehouse, which contains extracted data from operational systems that are optimised for flexible, read-only analysis and reporting, often referred to as OLAP (OnLine Analytical Processing). The use of dedicated reporting databases (data warehouses) ensures that the use of reporting and OLAP tools does not affect the performance of the 'live' operational systems.

## System to system data interchange

So far, we have considered I/O design in the context of communications between humans and computers. However, as more and more source data is being shared between systems, the I/O design task often needs to consider how the data will be extracted from a source system and be transmitted to a destination system, and then converted into a form that can be used by the system.

The functional model for the new system (such as the use case diagram in Figure 8.8) should identify the system boundary and define any interfaces with other systems. The ability for systems to interface with each other is referred to as interoperability and, traditionally, systems exchanged data using a mechanism known as EDI (Electronic Data Interchange). However, more recent developments use standard protocols to effect a point-to-point exchange of data using XML data files and schemas, often with the aid of a specialist piece of software referred to as middleware.

## PROCESS DESIGN

The principal objective of process design is to specify how the functional requirements defined during requirements engineering will be realised using a series of individual programs or software components that will be built and will interact with each other in order to deliver the required system behaviour. Process design is often sub-divided into two discrete activities:

- **High-level system design.** This is concerned with identifying the discrete components needed to realise the functional requirements, and the interfaces necessary to enable them to communicate with each other.

- **Detailed program specification.** This defines how each component identified in the high-level design is to be internally built. This activity corresponds to the unit/component design stage in the 'V' model lifecycle in Figure 8.4 and is also referred to as module design or component engineering.

Furthermore, the objectives identified earlier come into play here, such as the need to produce reusable code and the desire for an efficient, reliable, expandable, maintainable solution.

As with I/O design, the start point for process design is the requirements catalogue and some form of functional specification. If we take the UML use case model in Figure 8.8, then this would identify five key system processes to be specified, one for each use case:

- Place order;
- Pick order;
- Despatch order;
- Record delivery;
- Raise invoice.

The approach that the designer takes from here depends on the target environment that the new system will be deployed in. For instance, if the system is for a stand-alone PC with a single user, then the design can be relatively straightforward, but if the target environment is a series of networked workstations that are geographically dispersed, with mobile users requiring access from their laptops, smartphones and tablet devices, then the task becomes significantly more complex.

## High-level system design

If we consider a very simple environment like a stand-alone, single-user PC, then the high-level design may determine that the system can be developed as a single executable component. Hence, the design may focus on a set of sub-modules (often referred to as sub-routines or functions) that are linked together to form a single executable program, as shown in the form of a simple module chart in Figure 8.10.

---

**Figure 8.10  Simple module chart for a stand-alone system**

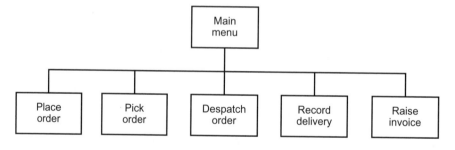

Having identified each of the high-level program modules, the designer would continue to specify each in more detail, using a technique known as **stepwise refinement**, which we shall consider later.

In contrast, we shall consider an example where the designer has identified a need to divide the functionality into a set of stand-alone components that can be deployed separately (for instance, on different servers within a local-area network), and where some common functionality is shared between components, as shown in the UML component diagram in Figure 8.11.

**Figure 8.11 High-level design showing separate components and their interfaces**

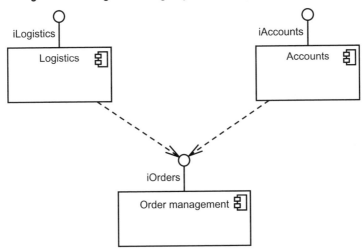

In Figure 8.11, we can see three separate components (Logistics, Accounts and Order Management), each providing a set of services defined in an interface (shown by the ball joint). Hence, iLogistics is the interface provided by the Logistics component, iAccounts is the interface provided by the Accounts component and iOrders is the interface provided by the OrderManagement component. Figure 8.11 also shows that the Logistics and Accounts components both have a dependency on the iOrders interface provided by the OrderManagement component, denoted by the dashed arrows.

Figure 8.11 does not include any indication of the technologies that will be used to build and deploy the components; it just shows, logically, which components will be needed and the required interfaces between them.

Figure 8.12 shows a UML class diagram that is being used to define the iOrders interface in more detail, by explicitly showing which services the interface will provide.

**Figure 8.12 UML class diagram showing a detailed definition of an interface**

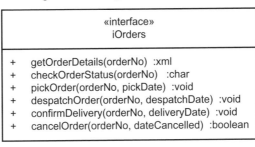

As can be seen from Figure 8.12, iOrders provides six services that can be invoked by the Logistics and Accounts components:

- getOrderDetails;
- checkOrderStatus;
- pickOrder;
- despatchOrder;
- confirmDelivery;
- cancelOrder.

Notice also that each service takes parameters that pass information (such as the order number in question and the pick/despatch/delivery/cancellation date) from the Logistics and Accounts components to the OrderManagement component, and returns information back to the component that invokes the service in the form of return values (such as an XML message containing the order details), returned by the **getOrderDetails** service or a boolean (true/false) value indicating whether the order has been successfully cancelled, returned by the **cancelOrder** service.

### Stepwise refinement

From a high-level view of the design, such as the module chart in Figure 8.10, the designer gradually breaks down each module into more detail, elaborating the requirements into a form detailed enough to enable a developer to produce a solution. This process is referred to as **stepwise refinement**. There are two common approaches:

- **Top-down.** An overview of the system is first formulated, specifying but not detailing any first-level sub-processes or sub-systems. Each sub-process/sub-system is then refined in yet greater detail, sometimes in many additional levels, until the entire specification is reduced to base elements.
- **Bottom-up.** The individual base elements of the system are first specified in great detail and these elements are then linked together to form larger sub-systems, which in turn are then linked, sometimes in many levels, until a complete top-level system is formed.

Figure 8.13 provides a de-composed view of the Place Order module from Figure 8.10 using a notation called a structure chart, as used with the Jackson Structured Programming (JSP) methodology.

In the example in Figure 8.13, the high-level module **Place Order** from the module chart in Figure 8.10 becomes the top-level driving module, which is then decomposed into three further modules: **Enter Details, Take Payment** and **Print Confirmation**. The **Enter Details** module is then de-composed into three further, more cohesive modules (the concepts of coupling and cohesion in process design are discussed later): **Enter Customer Details, Select Products** and **Enter Delivery Details**, and so on. The modules **Take Payment, Print Confirmation, Enter Delivery Details, Identify Existing Customer, Register New Customer** and **Enter Product Details** are at a base level, where further de-composition within the same diagram would render the diagram unusable. These

**Figure 8.13 Structure chart showing the de-composition of the Place Order module**

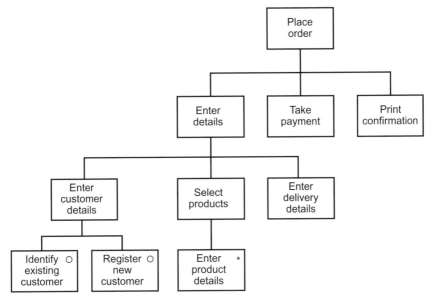

base level modules are best de-composed using a simple flow chart (such as a UML activity diagram) or a textual notation such as Structured English (also referred to as pseudocode). The module/structure charts, as the name implies, define the structural elements of the system processing, whilst the flow charts and pseudocode define the detailed behaviour of the modules.

### *Programming constructs*

The JSP structure chart in Figure 8.13, as well as showing the de-composition of the high-level module **Place Order** also explicitly identifies the three fundamental constructs supported by all programming languages: **sequence, selection** and **iteration**.

- **Sequence.** Steps in a process (or program source code statements) are executed in sequence. The sequence never changes and all steps are executed every time the process runs. In Figure 8.13 the modules **Enter Details, Take Payment** and **Print Confirmation** form a sequence construct, as do **Enter Customer Details, Select Products** and **Enter Delivery Details**.

- **Selection.** Steps in a process are selectively executed dependent on certain conditions. In Figure 8.13 the modules **Identify Existing Customer** and **Register New Customer** form a selection construct, as only one of those modules will be executed (not both) dependent on some condition, which would be evaluated in the module **Enter Customer Details**. In JSP, a selection is denoted by using the symbol ° inside the module box.

- **Iteration.** Steps in a process are executed a number of times, dependent on some condition. In Figure 8.13 the module **Enter Product Details** is an example of an iteration, as it would be repeated for each product being ordered. In JSP a selection is denoted by using the symbol * inside the module box.

167

### Coupling and cohesion

When identifying and defining the high-level modules of a system the designer must take into account the principles of good modular design, such as reusability and maintainability. Both of these principles are addressed by two design concepts: coupling and cohesion; these place constraints upon the modules by requiring them to be **loosely coupled** and **cohesive**.

Coupling is effectively a measure of the independence of the modules. Loosely coupled modules are relatively independent of one another, so that one module can be modified with little or no impact on the other. However, there must always be coupling, and hence, dependency, between two modules if one uses the services provided by the other, as in the example in Figure 8.11. We have already considered the concept of an interface (as shown in Figures 8.11 and 8.12), which is the mechanism designers use to achieve loose coupling.

Cohesion is a measure of how closely related all the aspects of a module are to each other. A module should have a well-defined role within the system and carry out a single, problem-related function. Hence, the designer breaks down a module that is not cohesive (in other words, covers more than one function), into a set of more 'single-minded' sub-modules, as shown in Figure 8.13, until all of the lowest level modules perform only one, well-defined function.

In general, loosely-coupled, cohesive modules can be more easily reused, as is the case of the **Take Payment** module in Figure 8.13, which could potentially be used in a number of systems. Furthermore, the designer may decide to use a ready-made component that provides payment functionality, or even a web service such as PayPal™.

## Unit/component design

The high-level design effectively treats the modules as 'black-boxes', where the internal workings are not visible but only the observable behaviour and any interfaces are determined. Once the high-level modular design is complete, the designer can turn their attention to specifying the detailed workings of each module. These specifications are often referred to as program specifications, as they effectively specify the work that the programmer needs to undertake. The most commonly used techniques for specifying these program units are flow charts (such as the UML activity diagram) and pseudocode (also called Structured English).

Figure 8.14 shows the **Enter Customer Details** module from Figure 8.13 de-composed into an activity diagram (flow chart) to show how the programmer should determine which of the lower-level modules **Identify Existing Customer** and **Register New Customer** should be invoked. On the diagram the solid circle denotes the start of the flow and the circle with a cross in it denotes the end. The actions performed are shown in rounded rectangles and the logical flow is shown by the arrows. The diamond symbol denotes that a decision is made at that point and which branch is followed is determined by the guard conditions shown in square brackets on their respective lines. The spectacle symbols shown in the two actions **Identify Existing Customer** and **Register New Customer** denote that these actions are de-composed in separate diagrams.

**Figure 8.14 Activity diagram specification of the Enter Customer Details module**

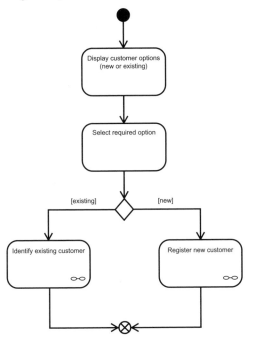

Figure 8.15 shows the same module specified using Structured English/pseudocode. Some of the words are in upper case, which denotes the key elements of structure. The DO and ENDDO at the beginning and end of the code denote the start and end of a **sequence** construct. The IF, ELSE and ENDIF define the key elements of a **selection** construct. The use of lines ties together key elements of the same construct. The underlining indicates that the items underlined refer to names of other modules that are defined using separate pseudocode.

## Object-oriented design

Object-oriented development (OOD) was introduced briefly in Chapter 6 as a programming paradigm (theoretical framework) based around the concept of an object. Objects are defined by their properties or characteristics (attributes) and their behaviour (the services that they provide to other objects). In object-oriented (OO) systems, the system requirements are realised by the interaction of objects, whereby an object invokes a service from another object in order to provide its own services and realise the required functionality of the system.

In software terms, an object is a discrete package of data and processes (operations), that typically relates to a particular real-world thing (such as a product), a conceptual idea (such as a skill that a person possesses) or an event that has (or will) taken place (such as a training course).

**Figure 8.15 Pseudocode specification of the Enter Customer Details module**

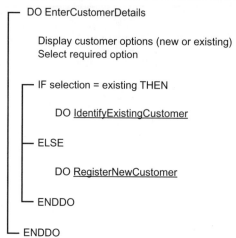

DO EnterCustomerDetails

    Display customer options (new or existing)
    Select required option

    IF selection = existing THEN

        DO IdentifyExistingCustomer

    ELSE

        DO RegisterNewCustomer

    ENDDO

ENDDO

Sticking with our theme of a sales order processing system, Figure 8.16 shows the definition of an **order** object, using UML class diagram notation. In OO theory, a class is a template for a kind of object.

**Figure 8.16 Definition of an order object**

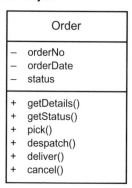

| Order |
| --- |
| − orderNo |
| − orderDate |
| − status |
| + getDetails() |
| + getStatus() |
| + pick() |
| + despatch() |
| + deliver() |
| + cancel() |

In this simple class definition there are three attributes (in practice there are likely to be more) and six operations (again, in practice there may be more). The attributes are prefixed with a minus sign and the operations a plus sign. This highlights a fundamental concept within OO design: **encapsulation**. This means that the inner workings of an object are invisible to outsiders, in other words, other objects. In UML the plus symbol (meaning public) and minus symbol (meaning private) are referred to as adornments and indicate the visibility of the elements that they prefix. Hence, the attributes of the object are said to be private (not visible to other objects) whilst the operations are public (visible to other objects).

An object can only access another object by sending a message to it. The message invokes the operation in the receiving object with the same name as the message. Consequently, when specifying OO processes, the designer produces some form of interaction diagram showing the explicit messages being sent between objects in order to realise the required functionality defined in a use case. Isolating objects in this way makes software easier to manage, more robust and reusable.

Other key concepts within OO design are **abstraction, generalisation** and **polymorphism**. These are all demonstrated within Figure 8.17, which shows a partial class model for an insurance policy administration system.

**Figure 8.17 Class model showing abstraction (generalisation) and polymorphism**

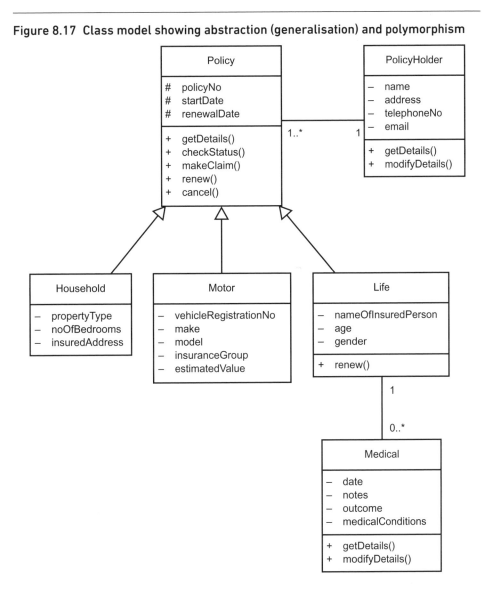

Abstraction captures only those details about an object that are relevant to the current perspective, as with abstract art, which hides irrelevant details. For example, when considering the vehicle insured by a Motor policy, as in Figure 8.17, although the vehicle has a colour, number of doors, engine capacity and gearbox type, none of these details is relevant to the policy administration system, and hence, they are not included in the class diagram.

Generalisation is a form of abstraction, whereby the common elements of a number of different types of 'thing' (such as a policy, as shown above) are grouped together into a super-class (called the generalisation) and the elements that are specific to each sub-type are shown as sub-classes (called specialisations). Hence, in Figure 8.17, **Policy** is the generalisation and **Household, Motor** and **Life** are the specialisations.

In OO design, sub-classes inherit characteristics (attributes, operations and associations) from their parent super-class. Hence, **Household, Motor** and **Life**, as well as having their own specific attributes, also inherit **policyNo, startDate** and **renewalDate** from the **Policy** class. The attributes of the Policy class are shown with the hash visibility adornment (#). This denotes that the attributes of the generalised class are visible to the sub-classes as well.

Similarly, the sub-classes also inherit the operations **getDetails()**, **checkStatus()**, **makeClaim()**, **renew()** and **cancel()** from the **Policy** class. Furthermore, although not immediately obvious from the class diagram, they also have an association with the **PolicyHolder** class, although the **Life** class also has its own association with **Medical**, which is not shared with any of the other types of policy.

Polymorphism (meaning literally 'many forms') is a technique used by OO designers and programmers to override the functionality defined at the super-class level within specific sub-classes. So in Figure 8.17 we can see that the operation **renew()** defined within the **Policy** super-class is overridden with a different implementation for the sub-class **Life**. This reflects the fact that the renewal process for life policies differs from all other policies, perhaps as a consequence of requiring a new medical each time.

## REFERENCES AND FURTHER READING

For References and Further Reading, please see the end of Chapter 9.

# 9    SYSTEMS DESIGN – 2

Peter Thompson

## CONTENTS OF THIS CHAPTER

This chapter covers the following topics:

- the objectives and principles of data design;
- the design of codes;
- the scope and principles of security and control design;
- logical and physical design;
- design patterns;
- references and further reading.

## DATA DESIGN

The objective of data design is to define a set of flexible data structures that will enable the realisation of the functional requirements agreed during requirements engineering, by supporting the input, output and process designs. The start point for data design is often a model of the data requirements, or a high-level business domain model, typically in the form of a UML class diagram or an entity relationship diagram. If no such analysis model is available, then the designer needs to start by producing their own model by identifying classes (or entities) from the requirements documentation (for example a requirements catalogue). One straightforward way to do this is to identify the key nouns from the narrative requirement descriptions, which become potential classes or entities. A detailed description of this process is outside the scope of this book.

Although an analysis data model is a good start point for data design, the model is typically not in a suitable format to enable a robust set of data structures to be created and, hence, requires normalising (see below). A further issue that the designer may encounter is that the analysis data model is incomplete. Additional data items (attributes), and even additional classes or entities are often required to support certain processing defined during the process design stage, or to enable future system flexibility in the form of configuration parameters.

From a normalised data model, the designer needs to agree the technology that will be used to store the data persistently. That is to say, some form of external data file(s) or even a specialist database management system (DBMS), where the data persists when the system is not running.

We shall now consider each of these aspects of data design in more detail.

## Normalisation

Normalisation is a technique that designers use to derive flexible, robust and redundancy-free data structures. This means that the data structures (tables, entities or classes):

- do not contain data that can be derived;
- only contain one copy of each logical data item;
- contain the very latest value for each data item;
- accurately reflect values as per the original source from which the data was derived or that are consistent with any changes made in the system;
- combine data items into logical groups based on underlying data dependencies.

A data structure that exhibits these data qualities is said to have good data integrity.

Let us take, for example, a simple spreadsheet that is being used by a business centre for managing room bookings, as shown in Figure 9.1.

### Figure 9.1  Spreadsheet showing un-normalised data

| Room bookings for week commencing 29th January | | | | | |
|---|---|---|---|---|---|
| **Day** | **Room** | **Time** | **Booker's name** | **Company** | **Hourly rate** |
| Monday | MR1 | 09:00–11:00 | Ben Peters | B.A.P. Consultants | 25.00 |
| | MR1 | 13:30–16:00 | Julie Knight | PJA | 25.00 |
| | MR2 | Free | | | |
| | MR3 | 08:45–11:45 | Jennifer Jones | Spring Clean | 20.00 |
| | MR3 | 13:00–14:00 | Mark Clarke | Polyphonic Technologies | 20.00 |
| | TR1 | 09:00–17:00 | Dave Thomson | Applied Data Training | 40.00 |
| | TR2 | 09:00–17:00 | Kevin Jones | Applied Data Training | 40.00 |
| | Conference suite | 08:00–19:00 | Helen Paterson | Keyvents UK | 50.00 |
| | | | | | |
| Tuesday | MR1 | 08:30–12:00 | Sarah Smith | Robert James & Co | 25.00 |
| | MR2 | 10:00–11:00 | George Jones | Spring Clean | 25.00 |
| | MR2 | 14:00–16:00 | Mark Clarke | Polyphonic Technologies | 25.00 |
| | MR3 | 09:00–11:00 | Ben Peters | B.A.P. Consultants | 25.00 |
| | TR1 | 09:00–17:00 | Dave Tomson | Applied Data Training | 40.00 |
| | TR2 | 09:00–17:00 | Kevin Jones | Applied Data Training | 40.00 |
| | Conference suite | Free | | | |
| | | | | | |
| ... | ... | ... | ... | ... | ... |

This spreadsheet highlights not only that there is redundant data in the spreadsheet (the hourly rate relates to the room that is being booked but is repeated for each booking), but that un-normalised data can become inconsistent, as is the case with the entries for training room 1 (TR1), whereby, although the same person has booked the room for Monday and Tuesday, the spelling of their name is different for each of the bookings (Dave Thomson on Monday and Dave Tomson on Tuesday). Just by looking at the data it is impossible to tell which spelling is correct. Furthermore, the hourly rate for meeting room 3 (MR3) on Monday shows as £20.00 but the same room on Tuesday shows as £25.00. Again, there is some inconsistency with the data and, again, it is not possible to determine which value is correct. We might surmise that the booking for Ben Peters in room MR1 on Monday was copied to Tuesday but MR1 was not available and, hence, the room was changed to MR3 but the user forgot to change the rate to the MR3 rate; however, it is impossible to tell from the data.

Figure 9.2 shows a set of normalised data structures derived from the un-normalised data in Figure 9.1. A detailed consideration of the process of normalisation is outside the scope of this book and interested readers are directed to some of the references listed at the end of this chapter.

## Figure 9.2 Normalised data structures

**Booker**

| Booker Id | Booker's name | Company |
|-----------|---------------|---------|
| 1 | Ben Peters | B.A.P. Consultants |
| 2 | Julie Knight | PJA |
| 3 | Jennifer Jones | Spring Clean |
| 4 | Mark Clarke | Polyphonic Technologies |
| 5 | Dave Thomson | Applied Data Training |
| 6 | Kevin Jones | Applied Data Training |
| 7 | Helen Paterson | Keyvents UK |
| 8 | Sarah Smith | Robert James & Co |
| 9 | George Jones | Spring Clean |

**Room**

| Room | Hourly rate |
|------|-------------|
| MR1 | 25.00 |
| MR2 | 25.00 |
| MR3 | 20.00 |
| TR1 | 40.00 |
| TR2 | 40.00 |
| Conference suite | 50.00 |

**Booking**

| Day | Room | Time | Booker Id |
|-----|------|------|-----------|
| Monday | MR1 | 09:00–11:00 | 1 |
| Monday | MR1 | 13:30–16:00 | 2 |
| Monday | MR3 | 08:45–11:45 | 3 |
| Monday | MR3 | 13:00–14:00 | 4 |
| Monday | TR1 | 09:00–17:00 | 5 |
| Monday | TR2 | 09:00–17:00 | 6 |
| Monday | Conference suite | 08:00–19:00 | 7 |
| Tuesday | MR1 | 08:30–12:00 | 8 |
| Tuesday | MR2 | 10:00–11:00 | 9 |
| Tuesday | MR2 | 14:00–16:00 | 4 |
| Tuesday | MR3 | 09:00–11:00 | 1 |
| Tuesday | TR1 | 09:00–17:00 | 5 |
| Tuesday | TR2 | 09:00–17:00 | 6 |
| ... | ... | ... | ... |

As we can see from Figure 9.2, the redundant replication of the hourly rate has been removed, so that hourly rate is only recorded once, against the room. This improves the integrity of the data because, whenever the system needs to access the hourly rate, it can look it up in the **Room** table and always find the latest value.

Similarly, there is only one record of each booker, so that the booker's name is only recorded once, and there is now no doubt that the correct spelling of Dave's surname is Thomson. However, notice that, in order to normalise the data, it was necessary to invent a new unique identifier called **Booker Id**. This is to ensure uniqueness, because the name of the booker cannot be guaranteed to be unique. In other words, we cannot assume that there will never be another Dave Thomson who books a room in future.

## Code design

In the normalisation example above, a new data item was invented to provide a unique identifier (also referred to as a **key**) for the Booker table. This is an example of a code.

Codes are invented data items that can be used to uniquely reference certain types of data. For example, a product code is used to uniquely reference data about a particular product and a customer code is used to uniquely reference data about a particular customer.

The simplest type of code is a sequential number, as with **Booker Id** in Figure 9.2. If we needed to determine the data about the booker from a particular booking (for example, who booked MR3 on Tuesday at 09:00–11:00, then we can use the **Booker Id** value in the **Booker** table (1) to look up the corresponding entry in the **Booking** table (Ben Peters, B.A.P. Consultants).

When designing codes, the designer must consider the following criteria:

- **Uniqueness.** The designer must ensure that there could never be two identical values of the code relating to different data records.

- **Stability.** A coding system should always have the same format for all possible code values.

- **Expandability.** A coding system should always allow for future growth in terms of the number of unique codes that can be generated.

- **Length.** This is an extension of the other considerations. If a code is not long enough (for instance, not enough digits or characters), then it may not provide enough unique values to allow for future growth, and hence, the format of future codes may need to change to allow for more unique values.

There are a number of high-profile examples where code designers have not fully considered these requirements. For example, when devising a code to uniquely identify any device connected to the internet, the designers used a four-part code (Internet Protocol version 4), which provides $2^{32}$ (4,294,967,296) addresses. However, the designers did not predict the phenomenal rise in demand for mobile devices that could connect to the internet, and hence, there was a need to devise a new code, Internet Protocol version 6. IPv6 addresses are represented as eight groups of four hexadecimal digits separated by colons, which provides for $2^{128}$, or approximately $3.4 \times 1038$ addresses, which is more than $7.9 \times 1028$ times as many as IPv4!

The Booker Id code used above is an example of using a simple sequential number. However, there are other types of code, including faceted and self-checking codes, that are worthy of further consideration.

### Faceted codes

A faceted code is one that is made up of a number of parts, or facets, such as vehicle registration identification numbers, an example of which is shown in Figure 9.3, courtesy of Wikipedia.

**Figure 9.3 Example of a faceted code (UK vehicle registration number)**

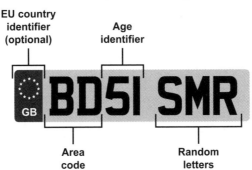

The reason designers use faceted codes is because they are intrinsically meaningful to users of the code. In our example, system users (staff at DVLA, the Driver and Vehicle Licensing Agency) can determine the local registration office that the vehicle was registered at without needing to look it up and other relevant stakeholders may also use this system (for example, drivers may use the above registration number to determine the age of a vehicle before purchasing it). Furthermore, a faceted code can also be more robust, as separate validation can be applied to the different facets of the code.

### Self-checking codes

The most common validation check performed on codes is to look up the code in some reference data table or file to determine whether it exists. If the code cannot be found then it is deemed to be invalid. However, if a code is made up of a sequential number, then it is possible for a system user to mis-type the code but still have entered a valid value. Under some circumstances, this may not be too much of a problem; for example, if the system displays back to the user some other data values associated with the code, such as the date and customer associated with a particular sequential order number. However, if we consider an online banking system, whereby a user wishes to transfer money from one account to the other, then the use of purely sequential bank account numbers could enable the transfer to go to the wrong account, which would be disastrous for the account holder making the transfer, and embarrassing for the bank. Consequently, banks use self-checking codes.

To understand how they work, let us consider the example of a bank account number as shown in Figure 9.4.

**Figure 9.4 Example of a self-checking code**

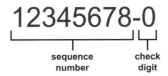

The main part of the account number is a sequential number, so the next available number is derived from the previously allocated number +1. However, a sequential number alone is not robust enough so a special digit, called a check digit, is added to the end. The check digit is calculated from the sequence number using a special algorithm. This algorithm needs to ensure that, for the same source number, only one possible value can be derived for the check digit.

Once the check digit has been calculated, it is appended to the end of the source number to form the code. From here onwards, the entire code is always used, including the check digit. So when a user enters the account number, they must enter the entire code including the check digit. The computer system then strips off the check digit and recalculates it using the same algorithm, comparing the calculated value with the entered value. If the calculated check digit matches the entered check digit then the user has correctly entered the code, otherwise the system rejects the entry as invalid. If the user inadvertently switches two of the digits of the account number, when the system recalculates the check digit it will not match the check digit value entered and, hence, the system will reject the entry.

## Database management systems

We have seen that data design is concerned with deriving a set of data structures to support the required inputs, outputs and processes. These structures are generally logical and independent of the target environment within which the system will be deployed. However, at some point the designer needs to decide how the data is to be stored persistently so that it is available the next time the system is executed. Traditionally, the data would be stored in a series of physical data files on a hard drive, which was perfectly adequate for single-user systems; but, with the advent of distributed, networked, multi-user systems, manipulating such files created performance difficulties and thus the new concept of the centralised database was born.

A database is a collection of organised data sets that are created, maintained and accessed using a specialist software package called a database management system (DBMS). A DBMS allows different application programs to easily access the same database. This is generally achieved by submitting a query defined using a special query language such as SQL (Structured Query Language) to the DBMS, which extracts, sorts and groups the data into a result set that is passed back to the relevant application program for further manipulation.

DBMSs may use any of a variety of database models, which define how the data is logically structured and, hence, how queries need to access the data. The most commonly-used models are: hierarchical, network, relational and object-oriented.

### Hierarchical databases

With a hierarchical database, the data is organised as a set of records that form a hierarchy, as shown in Figure 9.5. In Figure 9.5, the inset diagram shows the basic structure of the database in terms of three record structures: **Region, Town** and **Branch**, where the **Region** record is made up of two data items (**region** and manager), the **Town** record is simply made up of the data item **Town**, and the **Branch** record is made up of three data items (**branch-id, manager** and **no-of-staff**). The main diagram shows sample data and links between the data records. The ellipsis (...) show that there is more data than can be shown on the same diagram.

**Figure 9.5  Example of a hierarchical database structure**

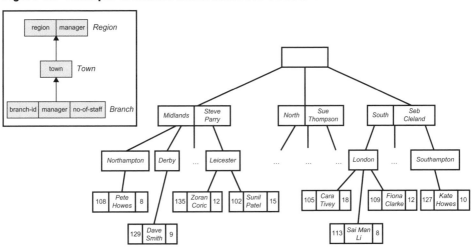

In Figure 9.5, each data node in the hierarchy has a single upward link (or parent node) and each parent node contains a number of links to its child nodes.

Hierarchical structures were widely used in the early mainframe database management systems, such as the Information Management System (IMS) by IBM, and now describe the structure of XML documents. Microsoft's Windows® Registry is another more recent example of a hierarchical database.

### Network databases

The network database model (also known as the CODASYL database model) is a more flexible derivation of a hierarchical database. Instead of each data node being linked to just one parent node, it is possible to link a node to multiple parents, thus forming a network-like structure, as shown in the example in Figure 9.6. This means that network databases can represent complex many-to-many relationships between the underlying data entities/classes, whereas hierarchical databases are restricted to simpler one-to-many structures.

**Figure 9.6  Example of a network database structure**

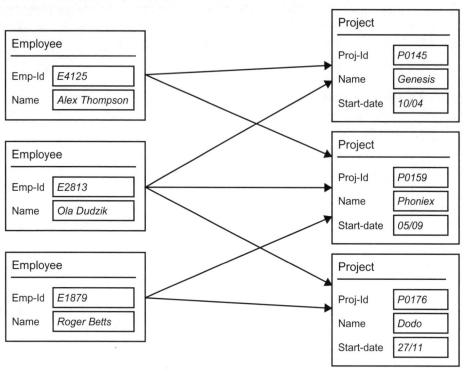

A network database consists of a collection of records connected to each other through links. A record is a collection of data items, similar to an entity in entity relationship modelling or a class in class modelling. Each data item has a name and a value. A CODASYL record may have its own internal structure and can include tables, where a table is a collection of values grouped under one data item name.

Probably the best known examples of a network DBMS are IDMS (Integrated Data Management System) and IDS (Integrated Data Store).

### Relational databases

Hierarchical and network databases have largely been superseded by relational databases, based on the relational model, as introduced by E.F. Codd (Ted Codd) in 1970. This model was devised to make database management systems more independent of any particular application and, hence, more flexible for sharing databases between different applications.

The basic data structure of the relational model is the table (also referred to as a **relation**), where information about a particular entity is represented in rows and columns. Thus, the 'relation' in 'relational database' refers to the various tables in the database. A relation is a set of rows (referred to as tuples). The columns represent the various attributes of the entity and a row is an actual **instance** of the entity that is represented by the relation. Hence, in the example in Figure 9.7, which is a relational representation of the same database as Figure 9.6, there are three relations (**Employee, Project** and **Employee-Project**), **Employee** contains two attributes (**Emp-Id** and **Name**) and three tuples (E4125, Bob Smart; E2813, Gary Blake; E1879, Roger Betts), and so on.

**Figure 9.7  Example of a relational database structure**

Employee

| Emp-Id | Name |
|--------|------|
| E4125 | Alex Thompson |
| E2813 | Ola Dudzik |
| E1879 | Roger Betts |

Project

| Proj-Id | Name | Start-date |
|---------|------|-----------|
| P0145 | Genesis | 10/04 |
| P0159 | Phoenix | 05/09 |
| P0176 | Dodo | 27/11 |

Employee-Project

| *Emp-Id | *Proj-Id |
|---------|----------|
| E4125 | P0145 |
| E4125 | P0159 |
| E2813 | P0145 |
| E2813 | P0159 |
| E2813 | P0176 |
| E1879 | P0159 |
| E1879 | P0176 |

In Figure 9.7, the relationships between the Employee and Project relations (as identified in Figure 9.6 as links between the records) have been represented in a separate table, which contains **Emp-Id** and **Proj-Id** as its columns. These columns show a * beside the column names, which identifies them as **foreign keys**. Relationships between tuples in different tables in a relational database are maintained by copying the **primary key** (one or more columns whose values can uniquely identify each tuple in a relation) from one table into another, where it becomes a **foreign key**. These foreign key values can be used to join the table to the original table, where the primary key values match the foreign key values. When accessing the data in a relational database, a query is issued to the DBMS, which then joins the necessary tables together, and if the query requires it, filtering and sorting the resultant table, which becomes the result set that is passed back to the query's originator (typically a program). Figure 9.8 shows the result set produced by joining the relations in Figure 9.7.

**Figure 9.8  Example of a result set from joining relations**

| Employee.Emp-Id | Employee.Name | Project.Proj-Id | Project.Name | Project.Start-date |
|-----------------|---------------|-----------------|--------------|--------------------|
| E4125 | Alex Thompson | P0145 | Genesis | 10/04 |
| E4125 | Alex Thompson | P0159 | Phoenix | 05/09 |
| E2813 | Ola Dudzik | P0145 | Genesis | 10/04 |
| E2813 | Ola Dudzik | P0159 | Phoenix | 05/09 |
| E2813 | Ola Dudzik | P0176 | Dodo | 27/11 |
| E1879 | Roger Betts | P0159 | Phoenix | 05/09 |
| E1879 | Roger Betts | P0176 | Dodo | 27/11 |

One of the strengths of the relational model is that, in principle, any value occurring in two different records (belonging to the same table or to different tables), implies a relationship among those two records. In other words, relationships between tables are established by the fact that the tables share common attributes.

There are a number of examples of relational database management systems (RDBMS) in general use, but perhaps the most common are Oracle (from Oracle Corporation®), SQL Server (from Microsoft®) and DB2 (from IBM®).

### Object-oriented

Many OO applications, whilst manipulating objects at run-time, need to hold a persistent copy of the data that is encapsulated within the objects, in some form of permanent store. Consequently, there is often a need to store the data in a database and then load it into a set of objects at run-time, saving the data back to the database before the application shuts down. Hence, many OO systems use relational databases to store their data persistently, a technique referred to as object-relational mapping.

Object-oriented database management systems (OODBMS) started to evolve from research in the early to mid 1970s, with the first commercial products appearing around 1985. These new database technologies enabled OO developers to retain the objects that they manipulated at run-time, reducing the need for object-relational mapping. However, perhaps more importantly, they introduced the key ideas of object programming, such as encapsulation and polymorphism, into the world of databases.

OO databases store data as a series of objects that are connected to each other by pointers. This means that the actual data can be directly accessed only through the invocation of one of the object's operations, which can then build in security and integrity rules to ensure that the data cannot be corrupted or accessed by unauthorised users. This is highlighted in Figure 9.9, which shows an OODB structure, by the use of visibility adornments against the attributes and operations. These same adornments were shown in the class diagram extract in Figure 8.16, but Figure 9.9 shows objects (instances of classes) rather than classes. (Note: the class diagram defining the structure for the objects and how they are associated is shown in the inset in Figure 9.9.)

In Figure 9.9, the objects are stored so that they can only be manipulated by their public operations; their attributes are shown as private. There are two main differences between object diagrams and class diagrams: first, the top compartment of the object box contains the identifier of the object as a prefix to the name of the class to which it belongs; and second, the attributes also include the values that relate to each object.

One common use of OODBMS technology is within environments that dynamically manage a large set of 'live' objects within limited memory resources, such as application servers. Objects are temporarily persisted into a local OODBMS, from which they can be quickly recovered when required.

## Figure 9.9 Example of an object database structure

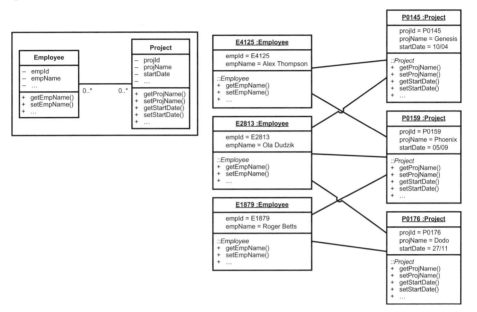

## Physical files

Although DBMSs are the most popular way to store data persistently because they create an interface between the application programs and the physical stored data, effectively de-coupling the data from the applications that manipulate it, they are not the only option. Some systems require that they directly manipulate data files stored on disk. This makes the system's designer's and developer's job more complex, but enables the use of proprietary data structures that are tailored to the specific needs of the application.

When designing data file structures, two fundamental factors must be considered:

1. how to physically organise the data on a disk (disk being the most utilised of permanent storage media);
2. how to access/retrieve the stored data.

### File organisations

The two most common data file organisations are serial and sequential.

With **serial** files, the records contained in the file are physically organised in the order in which they are created (in other words, in no logical sequence), as in Figure 9.10, which shows a simple file of employee records, with only two data items (known as fields); the first containing the employee Id and the second the employee name.

**Figure 9.10 Example of a serial file organisation**

| Rec | Emp.Id | Surname | First-name | ... |
|-----|--------|---------|------------|-----|
| 1 | E4125 | Thompson | Alex | ... |
| 2 | E1978 | Cho | Sam | ... |
| 3 | E2813 | Dudzik | Ola | ... |
| 4 | E3763 | Harris | Tim | ... |
| 5 | E3367 | Patel | Meena | ... |
| 6 | E1879 | Betts | Roger | ... |
| 7 | E5031 | Marshall | Jackie | ... |
| 8 | E2531 | Barnett | Robert | ... |
| 9 | E4656 | Richardson | Claire | ... |
| ... | ... | ... | ... | ... |

In Figure 9.10 none of the data fields are in any particular order. This organisation, whilst being more difficult to gain access to the data (as discussed later), is simple to add to. This is because, when a new record needs to be added to the file it is simply appended to the end of the file, requiring no re-organisation. However, if an application program needs to access the data in any sequence other than the sequence in which the records were created (for instance in **Surname, Firstname** or **Emp-id** sequence), then the program would need to start retrieving the data with the first record and then keep skipping through the records until the required data had been found. This is generally a very time-consuming task, especially if there is a large number of records in the file, and/or each record is quite large, in terms of the number and size of the data items recorded.

An alternative to the serial file is the **sequential** file. As the name implies, with a sequential file, the data records are physically stored on disk in some particular sequence (such as **Emp-id** sequence, as per Figure 9.11).

Like the serial file, the sequential organisation has both advantages and disadvantages. On the positive side, records in a sequential file are much easier to access/retrieve. This is because the application knows the sequence and can therefore perform some form of search algorithm to help reduce the time that would have been spent skipping through each record one at a time, if the file were serial. A relatively simple algorithm is the **binary chop**, whereby the program continually narrows down the scope of records to check on the negative side; adding new records to a sequential file necessitates a complete re-organisation of the file each time, which can be extremely time-consuming.

## Figure 9.11  Example of a sequential file organisation

| Rec | Emp.Id | Surname | First-name | ... |
|-----|--------|---------|------------|-----|
| 1 | E1879 | Betts | Roger | ... |
| 2 | E1978 | Cho | Sam | ... |
| 3 | E2531 | Barnett | Robert | ... |
| 4 | E2813 | Dudzik | Ola | ... |
| 5 | E3367 | Patel | Meena | ... |
| 6 | E3763 | Harris | Tim | ... |
| 7 | E4125 | Thompson | Alex | ... |
| 8 | E4656 | Richardson | Claire | ... |
| 9 | E5031 | Marshall | Jackie | ... |
| ... | ... | ... | ... | ... |

### File access/retrieval mechanisms

We have already considered the issues with accessing data from a serial file, and the fact that it is much quicker to retrieve data from a sequential file. Consequently, the most popular approach to manipulating data in physical files is to store the actual data in a serial file, whilst using a sequential file as an index into the serial file, as shown in Figure 9.12.

## Figure 9.12  Example of an index file

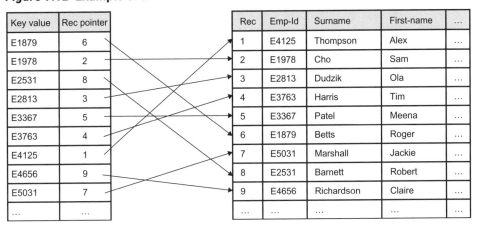

| Key value | Rec pointer |
|-----------|-------------|
| E1879 | 6 |
| E1978 | 2 |
| E2531 | 8 |
| E2813 | 3 |
| E3367 | 5 |
| E3763 | 4 |
| E4125 | 1 |
| E4656 | 9 |
| E5031 | 7 |
| ... | ... |

| Rec | Emp-Id | Surname | First-name | ... |
|-----|--------|---------|------------|-----|
| 1 | E4125 | Thompson | Alex | ... |
| 2 | E1978 | Cho | Sam | ... |
| 3 | E2813 | Dudzik | Ola | ... |
| 4 | E3763 | Harris | Tim | ... |
| 5 | E3367 | Patel | Meena | ... |
| 6 | E1879 | Betts | Roger | ... |
| 7 | E5031 | Marshall | Jackie | ... |
| 8 | E2531 | Barnett | Robert | ... |
| 9 | E4656 | Richardson | Claire | ... |
| ... | ... | ... | ... | ... |

The concept of an index file is essentially the same as using an index in a book. To find the entry that you are looking for, you first look it up in the index to find the corresponding page number, and then you can skip quickly to the required page. The same is true when accessing data using an index file.

The index file is a sequential file where the records are physically organised in the order of the key values. The key represents the value that is being sought (in the case of Figure 9.12, the key contains **Emp-Id** values). Consequently, the index file can be quickly scanned using an algorithm such as the binary chop, mentioned above, so that a pointer to the actual data record can be obtained. For example, if the index file in Figure 9.12 is scanned for the key value E2531, then this would result in a pointer to record number 8 in the serial data file.

Although indexed files tend to be the most common, some applications use a more specialist form of file retrieval whereby the actual location of the required data on the disk (known as the disk address), can be derived by applying a special algorithm to the key value. These files are collectively referred to as **direct files**.

## SECURITY AND CONTROL DESIGN

System controls are mechanisms used by the designer to ensure the integrity of the system from both a data and process perspective. There are several reasons why this is important, including:

- to comply with legislation or industry regulations (for example, data protection legislation requires that any data relating to individuals is protected from unauthorised access, and is correct and up to date);
- to enforce business rules and policies (for example, an organisation may have a rule that all purchase invoices must undergo an authorisation process before they can be paid);
- to protect an organisation's intellectual property and commercial interests (for example, access to an organisation's customer database and sales data may enable a competitor to poach customers by undercutting their prices);
- to ensure the accuracy of any data used to inform management decision-making (for example, (1) an organisation's senior management may decide to invest in a product based on previous sales figures, which, if they are incorrect may lead to heavy losses, or (2) inaccurate data about a customer's order may lead to dissatisfaction and loss of business).

The designer may devise a range of different controls aimed at complying with rules and regulations and ensuring system integrity. Some system controls are designed to prevent user errors during data input and the execution of system processes, whilst others prevent the unauthorised use of the computer system or unauthorised access to data.

Systems controls can broadly be categorised as:

- input and output controls;
- data controls;

- process controls;
- security and audit.

In practice, there are significant overlaps between each area.

## Input controls

Input controls are devised by the designer during I/O design to ensure and enforce the accuracy of data input into the system.

Input controls fall into two categories: **verification** and **validation**, which have already been briefly discussed but are expanded upon below. A further set of controls, referred to as clerical controls, may also be devised to ensure that any manual data entry activities are robust.

Whilst we have classified verification and validation as input controls, the likelihood is that they will actually be enforced within the processes that sit behind the data entry forms. Furthermore, some of the validation rules may well be implemented as part of the physical data design, as constraints within a database schema definition.

### Verification of input data

One of the biggest issues facing the designer when designing input mechanisms, particularly those that rely on keyboard data entry, is that of detecting and preventing transcription errors. In the context of keyboard data entry, this is where the user inadvertently transcribes (changes the order of) the characters being entered. The process that the designer implements in order to detect or prevent transcription errors is called verification and the most popular techniques used are:

- **Double-keying.** The user is asked to type the same data field twice and the two entries are compared. If the entries do not match, then one has been input incorrectly and the user is asked to re-key. This is used for critical entries such as email addresses (where email is the main source of communication with the data subject) and when creating new passwords.

- **Self-checking codes.** Covered earlier in this chapter, check digits are used for critical codes such as account numbers where, if the user types the entry incorrectly, the result may still be a valid code and cause critical integrity issues.

- **Repeating back what the user entered.** Data entered is displayed back to the user (or for voice-recognition inputs, the spoken inputs are converted into audio outputs) for confirmation by the user.

### Validation of input data

- **Existence checks.** The most effective way to check the accuracy and validity of a piece of data is to check if the value exists in some kind of reference file. However, this only works for certain kinds of pre-defined data, such as product codes and customer account numbers, where there is a set of pre-defined values held in a reference file.

- **Range checks.** For certain types of data, it is possible to check that the data value falls within a range of valid values. For example, the month part of a date must between 1 and 12.

- **Cross-field validation.** Often there are relationships between different items of data. For example, in a sales order processing system, the date an order is despatched cannot be prior to the date the order was placed.

## Output controls

Output controls are devised by the designer to ensure that the output from the system is complete and accurate and that it gets to the correct intended recipients in a timely manner.

Output controls include:

- **Control totals.** Used to check whether the right number of outputs have been produced and detect whether, for example, some outputs have gone missing or have not been produced. Furthermore, where outputs take the form of data files for transfer to another system, it is common practice to include special header and/or footer records containing control totals so that as the receiving system processes the file, it calculates the totals and compares the calculated totals against the values stored in the header and/or footer record(s). If the two do not match, then the file has either become corrupted or a problem has occurred when reading or processing the data.

- **Spot checks.** Used where output volumes are very large and it is not feasible to check every item produced. For example, spot checks could be conducted on a sample of payslips produced by a payroll bureau, to ensure that the correct amounts have been calculated for the correct employees. Spot checks can also be conducted for abnormally high values, as identified using an exception report. For example, checking any payslip where the amount paid exceeds £10,000 in any one month.

- **Pre-numbering.** Some outputs are produced on special pre-numbered stationery, such as invoices or cheques. Clerical controls could be put in place to ensure that there are no gaps in sequence numbers, or that where there are gaps, they are accounted for (for example, documents that were spoiled during printing).

## Clerical controls

Clerical controls can be used for both inputs and outputs and are essentially processes that are implemented and carried out manually to eliminate user errors and loss or corruption of the source data prior to data entry, or after the production of a system output. These kinds of control are particularly common in accounting systems where the accuracy of data is paramount.

A common form of clerical control is the use of some form of batch control document. When a batch of input source documents is received at a data processing centre, a member of staff prepares the batch for keying by a data entry operator. This preparation usually involves physically collating the documents together and completing the batch control document, which typically contains the following information:

- **Serial number of the batch.** To enable checking to determine whether the batch follows the previous batch received. This can help identify if an entire batch has gone missing.

- **Count of batch contents.** The number of forms that should be in the batch. This can be checked against the number of forms keyed by the data entry operator and can identify if one or more forms within the batch go missing.

- **Serial numbers of forms in the batch.** The serial numbers or number range(s) of the enclosed forms. Again, this may identify if forms within the batch go missing.

- **Batch control totals.** One or more values on each form can be added together to provide an overall total for the batch. For example, a common control total for a batch of purchase invoices is the total value of all of the invoices added together. This can help identify if any of the documents have been mis-keyed.

- **Hash totals.** A form of batch control, but instead of producing a meaningful total, such as total invoice value in the batch, a meaningless value is produced by totalling a field such as the invoice number.

Clerical controls are particularly important where source documents are posted – either from location to location or via the internal post within a specific site – as it is very easy for documents to be lost in transit, with the result that certain transactions do not take place.

## Data controls

We have already considered certain data controls in terms of validation, discussed under I/O controls. Validation rules are typically applied at individual data item level, or across two data items, in the case of cross-field validation. For example, an order date cannot be blank and cannot be later than the delivery date. Further rules relating to each data item are often defined by the analyst, but some may need to be specified by the designer during data design, typically in a document called a data dictionary, or within the repository of a software-based modelling tool. The data dictionary would define the following information about each data item, which effectively imposes constraints on the data items that must be enforced by system controls and tested during systems testing:

- **Data type.** During system development, when databases/data files are created, and during programming, each data item that is created must be assigned a data type. The data type determines which data values can be stored in the data item. Some data types are generic (such as alphanumeric, character, numeric, date, logical) whilst others are specific (native) to a particular DBMS or programming language.

- **Length.** The length of the data item is also specified, which, again, constrains the valid values that the data item can hold.

- **Format.** Some data items may also have additional constraints imposed upon them in terms of the format that valid values may take. For example, the Emp-Id data item in Figures 9.6 to 9.12 would have a data type of alphanumeric (meaning that it can contain a mix of alphabetic and numeric characters), a length of four, and the first character must be alphabetic; the remaining three characters must be numeric.

- **Value range.** Some data items may be further constrained by specifying that valid data values must fall within a specific range. For example, the **Emp-Id** data item may be constrained so that it may only take on values between E1000 and E5000.

- **Mandatory.** Identifies whether the data item must contain a value or can be left blank/empty. This is generally checked during data entry as part of the validation of input data, but can also be checked by a DBMS when new data is added to the database.

- **Default value.** Some data items may be defined with a default value(s) – a value that will automatically appear in the data item when the data is input or added to a database.

- **Visibility.** In some data dictionaries – for example, those defined using a UML modelling tool – it is also possible to define the visibility of each data item. This then constrains how the data item can be used, as further controls can be built into the definitions of operations that are used to access the data. As we saw earlier, the attributes of an object can be specified in a UML class definition as being private (their visibility is set to private), which means that the data cannot be accessed directly and, hence, can only be accessed via the object's operations. Figure 8.16 shows a class with private attributes and public operations.

In addition to these field-level data controls, additional controls can be derived from the logical data model (entity relationship diagram or class diagram), produced during data design. The data model defines some of the business rules of the organisation, and so, by default, determines some of the controls that must be implemented and tested. For example, the class model in Figure 8.17 states that a **Medical** can be associated with one (and only one) **Life** policy but a **Life** policy can exist without a corresponding **Medical**. Such rules preserve the integrity of the data as well as forming the basis for subsequent systems testing.

Code design can assist in data control. It may be feasible to implement a code design which has elements of self checking. Thus the first facet of the code (say the first three numbers) may be split off and certain checks performed. This might include consistency checks against other parts of the code.

## Process controls

We have already discussed the fact that system controls are devised to enforce business rules, which can be defined within a data model. However, there are other models produced both during systems analysis and systems design. For example, many systems enforce some form of process workflow, which can be explicitly captured in some form of state model, such as a UML state machine diagram or a state transition diagram.

Figure 9.13 shows a UML state machine diagram that represents the states that a purchase invoice object can pass through within its life.

**Figure 9.13  UML state machine diagram showing the lifecycle for an invoice object**

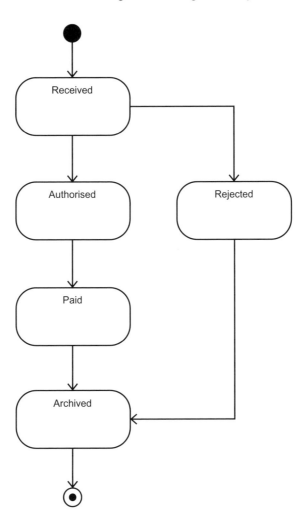

Figure 9.13 clearly shows that, once an invoice has been received, it can either be authorised or rejected, and, more importantly, only authorised invoices can be paid (as there is no transition between the states **Rejected** and **Paid**. This rule would be implemented using a system control built into the Pay Invoice process, by checking the status of the invoice object to ensure that it is **Authorised** and, if not, cancelling the payment process.

## Security and audit

Security is a special kind of system control that is devised to prevent unauthorised access to the system or to certain functions or data held within the system, and prevent loss of, or corruption to, system artefacts as a result of a range of risks including fire, flood, terrorist attack and Acts of God.

In terms of security, the options available to the designer can be broadly categorised as physical or logical security. However, there is a further aspect to security design that is not about the prevention of access or loss of system artefacts, but concerns the traceability of user activity: systems audit.

Apart from the fact that organisations hold sensitive data relating to their operations, which could be used to their detriment by their competitors, there are also legal imperatives in having a robust security design, in the form of data protection and computer misuse legislation.

### Physical security

Physical security measures prevent direct access to computer equipment, including workstations, servers and backing storage. The most common mechanisms used are:

- **Locks.** Including key-based locks, combination locks and swipe card activated locks. Also, biometric options are becoming more commonplace, including fingerprint and retina recognition to activate the lock.

- **Barriers.** Similar to locks, but where a barrier of some kind blocks the entry into a building containing computer equipment. Again, these can be activated either using swipe cards, combination codes or biometrics, or a combination of these mechanisms.

- **Safes.** Safes are often used as part of a backup and recovery policy (see below) to provide physical protection to computer media (like CDs, DVDs, magnetic tape, microfiche) from theft or damage/destruction by a range of risks identified above.

- **Security personnel.** Often combined with the use of barriers to check that any personnel attempting to gain access to a building have the appropriate authorisation to do so.

- **Backup and recovery.** There are a variety of measures that can be taken to ensure that copies of the system artefacts, including hardware, software components and data, are available to enable the system to be recovered/restored following loss as a result of the risks identified above. Considerations of the various options available are outside the scope of this book.

### Logical security

Logical security measures involve aspects of the software that make up the system in order to protect the system and its data from unauthorised access, destruction or corruption. The most common mechanisms are:

- **Access controls.** The most common form of logical access controls are passwords and PINs (Personal Identification Numbers), which must be correctly entered via a computer keyboard or keypad. These are often combined with physical security mechanisms in a multi-stage process that includes identification, authentication and authorisation:

  1. **Identification** – the user enters a user name to identify themselves.
  2. **Authentication** – the system checks that the user is who they say they are, often using a 'three-factor' approach which comprises:
     a. Something they know (such as a password or PIN).
     b. Something they have (such as a card or key).
     c. Something they are (such as a fingerprint or other biometric).
  3. **Authorisation** – the system checks what level of access (permissions) the user has been granted, both individually and as a member of one or more groups.

- **Firewalls.** Firewalls are special software locks that filter incoming access to a computer network to ensure that the access originates from a trusted or authorised source. Firewalls are used in addition to other logical and physical security mechanisms because traditional security mechanisms are not sufficient in a world where more and more computers and systems are connected to one another via the internet and by wide area networks, and hackers can gain remote access to systems almost undetected.

- **Encryption.** Encryption provides an additional level of security, above and beyond the traditional logical and physical mechanisms, to ensure that any data being transmitted from one system to another cannot be read, even if it is intercepted by an unauthorised party. Only the intended recipient of the data can read it using a special 'encryption key' to de-crypt the encrypted data. As well as being used to protect data in transit, encryption is also used to protect data stored in databases or local hard drives, so that only authorised users can read the data.

- **Anti-malware software.** The advent of open systems and the internet has increased the risk of systems being targeted by malware (malicious software), such as viruses, trojans, worms, spyware to name but a few. This specialist software is used to detect such malware and eradicate it before it can corrupt any software artefacts or data.

### System audit trail

Audit trails are implemented to maintain traceability of activities that take place within a system. An audit trail logs system activity in terms of who did what, when and on which piece of equipment. They are commonly used for four different purposes:

- To check the integrity of the system data by tracing through transactions that have taken place. This is often a requirement of annual audit reviews by internal and external auditors.

- To provide a record of compliance. For example, UK data protection legislation requires that personal data (data relating to individuals) is obtained fairly and lawfully. Consequently, systems often include a tick box for the data subject to indicate their approval for the data to be used in a certain way. A record of this permission is then logged in the audit trail to provide evidence of compliance with that requirement.

- To detect and recover from failed system transactions in order to maintain data integrity, for example a payment without a corresponding invoice. It may be possible to find the original transaction and re-apply it to correct the data.

- To identify any unauthorised or fraudulent activity that has taken place within the system.

Although audit information will vary from system to system, most audit records include the following information:

- unique sequence number;
- date of the transaction;
- time of the transaction;
- user ID of the person making the transaction;
- machine ID of the device used to make the transaction;
- type of transaction (such as Payment, Credit Note, Invoice, and so on);
- transaction value(s);
- data value(s) before transaction;
- data value(s) after transaction.

Sometimes auditors use specialised audit review tools, and hence the designer may need to ensure that the audit trail is maintained in a format compatible with such tools.

## LOGICAL AND PHYSICAL DESIGN

Design activities can be divided into two separate stages of design: logical design and physical design. The former is 'platform-agnostic' insofar as it makes no specific reference to the implementation environment or technologies, and the latter defines how the logical solution elements (inputs, outputs, processes and data) are to be built and deployed using specific technologies and infrastructure of the target implementation environment.

Although some designers may not perform a separate logical design stage, jumping straight to environment-specific implementation specifications, a common approach is to start with a platform-agnostic solution design that is then 'tuned' to take advantage of the specifics of a particular technological implementation environment. A benefit of splitting design into these two separate stages is that a generic solution can be proposed that can be adapted for implementation in a range of different environments. This is how the design objective of portability is achieved.

Much of this chapter has been about logical design, but there are areas that relate to specific technologies. I/O design in particular is difficult to achieve without making reference to specific technologies because use of particular technologies is an integral design consideration in order to achieve the I/O requirements of a system.

We shall now briefly consider some of the issues facing the designer when undertaking physical data design and physical process design.

## Physical data design

Physical data design involves taking the normalised data model produced during logical data design and 'tuning' it for implementation using specific data storage technologies and media. We have already considered some of the options available to the designer in terms of DBMSs and physical file structures. During this logical-to-physical mapping exercise, it is common to 'de-normalise' the logical data model in order to improve system performance. De-normalisation re-introduces data redundancy that was removed during the normalisation process (as described earlier in this chapter).

## Physical process design

We have already considered approaches to logical process design and specification, in particular, identification and definition of logical software components. Physical process design then considers which technologies to use in order to build the components and how they should be deployed within the implementation environment. Figure 9.14 shows an example of a UML deployment diagram that can be used to specify how physical components are to be deployed.

In Figure 9.14, each component has been stereotyped with the technology used to build/deploy it, such as <<iPad app>> and <<java servlet>>. Furthermore, the diagram shows the physical devices (referred to as nodes in UML), denoted by the three-dimensional cubes, where each component will be deployed in the target implementation environment. Also note that some of the nodes are referred to as <<execution environment>>. These represent special software environments such as the Oracle 11i DBMS, web browser and web server.

## Figure 9.14 UML deployment diagram showing physical components

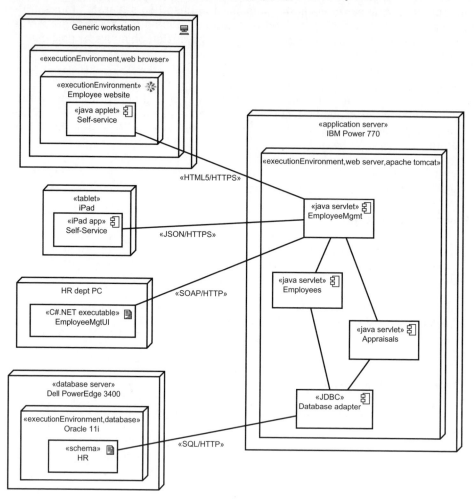

## DESIGN PATTERNS

Designers are often faced with similar challenges to those that they have already solved in the past. Rather than 're-inventing the wheel', they go back to a previous design with similar challenges to the one they currently face and use that as a template (pattern) for their current design. This approach has continued in an informal way for many years, but became more formalised with the advent of the seminal book *Design patterns: Elements of reusable object-oriented software* by Erich Gamma and others (1994).

In general, formally defined patterns have four essential elements:

- **Pattern name** – a handle for describing the design problem.

- **Problem** – this describes when to apply the pattern by explaining the problem and its context.

- **Solution** – this describes the elements that make up the design, their relationships, responsibilities and collaborations. The solution is a template, an abstract description of a design problem and how a general arrangement of elements can be used to solve it.

- **Consequences** – are the results and trade-offs of applying the pattern and help the designer to understand the benefits and disadvantages of applying the pattern.

The Gamma book introduced a set of template solutions to address common design problems. Each pattern is named, leading to the adoption of a common vocabulary for designers, who can simply refer to the names of design patterns rather than having to explain them to their peers. This has also led to a more standardised approach to systems design across the IT industry.

Gamma and his co-writers acknowledge that their book only captures a fraction of what an expert might know. It does not have any patterns dealing with concurrency, distributed programming or real-time programming. It does not include any application domain-specific patterns. However, since the publication of the book, the concept of patterns has been extended to other IT disciplines and now architectural patterns and analysis patterns are commonplace.

Design patterns make it easier to reuse successful designs and architectures. The patterns presented by Gamma *et al.* are independent of programming language and hence can be adopted during logical design and tuned during physical design. Most of the patterns are concerned with achieving the design objectives of minimising coupling and maximising cohesion, introduced earlier in this chapter. They achieve this through abstraction, composition and delegation, in turn fundamental principles of OO design.

Design patterns were originally grouped into three categories: creational patterns, structural patterns and behavioural patterns. However, a further classification has also introduced the notion of architectural design pattern, which may be applied at the architecture level of the software, such as the Model–View–Controller pattern. Table 9.1 provides a summary of the most commonly-used design patterns, although a detailed explanation of each pattern is beyond the scope of this book.

**Table 9.1 Common design patterns (after Gamma *et al.*)**

| Category | Pattern name | Description |
| --- | --- | --- |
| Creational | Abstract factory | Provide an interface for creating families of related or dependent objects without specifying their concrete classes. |
| | Builder | Separate the construction of a complex object from its representation, allowing the same construction process to create various representations. |
| | Factory method | Define an interface for creating a single object, but let sub-classes decide which class to instantiate. |
| | Virtual Proxy/Lazy initialisation | Delaying the creation of an object, the calculation of a value, or some other expensive process until the first time it is needed. |
| | Prototype | Specify the kinds of objects to create using a prototypical instance, and create new objects by copying this prototype. |
| | Singleton | Ensure a class has only one instance, and provide a global point of access to it. |
| Structural | Adapter (Wrapper or Translator) | Convert the interface of a class into another interface clients expect. An adapter that lets classes work together that could not otherwise because of incompatible interfaces. |
| | Bridge | De-couple an abstraction from its implementation, allowing the two to vary independently. |
| | Composite | Compose objects into tree structures to represent part-whole hierarchies. Composite lets clients treat individual objects and compositions of objects uniformly. |
| | Decorator | Attach additional responsibilities to an object dynamically keeping the same interface. |
| | Façade | Provide a unified interface to a set of interfaces in a sub-system. Facade defines a higher-level interface that makes the sub-system easier to use. |

*(Continued)*

**Table 9.1 (Continued)**

| Category | Pattern name | Description |
| --- | --- | --- |
| | Flyweight | Use sharing to support large numbers of similar objects efficiently. |
| | Proxy | Provide a surrogate or placeholder for another object to control access to it. |
| Behavioural | Chain of responsibility | Avoid coupling the sender of a request to its receiver by giving more than one object a chance to handle the request. Chain the receiving objects and pass the request along the chain until an object handles it. |
| | Command | Encapsulate a request as an object, thereby letting you parameterise clients with different requests, queue or log requests, and support undoable operations. |
| | Interpreter | Given a language, define a representation for its grammar along with an interpreter that uses the representation to interpret sentences in the language. |
| | Iterator | Provide a way to access the elements of an aggregate object sequentially without exposing its underlying representation. |
| | Mediator | Define an object that encapsulates how a set of objects interact. Mediator promotes loose coupling by keeping objects from referring to each other explicitly, and it lets you vary their interaction independently. |
| | Memento | Without violating encapsulation, capture and externalize an object's internal state allowing the object to be restored to this state later. |
| | Observer (publish/subscribe) | Define a one-to-many dependency between objects where a state change in one object results in all its dependents being notified and updated automatically. |

*(Continued)*

**Table 9.1 (Continued)**

| Category | Pattern name | Description |
| --- | --- | --- |
| | State | Allow an object to alter its behaviour when its internal state changes. |
| | Strategy | Define a family of algorithms, encapsulate each one, and make them interchangeable. Strategy lets the algorithm vary independently from clients that use it. |
| | Template method | Define the skeleton of an algorithm in an operation, deferring some steps to sub-classes. Template method lets subclasses redefine certain steps of an algorithm without changing the algorithm's structure. |
| | Visitor | Represent an operation to be performed on the elements of an object structure. Visitor lets you define a new operation without changing the classes of the elements on which it operates. |

## REFERENCES

Gamma, E., Helm, R., Johnson, R. and Vlissides, J. (1994) *Design patterns: elements of Reusable Object-Oriented Software.* Addison-Wesley, Boston, MA.

## FURTHER READING

Arlow, J. and Neustadt, I. (2005) *UML2 and the unified process: practical object-oriented analysis and design* (2nd edition). Addison-Wesley, Boston, MA.

Codd, E. F. (1990) *The relational model for database management, version 2.* Addison-Wesley, Boston, MA.

Date, C. J. (2004) *An introduction to database systems* (8th edition). Addison-Wesley, Boston, MA.

Pressman, R. S. (2010) *Software engineering: a practitioner's approach* (7th edition). McGraw-Hill, New York.

Rumbaugh, J., Jacobson, I. and Booch, G. (2005) *The Unified Modeling Language reference manual* (2nd edition). Addison-Wesley, Boston, MA.

Skidmore, S. and Eva, M. (2004) *Introducing systems development*. Palgrave-MacMillan, Basingstoke.

Yeates, D. and Wakefield, T. (2003) *Systems analysis and design* (2nd edition). FT Prentice Hall, Harlow.

# 10 SOLUTION-RELATED ARCHITECTURES

## Julian Cox

### CONTENTS OF THIS CHAPTER

This chapter covers the following topics:

- what is architecture?
- architecture patterns;
- enterprise architecture;
- solution architecture;
- software architecture;
- stakeholders and roles in architecture;
- architecture management;
- references and further reading.

### INTRODUCTION

Anything that we can classify as a system has an architecture, including buildings, living organisms (including humans), organisations, complex enterprise IT systems, software applications and individual components of those. When referring to IT systems, a core definition of what is meant by the term 'architecture' is provided by the ISO/IEC 42010:2011[1] 'Systems and software engineering – Architecture description' standard:

> 'The fundamental organization of a system embodied in its components, their relationships to each other, and to the environment, and the principles guiding its design and evolution.' (ISO, 2011)

This standard considers an architecture to be 'a conception of a system', in other words it is in the human mind, which can exist without being written down. This abstract idea of an architecture can be captured and communicated in the form of an architecture description.

---

[1] You will still find some people referring to this standard as IEEE 1471, which is its original form before being adopted as a broader standard.

The ISO standard also reinforces the idea that no architecture exists in isolation; it exists in a context which needs to be understood so that the architecture's relationship with its context can also be described.

The objective of anyone working on architecture is to determine the appropriate way in which to represent this architecture description; and this is often in the form of documentation containing an appropriate set of models.

In many respects, this chapter is an extension of Chapter 7 ('System modelling techniques') in that a lot of architecture is about modelling and so much of the theory about forms of abstraction and levelling contained therein applies equally apply to this chapter. It is therefore recommended that you read Chapter 7 before this one unless you are familiar with these concepts:

- abstraction; classification, idealisation, composition and generalisation;
- black- vs white-box models;
- the difference between a model and a diagram.

### Architecture is more than just structure

It is worth re-reading the ISO 42010 definition again, particularly the last part; '... and the principles guiding its design and evolution'. This emphasises that an architecture includes aspects such as requirements and constraints (in particular architecture principles) that inform what that architecture needs to be to satisfy key concerns of major stakeholders.

While the ISO 42010 standard is specifically aimed at systems and software engineering, the definitions contained are used consistently to refer to related types of architecture.

### Types of architecture

Many related architecture disciplines have evolved over the last 20 years, each focusing on different forms of systems. This chapter begins with the broadest and then focuses in on more specific architectures. The chapter will consider three levels of granularity:

- Enterprise Architecture;
- Solution Architecture;
- Software Architecture.

Before these are described, the following section explains some common patterns that all of these architecture types share.

## ARCHITECTURE PATTERNS

Architecture structures are typically models and there are some fundamental patterns that apply in various contexts, as will be discussed later in the chapter.

## Modular architecture

In the early days of information systems, monolithic software architecture (where various aspects such as data input and output, data processing and the user interface were not architecturally separated into modules or components) was common. This was not such an issue, as the technical architecture was somewhat simpler (often a single physical node) and much of the data processing was batch-driven and managed by job control software; each executable program tended to be limited in functionality.

There would, however, be issues associated with applying certain aspects consistently across the suite of executables where a change to a single business rule or to the structure of a data element might typically require multiple changes to ensure consistency and prevent processing errors.

Structured programming languages and tools introduced the ability to write software library modules containing routines that dealt with such issues that could be shared and invoked by multiple executables, although these would often be statically linked into a single executable during compilation and linking; this meant that a change to one of these modules would require that all executables that used it would need to be recompiled.

The introduction of dynamically linkable modules, or libraries, meant that this static, compile-time dependency could potentially be broken. The library modules could be updated independently of the calling modules, although these often needed to be updated too. Issues would frequently arise when a developer changed a library module to support their program's requirements without realising the impact on other programs.

Configuration and version management was key to prevent chaos. It was not until independently defined interfaces were available that these modules could be loosely coupled (see below), allowing them to be maintained independently. Software architectures, and consequently the physical architectures, could become truly modular and flexible. Modules began to possess properties that led them to be called components to distinguish them from their predecessors.

### Loosely coupled architecture

Coupling is a term used to refer to the level of dependency between two software components, although the term applies equally to hardware components. The earlier modules described above tended to have a high level of dependency, in other words they were tightly coupled. Table 10.1 compares some features of loose and tight coupling.

It should not be assumed that loose coupling is always preferable to tight coupling; there are situations where tightly coupled components are required, for example to achieve demanding performance levels.

**Table 10.1 Features of loose and tight coupling**

| Tightly coupled modules | Loosely coupled components |
|---|---|
| Changing one module requires that others need to be updated. | Components can be updated or even replaced without significantly impacting on others. |
| Dependencies typically exist in both directions on any pair of modules; otherwise known as cyclic or circular dependency. | Dependency is typically one way, or acyclic. Where cyclic dependency does exist this can be broken by employing a suitable design pattern, such as the observer pattern. |
| One module is dependent on how the other is implemented, for example by programming language. | Components[2] are not dependent on any technical aspect of the other. |

The fundamental structural element that enables loose coupling is an interface that is abstractly defined separately from the module's implementation code, this defines the signatures of the module's functions, operations, methods, algorithms, strategies or services (these terms are interchangeable depending on context). Clients should ideally be dependent on the abstract function definition rather than the implementation. This allows the implementation of the module to be updated, replaced or dynamically interchanged providing that the interface is supported.

The important role of interfaces means that their definition is a key focus of architecture. When modelling how 'black-box' modules can be assembled to create a system, the functional requirements of those modules can be defined through defining the system's interfaces, both at a logical and physical level. Once these requirements are defined, then the modules can be implemented in the most suitable way for the solution to meet all requirements (including non-functional requirements).

When coarse-grained components or sub-systems are being referred to, then the term 'Application Programming Interface' or API is commonly used.

'Coupling and cohesion' are often used in the same phrase. As we have seen, coupling relates to how dependent modules are on each other. Cohesion looks at how closely modular elements need to operate or be changed together; where this is the case, then there is high cohesion (and probably tight coupling). It is less problematic if these modules are co-located within the same coarser-grained component, which means that they will be deployed and maintained together.

---

[2] The Observer Pattern is a well-documented, core pattern and is one of those described in the 'Gang of Four' design patterns book by Erich Gamma and others (Gamma, Helm, Johnson, and Vlissides, 1994).

## Tiered/layered architecture

There are different kinds of functional elements in any solution or software architecture based upon its responsibilities; for example, those that represent and manipulate data as compared with those that handle the system's interface. These can be organised into distinct layers or tiers of modules with similar responsibilities.

## Hierarchical architecture

It is preferable in layered architectures the higher layer is dependent on the services provided by the layer below, but not vice versa. This provides flexibility in that components at one layer can be servicing multiple clients at the layer above; for example, application components sharing common infrastructure services (and their underlying components).

Specific examples of layered and hierarchical architectures are provided later in the chapter when discussing Solution and Software Architecture, for example Figure 10.2.

## COMMUNICATION AND INTEROPERATION PATTERNS

An architecture composed of, or assembled from, discrete components or sub-systems needs those components to communicate and interoperate. Some basic patterns are evident at both logical and physical views of business, application and infrastructure architectures.

## Point-to-point

This is the most direct and, in many respects, simplest pattern and can range from logically indicating that a particular client communicates directly with a specific server to physically laying a cable between two geographic locations or attaching a mobile device to your computer via a USB cable. Point-to-Point tends to be tightly coupled, as the components are specifically linked logically or physically and they need to share common protocols, data formats and so forth.

Problems arise when multiple point-to-points are required to connect a number of nodes, as the number of links required potentially increase exponentially when new components are added.

## Hub-and-spoke

Where a significant number of components need to interoperate, this can be set up as a set of point-to-point connections between each component and a single hub component. This component primarily exists to provide the means of connecting any component with any other. In doing so, the hub is potentially de-coupling each component pair to some extent and it can achieve this, first, by acting as an introduction broker or discovery agent, dynamically linking client to server component pairs on demand.

The hub can also offer other brokering services such as determining whether the client has security access to the server or by performing translations of communication protocols or data structures. It can even take over some of the logic processing and manage complex distributed transactions, at which point it has become a processing server component in its own right.

## Service-oriented architecture

The service-oriented model is fundamentally about how components can be defined by the services they require as a service consumer (or client) and provided as a service provider (server). These components are typically as de-coupled as possible in all aspects,

This model also applies to how we organise our business functions and it is the model that allows organisations to outsource certain functions, where they are defined, and interoperate according to the services they provide rather than according to how they perform the service. If done properly, it should not be evident to a service consumer whether the service is provided by an internal or an outsourced provider.

In a service-oriented IT architecture, there is typically a broker hub, often in the form of a service bus, that allows:

- service providers to register their services with a service registry held by the hub;
- service consumers to 'look up' or discover service providers as required.

The consumer and provider can then interact in one of two ways:

- a temporary point-to-point connection may be set up between them, across which they communicate directly;
- the interactions are conducted through the hub acting as a broker.

## ENTERPRISE ARCHITECTURE

For many organisations, a significant development has been the adoption of enterprise architecture (EA) as typically the highest level and most holistic form of architecture developed and evolved about the organisation (the enterprise) over a strategic timeframe. The organisations in question can be massive, global multi-nationals employing hundreds of thousands of employees all over the world and operating in many geographical marketplaces; or they can be a small businesses run by families. One is clearly a lot more complex than the other, but fundamentally both are systems with similar features. For example, both have:

- a context or environment within which they exist;
- a mission, the reason why they exist;
- a set of products and/or services that they provide to a customer base;

- an organisational structure with individuals fulfilling roles;
- a set of processes that they execute to conduct their operating model;
- information and data that they process and maintain about their organisation (and all the above) for either their own purposes or to meet legal and compliance requirements.

## Strategy versus tactics

Most important of all, any organisation should have:

- a vision of what their future context or environment is likely to be and what they want to be in the future to remain relevant to that future:
- the need therefore to evolve through changes to meet the challenges presented by their constantly changing context or environment:
- a strategy to achieve that over a period of time.

Enterprise architecture is primarily concerned with these highest-level, long-term, strategic issues. The individual changes conducted to support this strategy can usually be seen as shorter-term, tactical changes, which include some business as usual activities intended to support the strategy; for example, a shift in the marketing messages to effect changes to customer perceptions and potentially alter the customer base.

These tactical changes are typically evolving and different aspects of the business, particularly its operating model, which includes:

- organisational units of people;
- business practices such as business processes;
- IT systems used by the business to execute its processes.

## Architecture domains

Enterprise architecture is usually broken down into distinct architecture domains. EA frameworks relevant to most business or government enterprises typically use the following four domains:

- Business architecture;
- Data and/or information architecture;
- Application(s) architecture;
- Infrastructure or technology architecture.

These domains each contain a subset of the overall EA; they are interdependant and there will be overlaps of interest between them (see Figure 10.1).

**Figure 10.1 Architecture domains in enterprise architecture**

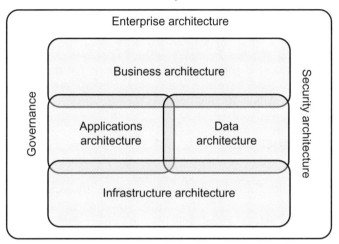

Organisations often employ other domains that cut across the main domains, the best example being security architecture, which is concerned with the consistency and completeness of security aspects across the whole enterprise. These domains will be discussed in more detail under solution architecture.

## EA processes, content models, organisation and frameworks

As with any development function, an enterprise architecture function needs to determine:

- **Organisation:** How it is to be organised internally into roles and responsibilities as well as how it will fit within the organisation as a whole.
- **Process:** What activities the EA function is going to perform and when.
- **Content:** What information about the enterprise will be recorded, how it is classified, organised and cross-referenced.

There are many frameworks available that organisations may adopt and/or adapt to fit their needs. Some well-known generic frameworks include:

- 'The Open Group Architecture Framework' (TOGAF), which covers all these aspects;
- 'Zachman Framework for EA', which focuses on classification of EA content.

There are frameworks specifically aimed at particular countries and organisations, for example:

- FEAF, the US government 'Federated Enterprise Architecture Framework', aimed at most US government departments and agencies;

- DODAF and MODAF are frameworks specifically for the US Department of Defense and the UK Ministry of Defence.

## EA governance

An important function of enterprise architecture is to put in place principles and policies that constrain any change in activities to ensure that the strategic objectives are met. These will obviously have an effect on any solution, software or infrastructure architecture and the resulting development work.

# ARCHITECTURE PRINCIPLES

Architecture principles are high-level constraints that are not directly actionable but that represent underlying rules and guidelines that drive the architecture.

> 'Principles are general rules and guidelines, intended to be enduring and seldom amended, that inform and support the way in which an organization sets about fulfilling its mission.'
>
> (from TOGAF 9.1)

'Architecture principles fill the gap between high-level strategic intentions and concrete design' (Greefhorst and Proper, 2011). Principles can be defined that relate to any domain or aspect; for example:

- 'business units are autonomous', is clearly a business domain principle relating to the organisational structure;
- 'routine tasks are automated', relates to business and application domains;
- 'primary business processes are not disturbed by implementation of change' relates to all domains;
- 'applications have a common look and feel', relates to application design;
- 'only in response to Business needs are changes to IT systems made', is actually an application and technology domain-focused principle.

These examples are taken from Greefhorst and Proper (2011).

## Policies

Policies are needed as a more actionable implementation of the architecture principles. These may include:

- policies that mandate that certain legislation, standards and industry regulations be complied with; for example compliance with data protection legislation, ISO 27001 security or an industry benchmark regulation;
- policies on how the change activities will be run; for example the role of project management and the involvement of relevant authorities to allocate and spend budget;

SOLUTION-RELATED ARCHITECTURES

- policies on supplier engagement; perhaps limiting choice to pre-approved suppliers or how a procurement exercise must be conducted;

- technical policy that limits the choice of technologies to be used to help with standardisation; this could include the use of certain tools, development languages and infrastructure elements (for example that a single sign-in service be used);

- development standards, such as processes to be followed or style guides to comply with.

All of these are put in place for the benefit of the organisation in the long term, even though – for some change activities – these may be inconvenient or even more expensive.

## Governance activities

It is the role of a specific authority (perhaps the EA function) to ensure that the policies are complied with through governance activities; although the ability to grant dispensation to be non-compliant for valid business reasons should always be considered.

## SOLUTION ARCHITECTURE

If EA is for long-term, strategic architecture then solution architecture is a shorter-term, tactical form of architecture. EA guides evolutionary changes to the whole enterprise over a period of time, whereas many of those individual changes will require the oversight of a solution architecture.

### Holistic solution

First, solution architecture should be distinguished from the conventional design activities described in Chapters 8 and 9 on systems design. Initially, the solution architecture will be a high-level description of the building blocks of the total, holistic solution architecture and how they interface and interoperate to meet the requirements.

### Driving and controlling design

This outlines the work for more detailed design and implementation which then needs to be overseen or governed by the solution architect; if any need to change any of the requirements or building blocks is identified, then they are best placed to analyse the impact across the architecture and resolve any issues.

### Architecture domains within solution architecture

The solution building blocks described above are not just IT software- and hardware-based. In most organisations, any solution should be regarded as a business solution. Even with organisations that are simply updating the IT infrastructure, there should be a business driver for any solution – in other words, a business issue that needs to be addressed. The domains described above apply equally, therefore, to solution architecture.

211

For example, any software applications that rely on the infrastructure will typically have service levels that the business needs to be met; and improvements to those service levels required by the business users (such as better performance, availability or reliability) typically involve improving the platform upon which the applications run – that is, the infrastructure and its components.

The domain seemingly missing from that description is the data architecture. This can be seen as cutting across or mapping into the other domains (as it does in Figure 10.1), with different views relevant to each. Simplistically, data might be considered at the conceptual level (meaning) for the business, logically (structure and rules) for the applications and physically for the infrastructure (how and where it is stored or persisted) although other abstraction forms will also be involved.

## Hierarchies of architecture domain services

An alternative view of the domains presented in Figure 10.1 is to consider how these domains describe layers of a hierarchical architecture where each layer provides services to the layer above (see Figure 10.2).

**Figure 10.2 Hierarchical domain services**

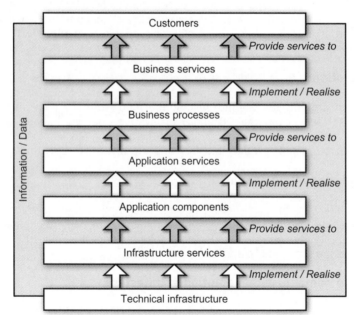

This layered architecture, where layers are offering services to the layer above, follows several of the patterns described earlier in the chapter, particularly the de-coupling of the hierarchical layers.

## Defining solution scope

Any solution needs its scope to be defined and there are three dimensions of scope to be considered (see Figure 10.3):

- focus;
- breadth;
- depth.

**Figure 10.3  Solution scope – focus, breadth and depth**

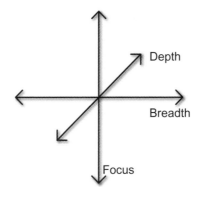

### *Focus*

The scope of a particular change that requires a solution architecture description may involve any or all of the domains discussed above; this reflects dependencies and the fact that the business requirements driving changes to the information systems are effectively from the business architecture. The solution may, however, be focused on changing aspects of the infrastructure architecture, whose requirements are driven by the application and data architectures' reliance on infrastructure services; thus, business architecture may not figure in this solution. It should not be forgotten, however, that non-functional requirements or the technology are ultimately reflections of business needs (for example for performance and availability).

### *Breadth*

Within each of the domains that are in focus, a solution is concerned with sets of architecture elements. Examples include business processes and people's roles within the business architecture as well as new application software and infrastructure components and changes to the services being offered and depended on at each layer.

The broader context of a solution architecture is the enterprise architecture. The breadth of the architecture needs to be clearly understood.

### *Depth*

For any solution architecture description, there comes a point where the architecture description stops and detailed design takes over; this is the depth. There are various ways of defining architecture levels; the perspectives of the Zachman Framework are worth considering as a classification.

## Architecture contract

As with any work specification, the solution architecture deliverables, related activities, roles and responsibilities should be defined before work begins. This is typically done in the form of an architecture contract. This can be considered as the architecture's terms of reference. The deliverables can be defined using the three dimensions of scope discussed above.

## Solution architecture governance

In our three levels of architecture granularity, solution architecture fits between enterprise architecture and software architecture. In terms of compliance, two issues are involved:

- Compliance: the solution architect needs to be aware of the constraints placed on the solution by the EA function (if one exists) as well as any placed by the solution specific requirements.

- Enforcement: the solution architect in turn creates constraints on the underlying detailed architectures and designs, for example the software architecture and design, where these need to comply with issues apparent in the holistic solution architecture.

Within this governance brief, the solution architect needs to be able to respond and react to issues that arise from the ensuing work, such as when technologies do not behave as expected or where non-functional requirements are not achievable without compromise or a change in the architecture.

## SOFTWARE ARCHITECTURE

Software architecture is fundamentally concerned with the purpose and structure of software applications, including software components, that may be considered to deliver platform services within the Infrastructure architecture. If operating within a described solution architecture, then its purpose is typically to break down the solution architecture functional building blocks or components into more granular, decomposed and eventually more physically implementable software components where appropriate.

The software architect incorporates more implementation-specific factors such as:

- choice of development languages and tools;
- structural constraints presented by platform technologies chosen for the solutions that already exist or need to be procured;

- identifying and employing appropriate logical and physical design patterns that encourage robust software design and implementation.

There is clearly a significant overlap between this level of architecture and the solution design activities described in Chapters 8 and 9.

## Tiered software architecture

The concept of tiered or layered architecture as a basic pattern was introduced earlier in the chapter. We now explore the concept in more detail.

---

**Figure 10.4  Client-server patterns**

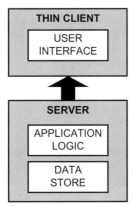 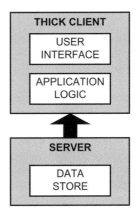

*Two-tier, client-server*

An early, basic version of this tiered pattern is a client-server arrangement, as illustrated in Figure 10.4.

In this arrangement we see:

- A server module the responsibilities of which are to read and write the data to and from storage, maintaining aspects of the data's integrity. It provides a defined set of services to a client.

- A client module, which is dependent on the services provided by the server. This could be an application run by users on remote devices that calls the services provided by the server, for example by sending queries to and from the server. As well as interacting with the users, this client application can apply business rules and logic.

This arrangement was common in the 1980s and 1990s, when PCs, as opposed to dumb terminals, became common on user's desktops. Typically in this arrangement, both the client and the server may each be performing different aspects of business logic. Where there was a lot of this business logic occurring on the part of the client, it would be referred to as a 'thick client'; where most of this was on the server, it would be called a 'thin client'.

### Hierarchical client-server

This arrangement has usually involved tightly coupled client and server components, where the client was dependent on that specific server and the server was in turn dependent on that specific client. This may have solved the immediate problem of deploying clients but it did not provide sufficient flexibility for future development.

This problem could be addressed by de-coupling the client from the server, where the server delivers its services in a more generic manner (typically through the interface pattern). Multiple alternative clients could be developed for different platforms, each of which could access the services. Typically, the servers became thicker and the clients thinner in order to 'centralise' as much business logic as possible on the server.

### Three-tiered software architecture

The client-server approach works well when the application exists within a silo; typically a single database dedicated to that application, even with its multiple clients. In most organisations, these silo-ed applications needed to be integrated – particularly where databases needed to be shared by multiple applications and clients potentially require data from multiple sources.

A third, middle tier provides the means to achieve this, where the business logic is de-coupled from the data sources and components within that layer can be shared by multiple clients. The concept of an application as a silo-ed set of software began to break down and the focus was placed instead on the application being defined by the services provided at the point of delivery to the business users via the user interface client. This is why, in enterprise and solution architecture in particular, application architecture that models and controls this complexity of dependencies across applications to deliver services to the business architecture is important.

Figure 10.5 illustrates how multiple applications can share a number of components at the middle and data tiers.

**Figure 10.5  Three-tier software architecture with components shared across clients**

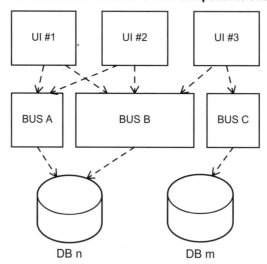

### N-tiered software architecture

The three-tier architecture is, however, simplistic. Typically, in modern architectures, these need to be sub-divided further (see Figure 10.6), for example:

- **System interface, boundary or presentation layer:** components at this layer provide the means for external entities, such as users or other systems, to interact with the system. Web technology in distributed architectures typically involves at least two sub-layers here:

  - A web-server layer that provides services to browser and other remote clients (for example, mobile apps) and interacts with the lower tiers to achieve this. It may be delivering the HTML or XML content to be rendered by the client, so is part of this presentation tier.

  - A client, which can either be simply the browser that renders the pages delivered by the web server or a client such as an app on a mobile device that exchanges XML or other specific data format through the web server.

- **Business logic layer:** this performs two roles as defined by the following sub-layers:

  - Process logic or controller layer – these coordinate sequences of logic performed by other components interacting with other to fulfil the system's functionality, usually supporting the interactions being performed through the system interfaces. Complex transactions involving a number of business entity components can be managed here.

  - Business entity layer – where the system manages representations of data dynamically. Components provide services and encapsulate functionality that apply business rules to particular data classes or entities as data is created, updated and deleted from the system. It interacts with the underlying data layer(s) to ensure the data is persisted on the system.

- **Data layer:** ultimately, this is the layer responsible for storing data in a persistent state, such as to disk, and retrieving it as required by various clients. In a simple, single database server environment, this may be seen as a single layer; in many complex architectures, however, this is divided into at least two layers:

  - Data services layer – components that provide a one-stop shop for data, hiding the complexity of multiple databases, nodes and data distributed between them. They can also be adapters that resolve different data retrieval protocols for different underlying database technologies.

  - Data management layer – typically Database Management Systems (DMBS) or file handling components.

## Figure 10.6 N-tiered software architecture

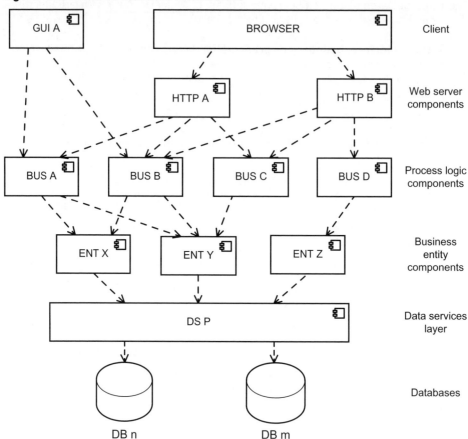

Not all of these tiers are needed all the time but, as organisations with complex IT systems begin to integrate their applications using enterprise technologies, then several are often required.

## Component-based software architecture

Today, most applications, no matter how many tiers are involved, are built as assemblies of components. By doing so they tend to be:

- more maintainable;
- more flexible in how they are deployed in distributed architectures;
- more consistent with each other through sharing components that enforce business rules and perform business logic.

### Systems as assemblies of components

The primary role of a software architect is to understand these complex software architectures and to be able to determine any specific solution:

- what software components already exist and whose services can be re-used in their current form;

- what software components already exist, but whose services may need to be added to or updated. In this situation, impact analysis must be performed on other applications that share those services to ensure that they are not disrupted. This conforms with the principle outlined earlier that 'primary business processes are not disturbed by implementation of change';

- what software components are not currently present, but which may be procured 'off the shelf' and configured to fit into the software architecture;

- what software components are not currently present and cannot be procured off the shelf, and so need to be specified to a sufficient degree that they can be designed and built by either internal or external development teams.

Component diagrams and models are available in the Unified Modelling Language (UML) and other notations to allow such an architecture to be modelled.

### Functionality provided through component interactions

Applications deliver their functionality and services through their software components interacting with each other. In Chapter 7, various forms of functional modelling are described, including system use cases, as a means of describing the application services provided to the users. The functional model map shows how system use cases can be realised through UML interaction models, particularly sequence diagrams that are commonly referred to as use case realisations. The participants within the software system in this top level of interaction modelling are typically components. Such modelling shows where existing components and their services can be utilised and where new functionality is required, either as new services on existing components or through new components.

### Component specification

Specification of software components at this level can typically be done at a 'black-box' level by specifying:

- what interfaces, services and functionality the component needs to provide to its clients (which may be other components) as identified within component interactions;

- what interfaces and services this component is dependent on that will be provided by other components in the architecture;

- any technical requirements including constraints for this component;

- any non-functional requirements that this component needs to meet.

The components can then be designed, built and tested to meet these specifications and the requirements behind them.

*Testing components*

The ability to specify components in this manner means that their behaviour and non-functional aspects can be black-box tested, providing confidence in them before they are integrated into broader systems for further testing, including regression testing of other components and applications (and even business processes) that may be effected by the change.

## STAKEHOLDERS AND ROLES IN ARCHITECTURE

If this chapter has revealed anything, it is that the amount and level of complexity within many organisations in terms of their business functions and the IT they utilise is difficult to manage when organisations are looking to make changes to any aspect. Therefore, a variety of roles can be recognised that contribute to this management.

### Enterprise, solution and software architects

Enterprise and solutions architecture can provide a holistic view of all these aspects as indicated in all the various architecture domains. Enterprise architects attempt to model the whole enterprise (at a high level of abstraction) to help specify and oversee long-term, strategic change to these domains in order to deliver the strategic vision; solution architects focus on a subset of the enterprise architecture to specify and oversee shorter-term tactical changes in order to deliver a solution.

Within a solution, the solution architects include software applications and their high-level building blocks, usually alongside business, data and infrastructure building blocks. Software architects typically focus on the software components at the next level of detail, particularly where those components may be reused across a number of applications.

### Domain architects

The specific architecture domains cut across these strategic and tactical architectures:

- Business;
- Application;
- Data;
- Infrastructure;
- Security.

Domain architects who work in these areas are typically involved in defining domain-specific standards and governing domain issues that ensure that all solutions are working in a consistent manner to deliver the vision. By doing so, they may also identify and be involved in the resolution of conflicts between different solution activities.

## Stakeholders

Each type of architecture needs to engage with the relevant stakeholders, internal and external. The following list is not exhaustive, but provides an indication of the range of stakeholder types that need to be engaged with.

### Organisation owners/board

The board is responsible for delivering both long- and short-term returns to the owners. They do this by ensuring that the organisation is fit for purpose to deliver its mission, not only today but also into the future. That requires the organisation to change to meet the challenges of the changing world around it as determined in its strategy.

Strategic change usually involves all aspects of the organisation and is where enterprise architecture becomes a tool for the organisation to understand the complexities involved and to determine how those changes can be delivered over time piece-by-piece, without breaking the organisation in the process. This involves significant investment in change decisions; the board are spending the owners' money and need to identify which change activities not only provide short-term gains but also support the long-term vision. EA can provide such information and advice.

### External legal, standard and compliance regimes

A common driver of change is the legal and compliance environment in which the organisation operates. New legislation and standards may require changes to how the organisation operates and this may require changes to business processes and/ or IT systems in order to comply. There are often agencies or other authorities that can be engaged with in order to clarify any compliance issues and minimise risk to the business of being fined, prosecuted or even disqualified from conducting business.

### Senior business management

Senior managers across the organisation are typically the 'owners' of business units and are responsible for ensuring that they operate effectively. Those units discharge various business functions involving business processes performed by their staff, often through the use of IT applications. Change activities may be funded through their delegated budget and they will be concerned that any outcomes are achieved after the change, particularly those that impact on their unit's key performance indicators (KPIs).

### Project, programme and portfolio management

Significant change activities are often managed by project and/or programme managers. Architects need to work closely with them to ensure that architecture activities are built into the plans, especially any governance activities.

### Operations managers

These are often mid-level managers responsible for ensuring that day-to-day business and IT operations are conducted properly. They need to ensure that the correct processes are performed and that the appropriate level of resources are available to meet any performance or other service level targets.

Changes to the operating model obviously have a significant impact on these stakeholders; they are often a key source of change requests, problem statements and requirements that require a solution and they will need to be satisfied that any changes are fit for purpose.

### Process workers and application users

Most solutions will struggle to succeed unless the users accept them. They may provide useful requirements that help ensure that any solutions are a good fit for their tasks. They may need to be re-organised and reskilled as part of any holistic solution.

### Suppliers

Components of a solution may be procured externally, whether it be software, hardware; or even business or application services. Business functions may be outsourced, but they need to be interfaced with correctly; many application services can be outsourced as cloud services or Software as a Service (SaaS).

### Solutions developers

This is a broad definition that includes business and system analysts, designers, programmers and testers. These may be internal, contracted or outsourced resources that will deliver parts of the solution.

## ARCHITECTURE MANAGEMENT

Given the wide range of architecture roles and related stakeholders, there are many organisational frameworks to determine where architecture functions are placed within an organisation, including reporting lines.

### Architecture planning

#### Strategic

Enterprise architecture should be a business-as-usual function, constantly helping organisations to manage strategic change. As well as maintaining the EA content, this function should be prioritising and planning tactical change activities, often communicated in the form of a 'road-map'.

The road-map should show how various streams of change activities will deliver change in the various business segments and domains, particularly where a number of these deliver a tranche of changes, synchronised at a milestone, which represent a significant holistic step change in the enterprise architecture. There will be key business events, such as strategic review cycles, or responses to significant unexpected changes in the environment, to which the EA function will need to respond and update the road-map.

#### Tactical

Enterprise and solution architects may be involved in a number of projects, such as a programme that delivers a number of changes as outlined in the EA road-map. Where there are a number of separate deliverables to be assembled to deliver a holistic solution, the programme plan can be regarded as a more detailed tactical road-map reflecting inter-project dependencies and synchronisation issues that need to be managed as risks. Day-to-day management of these plans and risks typically falls to programme and project managers, supported by the architects as the governors of the architecture behind these risks.

Other architects, such as domain architects and software architects are also involved in the definition, planning and governance of these changes.

## Architecture governance

Governance has been mentioned throughout this chapter. It is a key function of an architect, as it is a crucial part of architecture management. Architecture without governance is like requirements without testing. There is little point in establishing policies, standards and architectures if there is no check that these are being followed and complied with; that is the role of governance.

This chapter began with the ISO 42010 definition of architecture as:

> 'The fundamental organization of a system embodied in its components, their relationships to each other, and to the environment, and the principles guiding its design and evolution'.

Governance therefore needs to oversee all these aspects, particularly through validation and verification of both the final structure and the adherence to principles and other constraints imposed on its development.

Governance therefore requires:

- **Something to govern.** In the context of architecture, this is mainly the architecture descriptions which define constraints on the outputs and activities of change activities, including:
  - an architecture contract that defines roles, responsibilities and authorities;
  - the target system organisation or structures (components and their relationships) as described at an abstract level in the architecture description;
  - requirements that include applicable legislation, standards, principles and policies should form part of an architecture description.
- **Defined governance roles with the authority to govern.** Typically, there are levels of governance from corporate, through enterprise architecture to solutions and Specific architecture levels.
- **Governance processes.** Including:
  - establishing the architecture contract at the outset to outlines roles, responsibilities and authority, including governance roles;
  - defining what will be reviewed through the process (see 'something to govern' above), when and by whom;
  - conducting reviews;

- reporting and acting on the outcomes of the reviews, which may include granting dispensations to those concerned allowing them to vary from the original description for valid reasons;

- taking action to correct any discrepancies or non-conformities.

## REFERENCES

Greefhorst, D. and Proper, E. (2011) *Architecture principles: the cornerstone of enterprise architecture.* Springer, London and New York.

ISO (2011) ISO/IEC/IEEE 42010:2011 – 'Systems and software engineering' – Architecture description. International Standards Organisation.

The Open Group (2011) *TOGAF® Version 9.1.* Van Haren, Zaltbommel, NL.

## FURTHER READING

Buschmann, F., Meunier, R., Rohnert, H., Sommerland, P. and Staf, M. (1996) *Pattern-oriented software architecture.* Wiley, Chichester.

Fowler, M. (2003) *Patterns of enterprise application architecture.* Addison-Wesley, Boston, MA.

Gamma, E., Helm, R., Johnson, R. and Vlissides, J. (1994) *Design patterns : elements of reusable object-oriented software.* Addison-Wesley, Boston, MA.

Lankhorst, M., *et al.* (2009) *Enterprise architecture at work: modelling, communication and analysis.* Springer, London and New York.

Larman, C. (2005) *Applying UML and patterns* (3rd edition). Prentice Hall, Indianapolis, IN.

Linthicum, D. S. (2004) *Next generation application integration.* Addison-Wesley, Boston, MA.

Op't Land, M., Proper, E., Waage, M., Cloo, J. and Steghuis, C. (2009) *Enterprise architecture: creating value by informed governance.* Springer, London and New York.

# 11  QUALITY AND TESTING

**Tahir Ahmed**

## CONTENTS OF THIS CHAPTER

This chapter covers the following topics:

- introduction;
- the quality triangle;
- the definition of software quality;
- the objectives and limitation of testing;
- the static test stages of the 'V' model lifecycle;
- the dynamic test stages of the 'V' model lifecycle;
- static testing;
- dynamic testing;
- re-testing (confirmation testing);
- regression testing;
- testing in the lifecycle;
- the test plan;
- references and further reading.

## INTRODUCTION

The quality of software is an important aspect of system development. Delivered software needs to be 'fit for purpose', reliable and maintainable to meet changing requirements. To achieve this, the software needs to be tested at various stages of its development to ensure that the final software product meets the desired level of quality.

The cost of poor quality software can be very considerable; for example, a faulty mechanism in an aircraft undercarriage could result in destruction of the aircraft and death to the crew and passengers. It is always more cost-effective to build quality into the design and development of a product than it is to correct faults after the product has been built.

Delivering good quality software is a vital objective of systems development, and different systems will require different levels of quality. For example, software for military aircraft will have different quality requirements than software for a stock-checking system.

Thus, injecting quality methods and controls right at the start of the system development process helps to ensure that the delivered solution works as required and is as fault free as possible.

## THE QUALITY TRIANGLE

When developing systems, there is inevitably a trade-off between time, cost and scope, and these factors have a direct impact on the quality of the system being developed.

The quality triangle shown in Figure 11.1 indicates that delivering quality is at the heart of systems development.

**Figure 11.1  The quality triangle**

For example if, when developing a software program, it transpires that the required deadline for completion will not be met, the options available using the quality triangle are:

**Time** – extend the deadline by, say, another week. This however, will incur additional cost, and with time pressure on the software developer, the quality of the code might reduce.

**Cost** – add another software developer to the task. However, the second software developer might be inexperienced in the particular type or area of the software, which again might result in poor quality code.

**Scope** – it might be possible to agree with the users and sponsor that the incomplete software program is used, with an acceptance of higher number of defects.

Understanding the impacts of changes to time, cost and scope on quality is a key skill for software development managers when negotiating with key stakeholders.

# THE DEFINITION OF SOFTWARE QUALITY

Defining and agreeing what 'good quality' means is difficult, and can be a rather subjective process. For example, one person might regard a particular restaurant as high quality, whilst another person might regard the same restaurant as low quality. If asked to define what they mean, each person is likely to list different criteria.

The same holds true for software. One user might consider that, for example, ease of use constitutes a 'good' quality characteristic, whereas another user might rate system availability as a much more important aspect of quality.

This means that setting up checks and procedures to ensure that the final software product is built in a quality manner and is of the required levels of quality can also be difficult to achieve.

Some terms that are sometimes used to describe quality include:

- 'excellence';
- 'fitness for purpose';
- 'conformance to requirements'.

Yet how can software be checked for excellence or for fitness for purpose or for conforming to requirements unless there are agreed definitions for these terms?

A rigorous definition is needed, and one such definition is given by ISO8402:1994 (International Standards Organisation). It forms the basis for most quality management standards such as ISO9001:

> The totality of features and characteristics of a product or service that bear on its ability to satisfy stated or implied needs.

However, even this definition can cause uncertainty and ambiguity – 'implied needs' can easily be misinterpreted. For example, a user requirement for a listing of products might imply that they should be shown in some kind of sequence, for instance by product category, whereas the system might show the products listed in product code sequence.

Good software would exhibit the following characteristics:

| | |
|---|---|
| **Meets functional requirements** | The system must do what it is specified in the requirements document. For example, if there is a requirement to display customer details, then the system must provide this feature. |
| **Meets non-functional requirements** | This includes characteristics such as reliability, response time, availability, ease of use, and security. |

| | |
|---|---|
| **Has inherent qualities** | This includes characteristics such as maintainability, efficiency, flexibility/expandability (scalability), reusability, testability, modularity, well-documented, portability, and so on. |

## THE OBJECTIVES AND LIMITATIONS OF TESTING

Once the required level of quality characteristics has been defined and agreed, the question then remains how to ensure, or test, that the software exhibits these characteristics.

Testing is a crucial activity in the Systems Development lifecycle, but many people mistakenly believe that software programs can be fully tested and that, with this complete testing, programs will work correctly and with all errors removed.

Complete testing is impossible because:

- there are too many paths and combinations of paths through the software to test completely;
- the domain of possible inputs is too large;
- user interface issues are too complex;
- there are too many layers of interconnecting hardware components and software applications and modules to replicate into a test environment;
- the budget, time and resources that are available limit the amount and extent of testing that can be carried out.

Consider, for example, the complexity in testing all of the components for an internet-based application running on a mobile phone. The layers of software and hardware include:

- the software application itself;
- the mobile phone's operating system;
- the user interface;
- the physical connectivity of key depressions, swipe, screen-touch sensitivity;
- connectivity to the local internet access points and routers;
- the hardware, software and operating system on the router;
- connectivity to the internet service provider, and onward connectivity to the host service provider, and all of the associated hardware and software.

While most hardware and software components nowadays are developed and tested using software tools, these tools themselves would have to be tested, and again complete testing is not possible for the reasons given above.

Therefore, a system cannot be guaranteed to be fault-free. This means that the users' expectations have to be carefully managed and the testing activity itself has to be focused towards identifying as many defects as possible, or picking up critical defects, within the time and budget available.

The ISTQB (International Software Testing Qualifications Board) offers the following seven principles of testing:

1. **Testing shows the presence of defects**

   Testing can show that defects exist, but it cannot prove that the software has no defects. Successive testing reduces the probability of defects, but cannot guarantee that all defects have been removed.

2. **Exhaustive testing is impossible**

   Even with enough time to allow every path through the software to be tested, the variety of user inputs, and complexity of layers of hardware and software components and interconnections makes exhaustive testing impossible.

3. **Early testing is beneficial**

   Errors and faults found earlier in the development process are easier and cheaper to fix than if found later in the process.

4. **Defect clustering**

   Defects are not evenly spread through a system – they tend to cluster together. This could be because modules have been written by a particular programmer or a particular software package or interface may exhibit similar defects.

5. **There is a 'pesticide paradox'**

   Using the same tests over and over again is unlikely to reveal new defects. To overcome this, test cases need to be reviewed and revised, and new test cases need to be written to test different paths and areas of the software.

6. **Testing is context dependent**

   The type of tests will depend on the system being tested. For example, the tests needed for an internet application mortgage application system will be different to the tests needed for an aircraft navigation system.

7. **Absence of errors fallacy**

   The system must meet the needs of the users; having a defect-free system is not in itself sufficient.

The ultimate aim of testing is to ensure that the quality of the final system is as high as possible by:

- removing **errors** – mistakes made by humans;
- removing **defects** – faults in software code, also known as bugs;
- preventing **failure** – preventing the system from failing to do what it should do, and preventing the system from doing something it should not do.

**Static testing** is the term used to identify and correct **errors**, that is, mistakes made by humans, such as in the production of documents, writing of program source code, creation of lists of data, and so on. Static testing specifically applies to any form of testing where the program code itself **is not** exercised.

**Dynamic testing** is the term used to identify and correct **defects**, and specifically applies to any form of testing where the program code **is** exercised with the use of test data.

In terms of the 'V' model of systems development, static testing is used in the left-hand side of the model, and dynamic testing is used in the stages on the right-hand side of the model (see Figure 11.2).

**Figure 11.2  Static and dynamic testing in the 'V' model lifecycle**

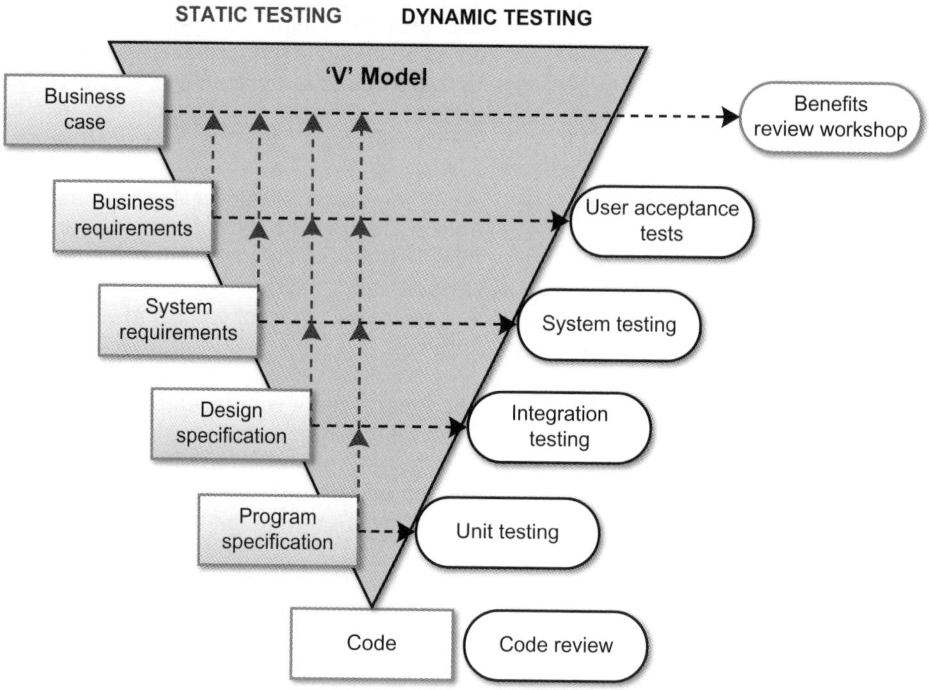

STATIC TESTING          DYNAMIC TESTING

'V' Model

Business case → Benefits review workshop

Business requirements → User acceptance tests

System requirements → System testing

Design specification → Integration testing

Program specification → Unit testing

Code → Code review

# THE STATIC TEST STAGES OF THE 'V' MODEL LIFECYCLE

Static testing uses techniques that do not exercise the program code, and as such can be applied early in the lifecycle before the code is even written. The purpose of static testing is to remove errors that could lead to defects in the software programs and failures in the delivered system.

Static testing primarily involves the use of reviews of documents and other artefacts as they are produced. These are compared against documents and artefacts produced in earlier stages of the lifecycle for completeness and correctness. The products that should be reviewed using static testing include:

**Requirements specification**

The requirements should be checked against the project initiation document (PID) or terms of reference (TOR), and against the business case, to ensure that they are clear, concise, unambiguous, and complete. Do they support the business case, and most importantly, are they testable?

As the requirements specification is the basis for subsequent user acceptance testing, a good check of its quality is to review whether or not acceptance criteria and test conditions can be produced from it.

**Functional specification**

The functional specification shows process and data models as well as the requirements. These should be checked against the requirements specification for technical correctness and feasibility, and to ensure that they correctly specify how the system is to be built.

The later stage of system testing will be based on the functional specification, and as such, the system test criteria, test conditions, test data, and so on should be able to be defined as part of the review of the functional specification.

**Design specification**

The design specification shows all of the program modules and data stores – how these fit together with each other and with the existing system (if there is one). It also shows the interfaces between programs and with other systems, both internal and external. It should be checked against the functional specification and requirements specification for technical accuracy and completeness and to ensure that the design will lead to the system features and behaviour as envisaged in the functional specification.

The design specification will be used as the basis for the later stage of Integration testing, and therefore it should be possible to produce integration test criteria, scenarios, data, and so on, from the design specification.

**Module or program specification**    The module or program specifications detail how each individual program should carry out the required processing. They should be checked against the design specification to ensure completeness, maintainability, efficiency, reliability, and so on. They should also be checked to verify that data is correctly passed to and from other programs.

Test data and test conditions for use in unit testing should be able to be produced as part of the review of module specifications.

The main types of review techniques for static testing are:

**Informal review**    This is usually a peer review, for example by one analyst reviewing another analyst's work, or one programmer reviewing a source code listing produced by another programmer. This type of review is relatively quick and cheap, and helps to identify any obvious errors. However, it is possible that the reviewer might not pick up some errors due to their own 'blind' spot.

**Walkthrough**    With this type of review, the product (for example, the requirements specification) is walked through line by line, section by section, or page by page, to identify any errors. This review could be undertaken by an individual, but more generally it is carried out by a small review group who meet specifically for the purpose of reviewing the product.

This review method is likely to identify more errors that the informal review method, particularly if the review group consists of people with different areas of expertise.

**Technical review**    In this type of review, the product is reviewed by a group of technical experts typically using checklists of common problems to identify errors.

**Inspection**    An inspection is a very formal review meeting, with clearly defined roles and objectives. The roles include:

- **Inspectors** – one or more qualified inspectors review the product in detail using industry standard quality management and review techniques.

- **Scribe** – the scribe has the responsibility to record all errors, actions, decisions, and so on.

- **Moderator** – the moderator is responsible for ensuring that the product is reviewed formally and in a structured way, that all points of view are taken into account and that conflicts are managed appropriately.

Inspections are rigorous and can identify very many errors in the product, but are expensive due to set-up and require careful planning and preparation beforehand, as well as follow-up on any actions and issues identified.

## THE DYNAMIC TEST STAGES OF THE 'V' MODEL LIFECYCLE

The purpose of dynamic testing is to check the quality of the software by executing the program modules to identify any defects found in them.

The software is executed in a number of progressive stages, with each stage building on the confidence of the system gained in preceding stages.

Figure 11.3 shows an example of an operational system, consisting of a customer system and a product system, each containing a number of program modules, some of which interact with other modules, and some of which access data stores. Each of the dynamic testing stages of the lifecycle will be discussed with reference to this figure.

The programs and data store marked with an X are to be changed as part of delivering new requirements.

**Figure 11.3 Dynamic testing**

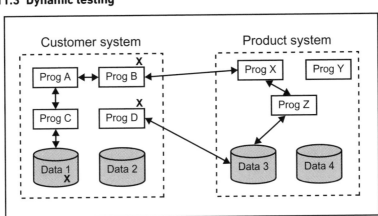

| | |
|---|---|
| **Unit testing, or module or component testing** | Each completed program module, or unit, is tested against its program specification to check that, in isolation, it does what it is supposed to do. Sometimes programmers produce their own unit test data, and unit test plans, and carry out the unit testing themselves, although a higher quality method is to have another developer produce data and carry out unit testing. |
| | In Figure 11.3, Program B and Program D are being changed, and these would be unit tested individually. Because Data store 1 is also being changed, Program C would also be unit tested with new test data to ensure that it still processes data correctly. |
| **Integration testing** | The individual modules are progressively integrated together and tests are carried out to ensure that, for example, the modules pass data back and forth between themselves correctly, and that they comply with the design specification. Integration testing is sometimes carried by developers, but sometimes trained testers are also involved. |
| | In Figure 11.3, Program B would be tested with Program A, and then Program B would be tested with Program X. |
| **System testing** | The system is tested as a whole by testers who check that the system does what it is supposed to do, and as detailed in the functional specification. Tests are designed to 'break' the system as well as to check its correct functioning, and include testing the system against non-functional requirements such as performance, reliability, security, and so on. |
| | In Figure 11.3, all programs in both the customer system and product system are tested. |
| **User acceptance testing** | In this final stage, the users test the system with the aim of ensuring that the system delivers the features needed to support business processes and data, and that the system conforms to the requirements specification. Business analysts often support the users in this stage. |
| | In Figure 11.3, all programs in both the customer system and product system are tested, but the tests and data will be different from that used in system testing. |

The techniques used in dynamic testing consist of:

| | |
|---|---|
| **Black-box techniques** | With black-box techniques, the item to be tested, for example, an individual program, is treated as if it were opaque, and the inner working are unknown, that is, as a 'black box', which takes inputs and produces outputs. |

The tester is not concerned with how the program works, but is only interested in whether the outputs are correct based on the inputs. For example, if the input is a customer account number, and the system displays the customer name and address, the tester would check if the correct customer name and address is displayed, rather than how the system carried out the processing.

Black-box testing is typically used in user acceptance testing, system testing, and integration testing.

**White-box techniques**   Unlike black-box testing, white-box testing **is** concerned with the internal working of the system. By examining the program code or module specification, the tester would design tests and test data that would exercise the program logic and data processing.

White-box testing is usually employed in unit testing.

**Experience-based techniques**   With experience-based testing, the experience of key stakeholders is used to identify areas of the system that are likely to uncover defects. For example, users may know of particular business processes and scenarios that are complex, or service managers may identify certain areas that impact service levels; designers might know of interfaces with external system that have proved problematic in the past.

## RE-TESTING

Re-testing is the term that is used to describe the test applied to any part of a system that has been changed. Its purpose is to check that changes have been made correctly.

In Figure 11.3, Program B and Program D are being changed, and therefore the tests associated with these programs would be referred to as re-testing. Re-testing is also known as confirmation testing.

Quite often, as a result of carrying out dynamic testing, programs need to be corrected and re-tested in order to remove any defects found. For example, if during system testing, a defect was found in Program D, Program D would need to be corrected and re-tested. The re-testing would need to include satisfactory unit testing and integration testing before the program could be considered to be ready for a re-test as part of system testing.

## REGRESSION TESTING

Unlike re-testing, which is concerned with testing the changed parts of a system, regression testing is concerned with making sure that the unchanged parts of the system have not inadvertently been affected and still function as they should.

In Figure 11.3, the only programs that are changed are Program B and Program D. Regression testing would be carried out on all of the other (unchanged) modules in the system to check that, for example, data passed from Program D is still processed correctly throughout the product system.

As regression tests are based on the unchanged parts of the system, they lend themselves to be designed and built once and then used repeatedly. Therefore, regression tests are ideal candidates for automation, using a test tool. The tests can be stored within the tool and executed whenever they are needed.

## PROGRESSION THROUGH THE DYNAMIC TESTING STAGES

The first dynamic test stage carried out is **unit testing**, which aims to achieve as high a level of quality as possible in the individual programs. Any defects found in a program at this stage are corrected and the individual program is then unit tested once again to verify that the defect has been removed.

Once unit testing of the individual programs is complete, meaning that no defects are found based on the unit tests carried out, the solution can then be tested in the next dynamic testing stage, **integration testing**.

In integration testing, any defects found with an individual program will require that program to be corrected and re-tested, and the program will need to go back into the unit test stage, possibly using different test scripts and data until the program has passed all tests. At this point, integration testing can be carried out once again but using the corrected program.

Once integration testing is complete with no defects found, the solution can then be tested in the next dynamic testing stage, **system testing**.

In system testing, all programs in the system, including the changed and unchanged ones, are tested. Again, if any defects are found, the errant programs will need to be corrected and unit and integration tested before being used in system testing again.

Typically, a complete pass through all of the tests is advised, as this will ensure that as many defects as possible are found and that several programs can be corrected at the same time rather than correcting programs as and when defects are found, which could be very time-consuming and costly.

Finally, **user acceptance testing** (UAT) can start once system testing is considered to be defect-free. Defects found during UAT will require the associated program to be corrected and tested in unit testing, integration testing and system testing before again being presented for inclusion in the user acceptance tests.

Whilst the aim is to have no defects at the end of a dynamic testing stage before progressing to the next stage, in reality some defects are considered to be less critical than others and therefore will not prevent the start of a subsequent stage. For example, an incorrect colour on part of a web form noticed during integration testing might not be critical to the start of testing of the system functions in system testing. However, not being able to display the web form at all would be considered critical and would need to be fixed before system testing could start.

This process of correcting programs successively through the stages and of passing individual and groups of programs that have been corrected through each previous stage helps to ensure that the final system is of the required levels of quality before being released for operational use.

## TESTING IN THE LIFECYCLE

This chapter has so far considered testing in the 'V' model, but testing is a crucial activity with any system development model (see Figure 11.4).

In the Waterfall model, testing is shown as a discrete stage, between development and implementation, indicating that all testing activity is carried out after the solution has been developed and before it is deployed for operational use.

In the Incremental model, testing also takes place at the stage between development and implementation but is repeated for each increment. This highlights some important considerations:

- Each increment is concerned with delivering a subset of the total requirements. The first increment might deliver the highest priority features required by the users. Testing can therefore be devised to focus on these high-priority requirements.

- Testing carried out in later increments might identify defects in programs tested successfully in earlier increments. This could mean that the previously implemented increment contains unexpected defects. Also, there is likely to be a great deal of further re-work, re-tests, and possibly re-implementation required to rectify these defects.

- Regression testing is the key type of test when checking the stability of previously tested increments; using an automated test tool would significantly reduce costs and improve quality.

- Test resources such as test analysts, defect managers, quality controllers and so on need to be retained for the duration of all the testing activity within each of the increments, and managing these resources could be a major challenge.

In the Agile model, testing is a continuous activity and, through the building of prototypes, is used to help develop an understanding of the requirements as well as the capability of the technology.

Successive prototypes are put through greater and more rigorous tests, which are based on two key principles:

- verification – that the system is being built in the right way; and
- validation – that the right system is being built.

**Figure 11.4 Testing in the lifecycle**

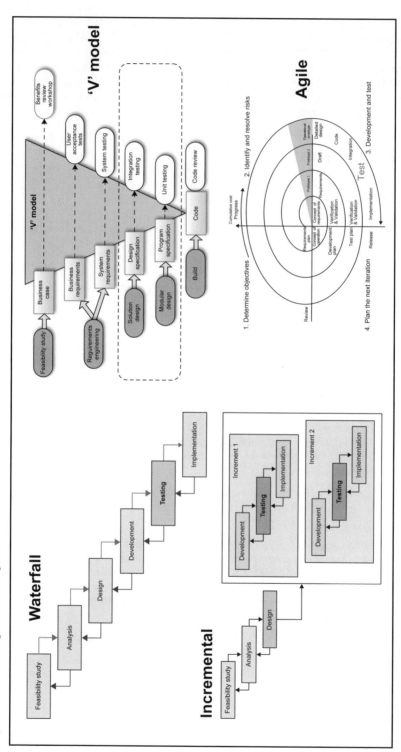

Once it is considered that the final prototypes are an accurate reflection of the required solution and have been approved, they form the basis for developing and testing the solution, or this particular part of the solution. This testing now involves all of the dynamic testing stages discussed earlier, and continues until the solution is ready to be deployed for operational use.

An important factor to consider for managers of Agile developments is how to ensure that testing is not compromised for the sake of speed of delivery of features.

Regardless of which system development model is being used, the testing activity needs to be planned and properly prepared for, and the information needed during the test stages needs to be documented in the test plan.

## THE TEST PLAN

The test plan is a key document in the system development lifecycle and is used by everyone involved in the testing activity to clarify what is to be tested and how the tests will be carried out.

A typical test plan includes:

| | |
|---|---|
| **Author and sign-offs** | States the author of the document, usually the test manager or project manager. Sign-offs to the document are required, usually by the sponsor, service manager, senior user, and other key stakeholders. |
| **Revision history** | Lists the various versions of the document to provide an audit trail of changes made. |
| **Purpose** | Describes the objectives of the testing, and what is to be achieved by carrying out the testing. |
| **System overview** | This is an outline of the system in terms of its major components, and it also describes which areas of the system are particularly high-risk or require greater testing. |
| **Stakeholders** | Lists all of the stakeholders who are impacted by, or have an interest in, the testing activity. |
| **Roles and responsibilities** | This details the roles and responsibilities of everyone involved in the testing, for example it might state that testers are responsible for running test scripts and raising defects, and that the test manager is responsible for the provision of test environments. It also shows the communication plan and points of contact and escalation at key stages during the testing. |
| **Test schedule** | The test schedule is a detailed plan of all testing activity and shows: |

- which dynamic test stages will be carried out;
- when each stage will start and end, and how long each stage is expected to last;
- how many cycles, or passes, are planned for in each stage;
- for each stage and cycle, a detailed schedule describes when each test will be carried out, and by who.

**Defect management**   This provides definitions for the categorisation of defects, for example, a critical defect is one which prevents testing from continuing. It also describes how defects will be recorded, and allocated to developers for correction.

**Test data**   This details what test data is required, and how the test data will be produced, for example by making modified copies of 'live' data.

**Test scenarios and test scripts**   This provides the scenarios that are to be tested, as well as details of the actual test scripts that will be run, and the expected results of the tests.

**Traceability**   This provides a cross-check between the tests and the requirements, and ensures that there are no gaps or inconsistencies.

**Test tools**   The tools to be used during testing are listed, for example where defects will be logged, which tool will be used for regression testing, stress testing, and so on.

**Test reports**   This describes the status reports that will be produced during testing, for example a weekly report that shows how many tests were run, how many tests failed, how defects were raised, how many defects were fixed, and so on.

**Entry criteria**   The entry criteria lists the detailed checks that must be successfully completed before each test stage can be given the go-ahead to proceed. The criteria includes readiness of test data, test scripts and the test environment, and sign-off of the requirements, design and program specifications.

**Exit criteria**   The exit criteria lists the checks that must be successfully completed before the each test stage can be considered to be complete. These include sign-offs from the test manager that all tests have been run successfully and that lessons learnt have been incorporated into subsequent test stages.

## REFERENCES AND FURTHER READING

Brian Hambling (1996) *Managing software quality*. McGraw-Hill, Maidenhead.

Brian Hambling (ed.) (2010) *Software testing: an ISTQB-ISEB Foundation Guide* (revised 2nd edition). BCS, Swindon.

Capers Jones (2000) *Software assessments, benchmarks and best practices.* Addison-Wesley, Upper Saddle River, NJ.

# 12 IMPLEMENTATION AND CHANGEOVER

## Tahir Ahmed

## CONTENTS OF THIS CHAPTER

This chapter covers the following topics:

- implementation in the lifecycle;
- planning for implementation and changeover;
- file and data conversion or creation;
- the principles and problems of data mapping;
- planning, testing and performing data conversion;
- migration of software modules;
- installation of hardware and infrastructure;
- the role of supporting documentation, including user manuals;
- approaches to training;
- defining training needs and training effectiveness;
- approaches to introducing a new system – 'big-bang', phased implementation, pilot implementation, parallel running;
- the implementation plan;
- references and further reading.

## IMPLEMENTATION IN THE LIFECYCLE

The purpose of the implementation stage is to make a new system operational. This is achieved through the transfer of the tested software modules to the operational or 'live' environment, along with setting up of the data required for the new system.

Implementation is carried out after the solution has been fully tested, accepted and signed off by the sponsor (see Figure 12.1).

**Figure 12.1 Implementation in the lifecycle**

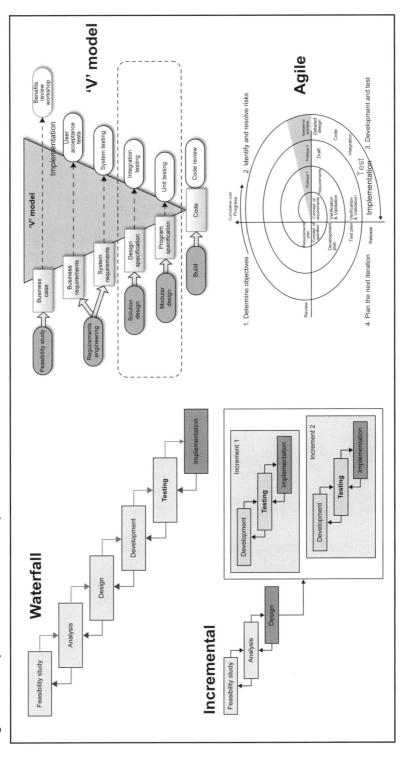

In the Waterfall model, the implementation stage is explicitly shown as the final stage, after the testing stage.

In the 'V' model, the implementation stage is sometimes not explicitly shown, but, like in the Waterfall model, it takes place after testing is complete.

In the Incremental model, implementation is the final stage in each increment, and is repeated for each increment.

With Agile delivery models, the implementation stage is carried out as the final activity of each spiral and delivers a shippable product into operational use.

## PLANNING FOR IMPLEMENTATION AND CHANGEOVER

Planning for implementation and changeover should begin as early as possible in the systems development lifecycle so that issues, timings, training, resources and so on can be considered and planned for. Failure to carry out a successful implementation can have severe consequences for the organisation.

Some of the planning considerations include:

- How to set up data in the new system – will this be newly captured data, or conversion of existing data, or maybe a combination of both?
- Which software modules should be migrated from the test environments to the operational environments, and when?
- What checks are needed to confirm that the migration has been successful?
- Exactly when will the implementation occur – should it be during a relatively 'quiet time', for example, avoiding weekdays, month-ends, and year-ends?
- How long will the implementation take – will it be a few minutes, or maybe several iterations of implementations spread over several months?
- What documentation will be needed to manage and operate the new system?
- What new skills and training will the users and operators of the new system need and what is the best mechanism for delivering this training?
- What is the best way of changing over to the new system from the old system?

Implementation planning is an important responsibility of the project manager. In order to determine all of the relevant factors, input will be needed from key stakeholders, including:

- **Service manager** – for understanding possible impact on service levels, optimum timings for the implementation, and which documentation will be needed;
- **Users** – for determining training needs and delivery, business and financial implications, user checking during the implementation, and how best to transition from using the old system to using the new system;

- **Sponsor** – for agreeing any business risks and impacts on expected business benefits;
- **Business analysts** – to support the users in the validation of business data and processes. Business analysts sometimes carry out user training;
- **Technical specialists** – for identifying the best methods for file and data conversion, assessing possible impacts on other systems and interfaces, and best methods of accessing system data.

These considerations are explored in more detail in the rest of this chapter.

## FILE AND DATA CONVERSION OR CREATION

Implementing a new system will inevitably require new data. If the system is entirely new, then data will need to be created manually or from paper records such as existing invoices or customer orders (see Figure 12.2).

**Figure 12.2 Data creation and data conversion**

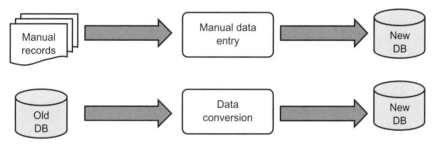

Nowadays, most implementations are an upgrade to, or replacement of, an existing system. The existing data will need to be converted to the new format, and a data mapping exercise is needed to determine how best to convert the old data to the new and to identify potential issues. In both cases, a great deal of work may be required – hence the need for early planning.

One question regarding historical data is whether it is sufficiently reliable and accurate, and whether the time and cost involved for correction is warranted.

The process for converting data from an old system to a new system can be automated, via bespoke software or a commercial off-the-shelf package (COTS). This is called ETL (Extract, Transform and Load), signifying the following steps in the conversion process:

1. Extract of data from the old system;
2. Carrying out some form of transformation of the extracted data making it suitable for the new system; and
3. Load of the transformed data into the new system.

Sometimes the costs involved in developing bespoke ETL software or purchasing a COTS may be excessive or might not be possible within time constraints. In this case, it may be quicker and easier to re-key data into the new system.

## THE PRINCIPLES AND PROBLEMS OF DATA MAPPING

Data mapping is the term given to the activity that identifies which data from the old system can be migrated to the new system (see Figure 12.3).

**Figure 12.3  Data mapping**

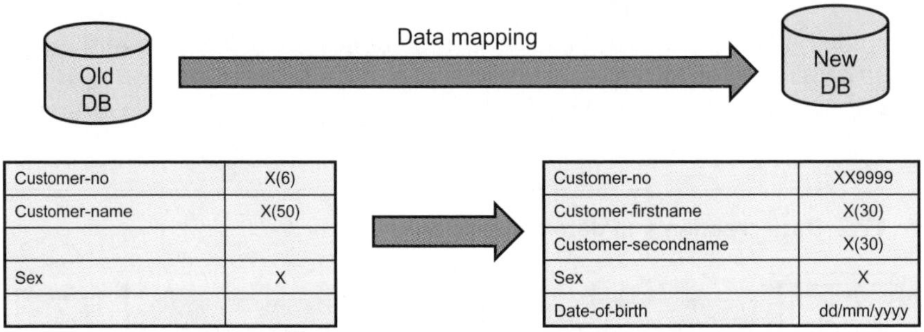

A number of issues can arise when carrying out this mapping, including:

**Field type**            The type of field in which the data is held may be different in the old and the new systems. For example, a product number in the old system might be held as an alphanumeric field (allowing both letters and numbers) whereas in the new system, a product number is held as numeric only.

**Field length**          The length of data fields may be different in the old and new systems. If the field in the new system is shorter than in the old system, then a business decision needs to be made as to whether truncated data is acceptable (for example, shortening of surnames) or whether human intervention is needed. Consideration should also be given to which part of the old data should be mapped to the new: the first part of the field, the last part of the field, or perhaps some other parts of the field?

If the field in the new system is longer than in the old system, then in theory, there shouldn't be any issues. However, care needs to be taken as to the placement of the old data into the new field, that is, left-filled, right-filled or some other placement.

Space characters can sometimes be an issue – fill them with noughts or leave empty? Some software modules expect noughts rather than space characters, and when an unexpected space character is encountered the software module could abnormally end, causing a system failure.

**Field structures**
Field structures in the old and new systems may be different. For example, a customer address in the old system may be held as a single address field, but on the new system it may be held as three address fields.

**Required fields**
Some data required for the new system may not be available from the old system. Consideration needs to be given as to whether the required data is needed before the new system is operational, in which case this data will need to be captured from elsewhere or manually entered, or if the required data can be captured after system implementation, as part of ongoing business processes.

**Semantics**
Semantics, or the meaning of the data, needs to be considered. For example when mapping the data for 'Title', in the old system this may include Mister, Miss, Ms, Doctor, Sir, Lord, Mister, Miss, etc. but in the new system 'Title' may mean a formal title only.

**Validation**
The conversion routines may include some tests to validate that the data on the new system has been converted correctly.

## PLANNING, TESTING AND PERFORMING DATA CONVERSION

Data conversion, like any other activity or project, is likely to be more successful if it is well planned. The planning activities should include:

**Identify steps**
All of the steps required for the conversion should be identified, including those needed to correct the data and to validate it.

**Decide timing**
The timing of when the data conversion should actually take place is a critical issue. If done too far in advance of system commissioning, then the data may become out of date, unless some method is devised to maintain the data. If the conversion is done to close to the system commissioning, then there may not be sufficient time to investigate and resolve any errors. The correct balance needs to be achieved.

**Writing or purchasing the conversion routines**
Whether the conversion routines are a bespoke development or a COTS, these software routines will need to be designed, developed or tailored, tested and managed just like any other IT systems development project. If data is to be captured from paper sources, then it may be necessary to develop data input forms or screens to convert the data into a standardised format.

| | |
|---|---|
| **Using automated test comparator** | Automated test tools could be used to compare the new data with the old data and to test the conversion routines. |
| **Actual file conversion** | The timing of the actual file conversion needs to be such that there is no disruption to the operational service. In practice, this usually means overnight, or weekends, or during a short 'window' during the early hours of a Sunday morning. Sometimes, though, there isn't a suitable slot to allow the conversion to be done in one step, resulting in the conversion being carried out in a series of shorter steps over a period of days, weeks or, sometimes, months. |

## MIGRATION OF SOFTWARE MODULES

As well as carrying out data migration, any new or changed software modules will also need to be migrated from the test environments to the operational environment (see Figure 12.4).

**Figure 12.4  Migration of software modules**

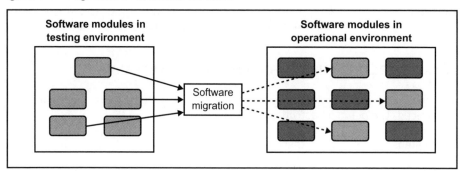

Failure to migrate the correct modules and, perhaps more importantly, the correct versions of the software modules, could result in system failure, which in turn can cause loss of business operations.

Some key considerations for software migration include:

| | |
|---|---|
| **Configuration management** | Configuration management is needed to ensure that only the correct versions of software modules which are relevant to the implementation are selected for migration. This is particularly relevant if one or more of the modules need to be 'backed out' in the event of implementation issues. Use of configuration management tools helps to ensure the accuracy of this selection. |

| | |
|---|---|
| **Release management** | Several implementations are typically packaged together into a 'release'. The release management activity checks that only compatible implementations are packaged together, and transferred to the operational environment in a single migration. |
| **Timing** | Sometimes it can be useful to migrate the software modules in a de-activated state, such that there is no disruption to business continuity, and to activate them only when needed. This separates the software migration step from their operational use, and reduces the risk of operational impact. |
| **Validation** | Validating that the migrated software works correctly can be carried out in stages, for example by checking that subsets of data are processed correctly by the modules before allowing the full set of data to be processed. |

## INSTALLATION OF HARDWARE AND INFRASTRUCTURE

Quite often, hardware and infrastructure components will need to be installed in the operational environment as a prerequisite to the migration of data and software. For example, the volume of data, the number of users, and the rate of user activity required for a new system might necessitate larger data storage devices, increased processing capability and larger network capacity.

Upgrades to, or replacement of, the existing hardware and infrastructure will need to be managed, planned, and tested just like any other IT project. Any planning and preparation for the implementation would need to include hardware and infrastructure requirements.

Sometimes, hardware and infrastructure changes are stand-alone projects in their own right as a precursor for implementation of business activity, for example, the roll-out of desktop computers, telephones and headsets to a new call centre.

## SUPPORTING DOCUMENTATION

As part of planning for the implementation, consideration needs to be given to the documentation that will be needed to support both the users of the new system, as well as the operators.

The users will need documentation to help them carry out their daily jobs and to provide some initial help in case of problems with using the new system.

Operations staff need documentation that helps them to support the new system, not only in terms of operating and routine maintenance, but also when unexpected problems or failures occur.

The main types of documentation for users include online help facilities and printed user guides, whilst documentation for operators includes operational manuals and technical documentation.

**Online help**  Making systems easy to use and intuitive helps users to carry out business processes more effectively. Online help facilities greatly support this by providing additional guidance to users if they encounter difficulties or are uncertain of the flows, content, context, and so on.

**Printed user guides**  Whilst online help facilities are useful when quick access to supporting information is needed, sometimes a more detailed and in-depth explanation of how to use the system is necessary. This detailed information is set out in printed user guides, and should be structured in the same manner in which users carry out their tasks. This allows users to readily find the relevant topics they need support with. Printed user guides are sometimes supplemented with quick reference cards, single-page diagrams, or 'crib cards'.

**Operational manuals**  Operational manuals are vital for the staff who are responsible for the day-to-day operation of the new system. The information needed will include how to start and stop the system, which routine maintenance activities are required and the tasks involved, how to backup and restore data, what to do when error messages are encountered, what to do in the event of system failure, how to carry out business continuity and disaster recovery, and so on.

**Technical documentation**  Sometimes, further information about the new system is needed to support the users and operators. For example, details of the data structures and system functions might be required to determine how best to deal with a particular error message or user problem. This information is held in the technical documentation produced as part of developing the solution.

Having ready access to the correct documentation becomes a vital aspect of supporting new systems, and many organisations have at times encountered situations where operational problems have taken some considerable time to resolve due to lack of up-to-date documentation.

These types of issues can be prevented if good configuration management and version control mechanisms and tools are in place to easily identify which are the relevant documents and which are the correct versions of these documents.

One of the challenges in an Agile development is that of documentation. Agile developments focus on creating working software rather than the production of documentation. Ensuring that the right level and amount of documentation is produced for the new system can pose a significant challenge to Agile project managers.

## TRAINING

In addition to having documentation to support their day-to-day activities, users and operations staff will likely need to be trained in the new system. There are various approaches to training, but the main elements to consider include:

### Identify competencies

The new system will have some new or changed business processes and operational procedures, which in turn will require new or changed competencies and skills to carry them out. Identifying which competencies the users and operational personnel will need to be trained in is the first step in the overall approach to training.

### Define training strategy

Having identified the competencies needed to use and operate the new system, the next step is to compare these to the competencies that the users and operational staff already possess. This comparison is known as the 'training needs analysis', commonly abbreviated to TNA. Once the TNA is understood, then the method of delivering the training and assessing the effectiveness of training can be planned.

### Deliver training

The key considerations when planning for training delivery include:

- How will the organisation be impacted by the training delivery? For example, it may be necessary to train small groups of staff in turn during periods of low activity to minimise disruption to service.

- How much training will be required? This considers, for example, if there are minimum changes to an existing system requiring 'on-the-job' training, or if there are new or changed processes requiring staff to be trained over several days.

- How complex is the new system? A more complex system will require more in-depth, perhaps face-to-face training by an expert.

- How skilled are the staff, and how quickly and easily can they acquire new competencies?

The main methods of delivering training include:

| | |
|---|---|
| **Traditional lectures and workshops** | These consist of face-to-face to training given to the potential users of the system by someone who understands the new features really well. This method is particularly useful when a |

COTS solution is procured from a software vendor – training is delivered by experts from the vendor.

Lectures and workshops require planning both in terms of scheduling least disruptive times for training delivery, and for roll-out of training across the user community. Other factors include the availability of suitable training rooms, equipment and the trainers themselves.

The main advantage with this method is that there is interaction between trainer and trainees, and opportunity to explore particular topics in detail. As such, this method of training can be relatively expensive compared with other methods.

**Remotely delivered training**

Remotely delivered training consists of, for example, webcasts and teleconferencing, whereby the trainer and trainees are brought together via technology, for relatively short periods of time.

This method is ideal for training large numbers of trainees at the same time, who are possibly geographically dispersed; however, the agenda and time require careful management. Communication tends to be one way – trainer to trainee. As such, the opportunity for trainees to ask questions and explore topics is very limited.

This method of training delivery requires the prior development and roll-out of software that users can themselves use to gain the competencies they need to use the new system.

Developing good Computer Based Training (CBT) and e-learning software is vital for this method to be effective, and the main considerations include:

- development or procurement of CBT and e-learning software could be expensive and time-consuming;
- trainees have the freedom (within limits) to gain training by themselves and at times and at a pace which fits in with their day-to-day tasks and work pressures;
- their needs to be some method of monitoring and assessment to ensure that the trainee has gained the required competencies within the required timescales.

**'Train the trainer'**

A popular approach is to use a training delivery method known as 'train-the-trainer', or 'cascade' training, whereby a small group of 'super-users' are trained in the new system, perhaps to a higher standard and level of expertise, and these 'super-users' then train the rest of the user community and or provide centres of excellence and support.

## Assess training effectiveness

Once training has been delivered, consideration needs to be given to the effectiveness of the training and whether or not any follow-up training will be needed:

- Post-course questionnaires (PCQs) are completed by participants at the end of training and are useful for capturing their views and impressions of the training content, the effectiveness of the trainer, the training environment, and so on. However, PCQs are not so good for assessing whether participants' competencies have been developed.

- Tests are good way of determining if the participants have gained the required competencies and knowledge. For example, participants could be asked to set up a new customer account to demonstrate they have gained both an understanding of the process, as well as the skills needed. Multiple-choice questionnaires are another method of testing if participants have gained the required knowledge.

## SYSTEM IMPLEMENTATION

An important consideration when planning for implementation is how to switch over, or 'changeover', to the new system from the old, that is, for deploying the new system into operation. There are four main options for changeover:

### Direct changeover or 'big bang'

The new system is brought straight into operation, and the old system (or manual system, if there isn't a previous system in place) is switched off. This direct changeover, or 'big bang', means that there is an immediate switch to using the new system and business processes without any gradual transition to the new system.

The timing of the changeover itself is often scheduled for a weekend or during a routine shutdown or some other quiet period in order to minimise disruption to business operations.

**Advantages**
- There is a 'clean break' from the old system to the new system.
- Users are forced to start using the new system straight away.
- This option is less expensive than the other options, as only one system is in operation at any one time – either the old, or the new.

| **Disadvantages** | • It is high risk – there is no fall back in the situation where the new system fails. |
| | • There may be reputational damage to the organisation if the changeover is seen to have been managed incompetently. |

Sometimes the 'big bang' approach is the only option for changeover, despite the high risks involved. In the banking sector, for example, where many banks need to pass data between each others' systems via third parties such as Visa or MasterCard, changes to interfaces at the third party would require all of the participating institutions to immediately switch over to the use of the new interfaces, otherwise some participants would 'lose' data or connectivity with others.

Minimising the risks of a direct changeover becomes crucial in the planning of the implementation. Factors to be considered include:

- allowing more time for thorough testing;
- ensuring there are sufficient steps in the cutover activity itself to check for the accuracy of the migrated data and software;
- identifying the key points during the cutover at which there are options to revert back to the old system;
- identifying the point in the cutover where there is no going back to the old system and that any errors encountered after this point will need to be fixed in situ (known as 'fix-forward').

## Parallel running

With this option, the old and new systems are both operated side by side until the organisation is confident that the new system is operating satisfactorily, and at this point the old system is switched off.

| **Advantages** | • There is less risk than with the direct changeover approach, as the old system can still support the organisations operations. |
| | • In the event that the new system fails or is unsatisfactory, the old system is a fallback. |
| | • Users can gradually transition from the old to the new system. |
| | • Data from the new system can be compared with data from the old system to validate the correct functioning of the new system. |
| **Disadvantages** | • It is more expensive that the direct changeover approach, as both the old and the new system have to be supported for a period of time. |

- Users may be reluctant to move to the new system, and to 'let go' of the old system, particularly if the new system is being 'imposed' on them or gaining their commitment and buy-in hasn't been managed well.

## Pilot implementation

A pilot implementation is where the new system is initially implemented in one or more sites, or with a subset of users, rather than being implemented across the whole organisation. Experience of using the new system during this pilot is used to make any corrections and final adjustments to the new system before it is fully deployed.

**Advantages**
- There is less risk than with the direct changeover approach, as any problems with new system can be resolved in a controlled subset of users before the full deployment.

- The new system is only deployed to the organisation as a whole when it is more stable and major problems have been eliminated.

- Operational use during the pilot enables the new system to be 'tuned' to be more effective – this is particularly useful for Agile and other incremental developments.

- It can be less costly to implement the new system and resolve any errors in a pilot than it would be to do so after full deployment.

**Disadvantages**
- The area chosen for the pilot might not be typical of the users and sites as a whole, and lessons learnt might therefore not be relevant.

- If the experience of the users during the pilot is poor, than this might undermine confidence in the new system.

## Phased implementation

With the phased implementation, the functionality of the new system is deployed in stages or increments such that, in the first phase, a subset of the total functionality of the new system is deployed, and then additional components and functionality are deployed in successive stages until the new system is fully operational.

**Advantages**
- Higher priority requirements and functionality can be delivered sooner than lower priority items.

- The risk is reduced, as the organisation isn't dependent on the new system at once.

- Users can gradually transition from the old to the new system in stages, and gain confidence with some system functionality before additional features are introduced.

- It is easier to fall back to earlier phases if problems are encountered with later phases.

**Disadvantages**
- Users might lose interest after their higher priority requirements are delivered in initial phases.

- Conversely, users might not adopt earlier phases if they are mainly interested in features being delivered in later phases.

- This approach can be expensive, as both the old and the new system will need to be supported over some period of time until the full functionality is delivered.

- Users might cling on to the old systems and ways of working.

## THE IMPLEMENTATION PLAN

The implementation plan is a key document in the system development lifecycle and is used by everyone involved in the implementation activity to ensure that all of the steps are detailed, understood and feasible. It also states what actions should be followed to validate that the implementation is being carried out successfully, and what actions and escalations should be triggered in the event of problems or issues.

A typical implementation plan includes:

**Author and sign-offs**
States the author of the document, usually the implementation manager or project manager. Sign-offs to the document are usually by the sponsor, service manager, senior user and other key stakeholders.

**Revision history**
Lists the various versions of the document to provide an audit trail of changes made.

**Purpose**
Describes the objectives of the implementation, and what is to be achieved by carrying the implementation.

**System overview**
This is an outline of the system in terms of its major components, and it describes how the implementation will affect the system.

**Stakeholders**
Lists all of the stakeholders who are impacted by, or have an interest in, the implementation.

**Points of contact**
This details the roles and responsibilities of everyone involved in the implementation. It also shows the communication plan and points of contact and escalation at key stages during the implementation.

**Implementation schedule**   The implementation schedule is a detailed plan of all activities during the implementation, and shows the timings of each task, who is responsible, the sequence and dependencies and the validation and escalation processes needed.

**Entry criteria**   The entry criteria lists the detailed checks that must be successfully completed before the implementation can be given the go-ahead to proceed. The criteria includes sign-off of testing, business readiness, IT readiness, operational readiness and sign-off of the implementation plan.

**Exit criteria**   The exit criteria lists the checks that must be successfully completed before the implementation can be considered to be complete. These include sign-offs from the business that business data has been validated and sign-offs from IT and operations that the data and software migrations have completed successfully; it also lists any implementation issues and lessons learnt.

Not all implementations are successful, and keeping a record of how well the implementation plan and schedule progressed is vital to ensure the success of subsequent re-implementation activity.

For example, by keeping a record of when tasks actually started and completed, and whether or not there were issues, delays, or interruptions will help to ensure that the next revision of the implementation plan and schedule are more realistic.

This is particularly relevant for pilot and phased approaches to changeover, and in Incremental and Agile development models, whereby the implementation plan for a previous implementation can be used as the basis for subsequent implementations.

## REFERENCES AND FURTHER READING

Skidmore, S. and Eva, M. (2004) *Introducing systems development*. Palgrave Macmillan, London.

Truelove, S. (ed.) (1995) *The handbook of training and development* (2nd edition). Blackwell, Oxford.

Yeates, D. and Wakefield, T. (2004) *Systems analysis and design* (2nd edition). FT Prentice Hall, Harlow.

# 13 MAINTENANCE AND EVALUATION

## Alan Paul

## CONTENTS OF THIS CHAPTER

This chapter covers the following topics:

- the place of maintenance in the lifecycle;
- corrective, adaptive and perfective maintenance;
- evaluation and types of review;
- the role and selection of metrics for evaluation;
- key performance indicators (KPIs) and service level agreements (SLAs);
- references and further reading.

## INTRODUCTION

Most of this book is devoted to the approaches and techniques used to develop a system. However, when the system is handed over for live use, it moves into a new stage – maintenance – and the project itself moves into an evaluation stage. A definition of the evaluation and maintenance stages is:

> to recognise the need to evaluate a delivered system and to enhance it through subsequent maintenance.

Maintenance and evaluation of systems are subjects in their own right and many books have been written on these topics, some of which are noted at the end of the chapter. This chapter provides an overview of some of the main aspects of maintenance and evaluation. It should also be borne in mind that work in the maintenance stage is generally (although not always) carried out by a different team from the team involved in developing the system. The maintenance team often operate within a different management structure and, of course, due to the different nature of the work, different techniques are required.

## MAINTENANCE IN THE SYSTEMS DEVELOPMENT LIFECYCLE

The term 'maintenance' can sometimes be misleading as it implies that it concerns only actions carried out to correct faults or to keep the system in good running order.

However, evidence suggests that, of all the work carried out in the maintenance stage, only around twenty per cent is actually corrective, with the remaining eighty per cent being related to system enhancements. This may reflect the current focus on delivering software in releases or increments. It is possible that, if a system undergoes significant enhancement over time, it may end up bearing little, or very limited, resemblance to the original system. It is also the case that the costs incurred during the maintenance stage are typically high in relation to the cost of the original development, if they are considered over the full life of the system; maintenance costs may account for several times the development cost. Obviously, this varies considerably from system to system, depending upon factors such as the lifetime of operation. For example, a pensions management system is likely to be in operation for many years, thus incurring high overall maintenance costs, whereas a system developed to help launch a new product may have a very short lifespan and require little maintenance before being abandoned.

Chapter 2 explained the different system development lifecycles and it is useful to look at how the maintenance stage is added to some of them.

## Linear approach

The first sets of lifecycles are linear in nature, and include the Waterfall and 'V' models. Figure 13.1 shows a conventional Waterfall lifecycle, with maintenance added as an extra stage at the end. However, this model doesn't provide any insight into what is actually done in the maintenance stage; it simply treats maintenance as another stage that starts when the Implementation Stage is finished.

**Figure 13.1  Maintenance in the Waterfall lifecycle**

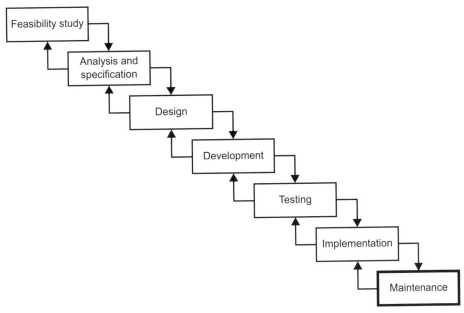

A better representation is provided by the 'V' model of systems development (Figure 13.2) as in essence it involves repeating the entire lifecycle. The maintenance stage of the system's life will consist of a series of iterations of the 'V' model stages. Each iteration will, of course, be on a smaller scale than the original development, encompassing a selected set of additional requirements. So, when user acceptance testing is finished, we return to the first stage (business requirements), and continue down and then up the 'V' as before. This sequence will probably be repeated many times in order to maintain the system during its lifespan.

**Figure 13.2 'V' model lifecycle**

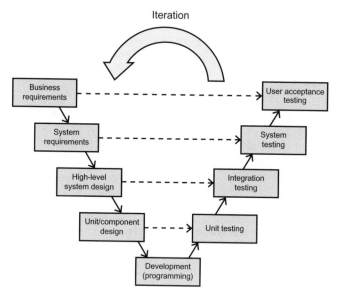

There is another variant of the Waterfall model that explicitly shows the maintenance stage and this – by reason of its shape – is known as the 'b' model. It is illustrated in Figure 13.3.

The 'b' model shows that, once the system is in live operation, there is a separate set of stages where the users and others carry out evaluation and maintenance:

• they evaluate how well the system works:

• they record things that are wrong with it and, with the benefit of their experience in using the system, think of additional things they would like it to do;

• these ideas may then be examined in a feasibility study and, if approved, give rise to a small development project to enhance and improve the system.

This sequence continues throughout the lifetime of the system.

**Figure 13.3 The 'b' model of systems development**

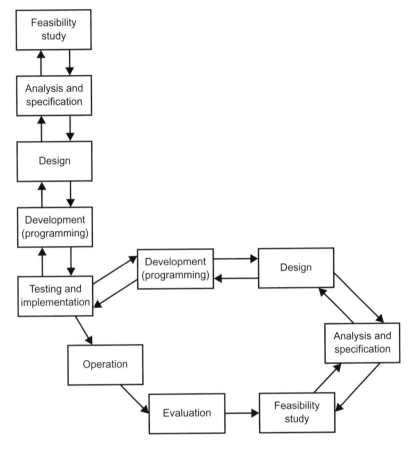

## Evolutionary approach

The second main approach concerns evolutionary systems development. This approach is based upon the Spiral lifecycle, which is used to some extent by many Agile approaches such as RAD, DSDM, SCRUM, XP, RUP, Kanban, ScrumBan, AgileUP and so on.

Figure 13.4 shows the original Spiral lifecycle proposed by Barry Boehm.

This model suggests that a separate 'maintenance' stage is not needed since the principles of continuous improvement and addition are inherent to, and built into, the approach. The essence of the model is that it is iterative using an evolutionary prototyping approach to develop a system release. Any further release of the system, following the initial deployment, begins at the heart of the spiral and is developed using the same approach.

However, it is possible, in practice, that a system is developed using an evolutionary approach, but when it moves into maintenance, it is passed into a maintenance pool where other standardised maintenance approaches are used.

**Figure 13.4 Spiral lifecycle (Boehm)**

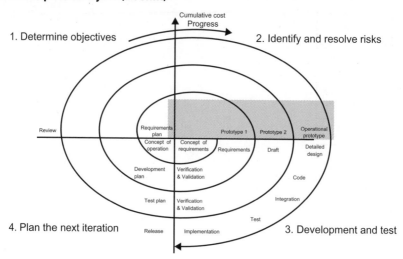

## MAINTENANCE CATEGORIES

The maintenance work undertaken after the system is implemented can fall into three broad categories:

### Corrective maintenance

Corrective maintenance fixes faults and failures discovered within the system. The system may have been exhaustively tested before being handed over to the users for live use, but faults may still be found when used in the real world and subjected to real situations. If problems have been discovered with the way requirements were defined originally, or in the way that the developers have implemented some requirements, putting the resultant problems right would also fall into this category.

### Adaptive maintenance

Adaptive maintenance (or enhancement) involves making changes to the system to meet new or changed requirements. The system is being **adapted** to cater for these changes. These usually result from changes to the way the organisation operates, sometimes caused by external forces such as new legislation. For example, if the rules for calculating National Insurance contributions are changed in the budget, adjustments would be needed to a payroll system to encompass them.

### Perfective maintenance

Perfective maintenance (optimisation) involves 'tuning' the system to make it work better. Often, perfective maintenance work is directing at improving the non-functional requirements, for example to make response times faster or the system more intuitive to use.

## Other types

Other categories include **preventative** maintenance – action taken on foreseeable or latent errors, but where the error has not yet caused any problems. A good historical example was the Year 2000 date format issue ('Y2K'), when a lot of software was modified to avoid possible problems where dates were held in dd/mm/yy format.

Sometimes part of adaptive maintenance is classed as **evolutive** – where the users decide to change the requirements as a result of their experience in using the system, as opposed to system modifications made necessary by changes in the external environment, such as new legislation or the need to interface with another system.

## TESTING IN THE MAINTENANCE STAGE

Whatever type of maintenance is being undertaken, there is a need to test the changes before they enter live running. The stages of testing involved here are basically the same as for the original development – unit (module) testing, integration testing, system testing and user acceptance testing – but maintenance also requires what is called regression testing.

Regression testing means, in effect, checking that the changes being introduced do not adversely affect something that previously worked correctly. For example, if there had been a module of the system that passed a field to another module, what would happen if the size of that field were increased? Would the receiving module be able to handle this larger field or would it fail in some way? It is possible that the receiving module may truncate the length of the field leading to an undesirable outcome, so regression testing is needed to ensure that these types of errors do not occur.

## EVALUATION

It is important that the 'evaluation' aspects of a system are carefully considered. Evaluation should always be carried out and has a number of different objectives.

Evaluation of a system may vary depending on the type of system and on how it is used. It is useful to bear in mind the 'CCP' model when considering evaluation reviews:

**Context:** Why is evaluation being carried out and who is to be involved? Which stakeholders are interested in the review and why?

**Content:** What is being evaluated? It may be the conduct of the project, or the performance of the software, or an aspect of the expected benefits.

**Process:** What is the timeframe for conducting the review, how is it done, and what is done?

Evaluation can take many forms and the terminology used for these can be misleading, as different organisations may use the same term to mean different things (and different terms to mean the same thing). The three major evaluation activities are post-project review (how well the project was conducted), post-implementation review (how well the delivered software meets the requirements) and benefits review (how well the benefits have been realised). The more common types of review are described below. Although organisations use different names for these reviews, those used below are the most common terms.

## Post-project review

The post-project review is a one-off exercise conducted at the completion of the development project. This review is likely to take place almost immediately after the start of live running and examines how well the development project was conducted, in terms of what was done well, and what could be improved. The output from this review is a Post Project Review Report, sometimes called a Lessons Learned Report. The review is not an opportunity to apportion blame for things that went badly, but to agree on 'what worked well' and 'what did not work well' during the project in order to use the findings to benefit future projects.

The review will look at a number of areas, including the following:

- **Project management:** How well was the project planned, monitored and controlled? How did the project perform against its constraints of time, cost and quality?

- **Estimating:** How good were the estimates and what useful software metrics were gained from the project?

- **Risks and issues:** How well were risks identified, analysed and dealt with?

- **User involvement:** Was there sufficient user involvement and how well were the users' expectations managed?

Members of the project team – user representatives, analysts, designers, developers and testers – are involved in this review as well as the project sponsor. Input documents may include project progress reports, cost reports, outstanding error lists, issues logs and so on.

## Post-implementation review

The post-implementation review looks at how successfully the software meets the requirements defined earlier in the project and typically takes place shortly after go-live – perhaps three to six months later (although this is not a fixed timescale). The post-implementation review (PIR) is concerned with reviewing the product produced by systems development, primarily the software, although other deliverables (user guides, training and so on) could also be included. It focuses on whether the product meets the objectives and requirements defined at the start of development in the project initiation document. It also addresses any unresolved issues still remaining with the product.

The participants in this review should include user representatives, business analysts and developers. The aim is to develop a 'snagging list' of items that require attention.

This list should be prioritised in some way, for example, whether the issue needs immediate attention or whether a fix can be incorporated in the next scheduled upgrade of the system, or even whether it can be lived with indefinitely.

In addition to the snagging list, another outcome of a post-implementation review may be changes to the software development and testing processes. This is designed to avoid the same software problems occurring in future projects, although this is more correctly dealt with in the post-project review. Some organisations combine the two types of review, although this is generally not a good idea as the objectives of the reviews are different.

## Benefits review

Benefits management is an ongoing process, which should have started much earlier in the lifecycle, at the point when the business case has been agreed and the predicted business benefits established. A benefits review may take place at any appropriate point after the system has been delivered and when enough time has elapsed for the benefits to have appeared (or at any rate where the likelihood of their appearance can be assessed). The main objective of investing in new IT systems is to deliver business benefits, and benefit reviews are carried out in order to check that this has actually happened. Once a system is in live operation, the benefits review is conducted to determine whether or not the business benefits have been realised.

It is important that the benefits are defined clearly at the outset of the project, otherwise it is impossible to determine whether the new system has been a success and whether it has delivered the intended benefits. The initial definition of the benefits should be contained in the business case, and this business case should be revisited throughout the development project to ensure that the benefits are still on track to be delivered. The business case may require to be changed as a result. Points at which the business case is reviewed may be pre-determined, for example, at the end of each stage, or may take place as a result of a major external factor, such as a significant change in legislation which affects the system under development.

The benefits review is concerned with benefits **realisation**, where the benefits are checked to see if those originally proposed in the business case have actually been delivered. Although the business benefits are often financial in nature, they may also be related to other non-financial aspects such as meeting legal requirements, increased quality of customer service, speedier responses to enquiries and so on. As a result, there may be many aspects to check in order to confirm (or otherwise) the realisation of a benefit. The place of benefits realisation as part of an extended 'V' model is shown in Figure 13.5.

## THE ROLE AND SELECTION OF METRICS FOR EVALUATION

In general, a metric is a quantifiable measurement used to track and assess the performance of a product, plan or process. For an IT system, metrics may be used to assess and monitor its performance during live running, or to help establish whether the business benefits are being met.

**Figure 13.5  Extended 'V' model showing benefits realisation stage**

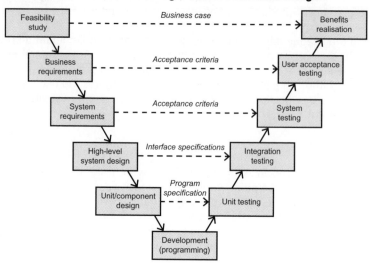

To be useful, metrics should be defined in line with the following characteristics:

**Quantifiable**   It should be possible to assign some value to the metric, for example that ninety-five per cent of the requirements were agreed to have been met during user acceptance testing or that transactions are processed twenty-five per cent quicker than previously.

**Relevant**   The metrics must be relevant to the business objectives for the project, for example, that they contributed towards increased sales or a better image for the organisation.

**Easy to collect**   The effort of collecting the data should not be disproportionate to its importance. Some very useful measures – such as customers' perceptions of a new product – may perhaps be collected through time-consuming methods such as one-to-one interviews. In some contexts, this may be considered worthwhile, but this may not be the case in other situations.

The metrics should be defined such that they focus on key aspects of the new system development. Examples include:

**Business objectives**   If the aim of the project was to improve profitability by replacing salespeople with a new website, data must be collected that enables the organisation to assess whether this has worked or not. This could include number and value of sales processed via the website, reduced cost of the salesforce and so on.

**Functional fit**

It is important that the software does what it was initially required to do. User acceptance testing provides some insights into functional fit by identifying how well the requirements have been met. However, another measure is the number of corrective maintenance changes requested after the initial implementation.

**Reliability**

Reliability is another important aspect to be considered when evaluating the success of a system. Measures such as the percentage availability of the system during working hours, or of the amount of 'downtime' experienced, fit into this category.

**Usability**

Usability is a key factor for ensuring the successful deployment of a system into the work environment. This can be difficult to measure, but such issues as how long it takes to train someone to use the system effectively and how well-defined the help facilities are, should be considered.

## Key performance indicators (KPIs)

Key performance indicators are used to measure vital aspects of the system's performance. Usually a number of KPIs are measured, which together provide an overall measure of how well the system is performing. KPIs should make use of SMART, that is they should be Specific, Measurable, Attainable (or Achievable), Relevant (to the business) and Time-based.

## Service level agreements (SLAs)

A service level agreement is generally an agreement between two (or more) parties where one party is the customer and the other party is the supplier of the service. In an SLA, there is a 'contract' between the parties where the provider agrees to provide the service to a pre-defined level or standard. This level of service is then monitored and, depending on the contract in place, penalties may be imposed on the supplier if the SLA is not met. In the case of a delivered system, there should be several SLAs in place. One SLA may state that the maintenance team will correct any high-priority faults and restore a full service with 24 hours. Another example SLA may be that the system will be available for use ninety-eight per cent of the total time within each calendar month.

## REFERENCES

Boehm, B. (1986) *A spiral model of software development and enhancement*. ACM SIGSOFT *Software Engineering Notes*, August.

## FURTHER READING

Grubb, P. and Takang, A. A. (2003) *Software maintenance: concepts and practice.* World Scientific Publishing, London.

Pigoski, T. M. (1996) *Practical software maintenance: best practices for managing your software investment.* Wiley, New York.

# 14 SOLUTION DEVELOPMENT TOOLS

## Julian Cox

**CONTENTS OF THIS CHAPTER**

This chapter covers the following topics:

- typical tool functions and benefits;
- tools through solution lifecycles;
- what's in a name?
- evaluating tools;
- benefits and pitfalls of adopting tools.

**INTRODUCTION**

As the capabilities of computer-based software applications have evolved over the last few decades, so have the complexities of the software and its environment. Whereas it was once possible to develop a whole application using a pen-and-paper design, coded and built using a text editor and a command line compiler, it is difficult to imagine doing so now for even the simplest application.

During unit design, the code and build activities for the different run-time environments (including operating systems, application servers and client-side web-browsers) require specific combinations of static and dynamically-linked libraries of components and objects to be incorporated into the application specific source code. The interdependencies between all these elements are so complex that they are almost impossible to manage without the aid of tools.

This Introduction has so far focused on how development tools are essential at the point of coding software, but their use extends well before that into the realms of business analysis and requirements and beyond into testing, release management and even supporting and monitoring the software in operations.

**TYPICAL TOOL FUNCTIONS AND BENEFITS**

The benefits of using computer-aided tools over more primitive approaches such as pen and paper or whiteboard is not due to simplicity, cost or general availability. So what can computer-aided tools provide that, if using primitive tools, can be done manually, but not as efficiently?

## Standardisation

The use of templates and specific notation and syntax is a critical element of any team-based activity such as developing and managing IT systems. This includes the use of forms for written documents and specific visual syntax for diagram notation.

## Storage

Creating computer-based files rather than paper documents means that they can be stored and backed up electronically – either as electronic equivalents of paper documents or as elements within a tool's repository. That repository could be as simple as a folder on a disk drive or a complex meta-model defining a tool-specific repository of element data.

## Availability

Depending on the nature of the technologies involved, electronic documents and repositories can be accessed and the information distributed to appropriate stakeholders inside and outside the team electronically, even across the world.

## Security

Opening up availability may lead to the need to control who can access these elements, and to specify those who can create and edit items, as opposed to who can have read-only access.

## Version control

Many elements need to evolve over time, so the ability to maintain multiple versions (allowing roll-backs to undo changes) while recording who made changes and when is a valuable function of any such tool.

## Change control

This includes light-touch change control that allows elements to be 'checked-out' while they are worked on as well as a formal level as part of change management, where elements can be baselined and locked unless the change is approved.

Most of the functions listed thus far can all reasonably be performed manually (even if not conveniently). The following functions show how specific tools begin to justify the investment in order to handle the complexities.

## Maintaining links and cross references

Any repository of elements of different types for different purposes is given greater value when those elements are linked in a meaningful way. These links can have various meanings within and between groups of related elements:

- cross-references;
- dependencies;
- mappings;
- shifts in abstraction:[1]
  - composition and decomposition;
  - specialisation and generalisation;
  - Conceptual, Logical and Physical.

Depending on the toolset employed, it is even possible for links to be established and maintained between distinct tools and their repositories, for example between a system modelling tool and a testing tool.

## Visual modelling

There is a level of visual diagramming using software that is not very different from using pen and paper, in other words using a tool that either simply draws the shapes or provides some basic syntax support.

A visual modelling tool is one that considers diagrams and other visual representations to be views on an underlying model or repository. As a visual element is added to a diagram, a corresponding element is either added to the underlying model or an existing element in the model is reused. These elements include the nodes (shapes) and the visual links themselves. UML and BPMN 2.0 are two standard modelling languages for which a range of tools, from diagramming to full modelling, are available from a range of tool providers.

## Traceability and impact analysis

These links and cross-references provide the ability for the tool to produce useful views and reports of the elements such as matrices and traceability reports. This is particularly helpful during change control to support impact analysis. If a change is requested or required on any particular element, tools are able to quickly identify other elements that may also need to change.

## Configuration management

A configuration is a set of related configurable items, each of which has specific values or settings which need to work in specific combinations; a configurable item could be any of the elements being managed by the tools.

Identifying these configurations, and being able to apply version and change control practices to each of them, allows more effective management of larger complex systems.

---

[1] See Chapter 7 for a description of these different types of abstraction.

## Documentation generation

The final feature possessed by some tools is the ability to generate meaningful documentation, accessible to a range of stakeholders, from the elemental data they contain. In this way, documentation becomes more of a valuable by-product of the main activities the tools are used for rather than being an activity in itself that is often perceived as an overhead.

## TOOLS THROUGH SOLUTION LIFECYCLES

Some tools specialise in specific aspects or phases of a solution's lifecycle, from business modelling tools through computer-aided software engineering, (CASE) tools linking through to IT service and support management (ITSSM) tools. Figure 14.1 shows the areas covered by tools.

---

**Figure 14.1  Areas covered by solution development tools**

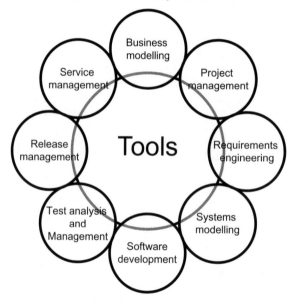

## Business modelling and architecture

Tools that support this area allow the business to develop, implement and maintain business models and architectures of an organisation's:

- context and links with the outside world;
- business functions and processes;
- products and services;

- internal structure and roles;
- information systems (IS) including information technology (IT).

In this context, the IS/IT are simply components that provide services to the business and perhaps direct to customers. As the organisation seeks to change its model in any respect, then that often requires a change in the IS/IT and the drivers for such a change are apparent as are the dependencies across the business architecture that need to be handled.

## Project management tools

Often, business changes – especially significant changes to the IS/IT – require formal project management. Although many project management tools tend to focus on planning, resource management and progress reporting, at the heart of any project is a definition of what that project is delivering as outputs and the benefits expected by the business as eventual outcomes. These are often encapsulated in the business case and/ or project initiation document as the high-level project and business objectives. These may be derived from the business modelling described above and form the basis for further requirements engineering.

## Requirements engineering tools

Computer-aided requirements engineering (CARE) tools are specialised tools; they sometimes operate as a stand-alone tool or as a function of a broader business modelling or CASE tool.

Requirements may be documented using pen and paper or by using generic word-processing and spreadsheet tools. There are, however, aspects of requirements engineering which specialised tools can make a lot easier, including:

- version control;
- team support and access security;
- change control;
- configuration management;
- traceability.

## System modelling tools

A fundamental element of many CASE tools is the ability to support model-driven engineering. That is, to move from abstract models of a system through to an implemented version of that model and vice versa. In Chapter 7 ('Systems modelling techniques'), the U-curve describes how:

- the current, 'as is' physical system can be documented (potentially through an automated tool process called reverse engineering)
- this can be abstracted to a logical 'as is' model. Business requirements and changes can then be applied leading to...

- the logical 'to be' model, which can then be designed into a...
- physical 'to be' design that can be implemented.

Chapter 7 also discusses how several different views (for example functional, data and event) can be used in combination to provide a more complete understanding of the system.

System modelling tools can often be used by a number of roles, from business analysts through system analysts and designers to developers, each evolving the models towards the solution. Testers can also take these models as a basis to analyse and design the testing; or in some cases, these tools integrate with the testing tools they employ.

## Software development tools

Fundamentally, development tools provide the ability for developers to take a design, and either write source code or use a visual notation that links components into an assembly for which source code is automatically generated.

Source code then needs to be able to be executed by the computer. There are various forms for this:

- **Interpreted code.** The source code is interpreted as a set of instructions at run-time. This includes older implementations of BASIC, COBOL and other procedural languages. More relevant in the twenty-first century, it also includes scripting languages such as JavaScript, which is interpreted server or client-side – for example, Javascript embedded in a web page and interpreted by a browser.
- **Compiled (and linked) native executable code.** The source code is taken through what is typically a two-stage process. It is first compiled into an intermediate link-code which is then linked to similar code in statically-linked libraries to produce a version of the code that is more directly executable by a specific platform.
- **Partially compiled code.** An example of this would be Java, which is compiled into a 'byte code' that can be executed by a Java run-time environment (which often performs the final linking just-in-time).

Modern development tools typically allow the developer to create and run these in real time, enabling a very incremental means of developing software, while performing some run-time tests.

Various features expected of development tools include:

- Syntax support: indicating an invalid syntax as it is typed.
- Checking references: although the syntax may be correct, the libraries, functions, variables may be incorrect. Tools can either highlight these before compile/link cycles and even provide valid choices as the developer types.

- Integration with team repository and version control tools: providing the ability to baseline software and undo changes.

- Model to source code support: converting design models into skeleton source code with features and dependencies carried over.

In many cases, the code development and system modelling functions are incorporated into a single tool.

## Testing tools

Whereas some unit testing features are often incorporated into development tools, the testing discipline typically employs specialist tools, often referred to as computer-aided software testing (CAST) tools. These do more than simply run automated tests on the software, and other features include:

- **Test management** – allows test managers to plan, review, evaluate and report on a testing programme.

- **Test design** – allows testers to analyse requirements and design in order to design an appropriate level of testing. This includes the design of test scenarios, sample data and boundary tests.

- **Automated testing** – allows the execution of automated, repeatable tests.

- **Test analysis** – allows testers to review the results of tests and to determine what feedback to provide to the developers about defects and what changes to make to the test designs to increase the effectiveness of the tests.

Elements of testing, such as evidence of testing, may be linked to earlier elements including traces back to the requirements that have been delivered.

## Release management

Release management occurs at the handover from development to operations. Many modern enterprise IS/IT solutions have a number of significant issues to manage at release, including the dependencies between different hardware and software components in a distributed architecture, the release and configuration of which has to be coordinated in order to avoid disruption to day-to-day business activities. These include:

- server hardware and software components;

- client-side hardware and software components;

- infrastructure components, such as networks and various middleware;

- a prepared user base, including provision of training and documentation;

- a prepared operations team, including support and management tools and processes (including help-desk services).

Through design, development and testing activities, specific combinations of configurations should have been planned and tested for release. This release could be through pilots, an incremental release or a 'big-bang' delivery. These tools may deploy updates out to clients either as a pull (clients specifically requesting updates) or push (updates deployed remotely) to a plan.

## Service management tools

Commonly referred to as IT Service and Support Management (ITSSM) tools. Once released, the solutions still require:

- monitoring against service levels;
- support through help-desk services;
- implementation of business-as-usual maintenance;
- documentation of what is deployed.

Configuration management is a major contributor of effective service management. The configuration management database (CMDB) is a key feature of any ITSSM tool.

One of the outputs from service management may be a set of change requests and other pressures for change that initiate a new solution development cycle.

## CONCLUSION

### What's in a name?

Throughout this chapter, there has been reference to a range of disciplines, activities and abbreviations.

For solution development tool support, the broadest term is CASE (computer-aided software engineering), which typically covers requirements through to testing. Within that space, we find specialist tools such as CARE (computer-aided requirements engineering) and CAST (computer-aided software testing) as well as the core software development tools that manage code and produce deliverable software components.

At either 'end' of this continuum, we have business tools and service management tools that are primarily focused on the business operating model; modelling, monitoring and looking for issues that drive change for business improvement.

### Evaluating tools

Precisely where one definition ends and another begins is often down to the tool supplier, who will often adopt a broad term for marketing reasons. Organisations or individuals need to assess and give careful consideration as to which tools are adopted, taking into consideration a number of factors:

- **Requirements:** precisely what does the organisation expect the tool to do? Produce requirements as one should for any COTS (commercial off-the-shelf) business application.

- **Functionality:** beware lists of 'features' in marketing collateral. Precisely what can various roles do with the tool and do these meet the organisation's requirements?

- **Suitability:** does the tool fit with the organisation's standards, processes and notations or will the organisation need to change to fit with the tool?

- **Compatibility:** the disciplines that utilise tools, as described above, may exist within their own silos, but tools will be more effective if they aid communication across the disciplines through tools being able to share information and interact effectively. Tools also need to be compatible with any existing operational applications and infrastructure if they are to monitor, reverse-engineer and maintain them. If part of the development is outsourced or offshored, the ability to communicate and interact effectively through tools' exchanging information may be of immense benefit.

- **Technical:** what are the technical requirements for the tools and is this compatible with existing hardware?

- **Skills:** what specific skills are required to use the tool? Do the tool users require tool specific or other training in order to be effective?

- **Costs:** including up-front and ongoing licensing costs, as well as costs of support and training to use the tool.

Ultimately, the choice should be determined through a business case as selecting and implementing the wrong tool can seriously damage an organisation's capability to develop solutions.

## Benefits and pitfalls of adopting tools

The development and operation of solutions that incorporate IS/IT elements are logically possible without the support of automated tools. However, the complexity and scale of such solutions often makes this unfeasible.

There is a massive marketplace where tools of all types, shapes and sizes are available. Different disciplines may choose their own tools, but even more benefit can be achieved where these tools integrate or share in order to provide a better quality of support.

The tools themselves are, however, only as useful as those who use them; users need to have the necessary skills and knowledge. If, for example, a systems analyst doesn't understand the syntax and appropriate use of a particular modelling language such as UML, then giving them a tool based on that language will not help. Indeed it risks the opposite.

There is also the danger of a misplaced perception and confidence that anything output by a tool must be 'OK' or correct. There's an abbreviation, GIGO, from the early days of computing, that rings true even more today with the widespread use of tools: Garbage In = Garbage Out!

## FURTHER READING

Avison, D. and Fitzgerald, G. (2002) *Information systems development: methodologies, techniques and tools*. McGraw Hill, Maidenhead.

Black, R. (2009) *Managing the testing process: practical tools and techniques for managing hardware and software testing* (3rd edition). John Wiley and Sons, Indianapolis, IN.

Reifer, D. J. (2012) *Software change management: case studies and practical advice*. Microsoft Press, Washington, DC.

# GLOSSARY OF TERMS AND ABBREVIATIONS

**Abstraction**   The thought process wherein ideas are distanced from objects. In the context of this book abstraction is the removal of detail unnecessary to that particular view. Four types of abstraction are useful in this context: Classification, Composition, Generalisation and Idealisation. In object-oriented programming, abstraction involves the definition of 'objects' that can perform work, change their state and communicate with other objects; each object is therefore a mini-system in its own right and larger systems are built up by combining objects in different ways.

**Acceptance testing**   See *User acceptance testing*.

**Activity sampling**   A quantitative *requirements elicitation* technique where an observer samples the work of a group of users over a period to find out how their time is utilised.

**Adaptive maintenance**   Maintenance undertaken to adapt a system to changing needs and circumstances.

**Agile (approach to development)**   A movement triggered by the creation of the agile manifesto in 2001 which promotes a lightweight and more collaborative approach to developing software.

**Agile Unified Process (Agile UP)**   A lightweight version of the Rational Unified Process. See also *Rational Unified Process*.

**Anti-malware software**   Specialist software designed to detect, quarantine and repair damage caused by malware (malicious software).

**Application**   A set of software components or modules that between them deliver a cohesive set of application services (see Software architecture). Some of these components may be distributed around the IT infrastructure and potentially shared with other applications.

**Applications management**   The support and enhancement of applications once they have been delivered initially.

**Architecture (systems)**   Noun: 'The fundamental organization of a system embodied in its components, their relationships to each other, and to the environment, and the principles guiding its design and evolution.' (ISO/IEC/IEEE 42010:2011 - Systems and software engineering). See also *Enterprise Architecture*, *Solution Architecture*, *Software Architecture*.

**Attribute**   An atomic item of data.

**Audit trail**   A record of the changes made to a computer system including when the change was made and who made it.

**BAU**   See *Business-as-usual*.

**Benefits realisation**   The process of checking, after a project has been completed, whether the expected benefits have been achieved and, if not, of identifying what further actions may be required to achieve them.

**Benefits review**   A formal review undertaken at some point after the end of a project to find out whether the expected benefits of a project have been realised.

**Big bang Implementation**   With a big bang implementation, the changeover to using the new system is done in one operation, completely replacing the old system in one go. Big bang implementation is also known as 'Direct implementation'.

**Binary chop**   A simple algorithm for searching sequential files to quickly access the required record.

**Black-box testing**   A method of software testing that tests the functionality of a software application (what the software does) without examining its internal structures or workings.

**Boolean**   Boolean is a data series made up of only two possible values: 0 and 1, or alternatively, true or false or yes or no. Programming languages and DBMS' often incorporate a Boolean data type to constrain the values that can be stored in variables or data fields of that type.

**Business analysis**   An internal consultancy role which has the responsibility for investigating business situations, identifying and evaluating options for improving business systems, defining requirements and ensuring the effective use of information systems in meeting the needs of the business.

**Business analyst**   One who carries out *business analysis* work.

**Business-as-usual (BAU)**   BAU refers to the normal day-to-day operations of an organisation, which have to continue with as little interruption as possible alongside the development of new and enhanced IT systems.

**Business case**   An examination of the courses of action available to address a business issue, together with its costs, benefits, impacts and risks, so as to enable senior management to make informed decisions on whether to proceed with a proposed initiative.

**Business feasibility**   An aspect of assessing the feasibility of project which considers whether it is feasible in business terms, for example will it fit with the culture or structure of the organisation?

**Business requirement**   A type of *requirement* identified by the IIBA® which documents the high-level goals, objectives and needs of an organisation.

**CASE (Computer-Aided Software Engineering)**   An automated tool that provides facilities to support the definition and development of a software-based information system. Typical features include the definition of system artefacts in a model repository, the rendering of diagrammatic model views and code generation.

**Change control**   A process for ensuring that changes in the objectives, timescale or budget of a project are made in a controlled way after due considerations of the impacts and risks of the changes.

**Changeover**   See *Cutover*.

**Check digit**   An additional character added to identification numbers/codes (such as bank accounts) to detect input errors. The character is derived by applying an algorithm (such as the modulus 11 algorithm) to the base part of the number/code.

**Class**   A *type* of *object* within an object-oriented system, not limited to software systems. A static definition of the roles and responsibilities that object possesses, or is required to possess, including its attributes (data) and operations (behaviour). In object-oriented software systems classes are units of source code that implement these. See *Classification*.

**Class model**   A type of *data model* defined in the *UML* whereby data elements are shown as *classes* of *object* and the relationships between them are shown as *associations*.

**Classification (abstraction)**   In general terms, classification is one of the major ways in which human beings make sense of the world and provide themselves with a mental map of it. In information systems, and particularly UML, it refers to the concept of putting objects into different categories.

**Closed Source**   See *Shared Source*.

**Cloud Computing**   An umbrella term used to refer to a set of technologies. See *IaaS, PaaS* and *SaaS*) that provide 'a model for enabling convenient, on-demand network access to a shared pool of configurable computing resources [...] that can be rapidly provisioned and released with minimal management effort or service provider interaction.' [Source: National Institute of Standards and Technology].

**Commercial off-the-shelf (COTS)**   A readily-available package that can be used to meet a business need more quickly and, in theory at least, more cheaply than developing a solution to meet the need.

**Component**   A component is something that can be deployed as a black box. It has an external specification, which is independent of its internal mechanisms. In software terms, a component is an executable software artefact that exhibits these characteristics.

**Component-Based Development (CBD)**    An approach to developing IT systems whereby they are assembled from, in the main, pre-existing components, the advantage being the speed of development and the fact that the new system is built largely from tried and tested elements.

**Composition (abstraction)**    A form of abstraction where an element is recognised as an aggregation or composition of other elements and is treated as a whole and the 'part' elements are hidden. Can apply to functional and data structures as well as real world objects (for example teams of people). The opposite is de-composition.

**Conceptual or Domain class model**    A form of *class model* that acts as a *data model* during analysis which focusses on the types of data-centric *business objects* within the system; where the class' *attributes* represent the individual *data elements* and *associations* between the classes are based on the need to link data *objects*.

**Configuration management**    A process for managing the versions of artefacts (for example, documents and software components) and understanding how the different versions fit together to make larger artefacts.

**Corrective maintenance**    Maintenance undertaken to correct faults found and reported in a system.

**Cost/benefit analysis**    The process of comparing the costs and benefits of a proposed business initiative over time to find out whether the benefits expected are greater than the anticipated costs.

**Cross-field validation**    The comparison of the contents of one data field with another to check for accuracy, for example that gender and title match or that someone's date of birth is not after their date of death.

**Cutover**    The transition from the use of one system to a new system. It is also called Changeover.

**Data conversion**    The conversion of data from one format to another, whereby the concerted data is suitable to be processed by a computer system. For example, conversion of data held in paper records to machine readable format.

**Data element**    The smallest piece of *data* (*datum*), usually containing a single fact, being considered in data modelling whether in the form of an *Entity Relationship Diagram* or a *Class Model*. Often given different names such as *data item* or *data field*.

**Data item**    See *Attribute*.

**Data mapping**    The process of determining how data held on one system needs to be modified for storage on another system. Sometimes data will need to be created on the target system in situations where the required data doesn't exist on the source system.

**Data migration**    The process of transferring data from one system to another system. This process typically consists of three steps known as Extract, Transform and Load. See *ETL*.

**Data model**   A model of the data elements that support a business or IT system and the business rules that govern then creation, amendment and deletion of those elements. One type of data model is the *entity relationship diagram* and, in the *Unified Modeling Language*, *class models* are used.

**Data warehouse**   A repository of corporate data, often drawn from many systems, that is used to support enquires and provide management information.

**Database**   An assembly of data organised so as to support searches and other uses.

**Database Management System (DBMS)**   A dedicated piece of software that is used to manage a database.

**DBMS**   See *Database Management System*.

**Default value**   The value that would be put in a data field in the absence of an entry by a user or as a starting point for future updates.

**Department of Defence Architecture Framework (DoDAF)**   An *architecture* framework for the United States Department of Defense. It provides visualisation of the infrastructure for the concerns of specific stakeholders organised into various views.

**Design pattern**   A reusable solution to a recurring problem or requirement.

**Design**   The process of mapping out how an information system is to be developed and implemented by the use of appropriate databases, software and hardware.

**Developer**   A role within systems development responsible for taking specifications (or, in the case of Agile approaches, users' needs) and meeting them through the writing of software *programs*.

**Development**   The process of creating software *programs* and other artefacts that constitute an operational information system.

**Dialogue**   An interaction between an IT system and its user.

**Direct file**   A file of data that can be accessed in any order.

**Direct implementation**   See *Big bang implementation*.

**Discounted cash flow (DCF)**   A approach to *investment appraisal* whereby future cash flows are discounted to adjust them to the present value of money, based on the principle that money received later is worth less than money received in the present.

**Document analysis**   An *requirements elicitation* technique where an analyst dissects the contents of a form, report or computer screen to find out where the information comes from, what format it is in, who gathers and uses it and so forth. It provides useful insights into the creation of *data models*.

**DoDAF**   See *Department of Defence Architecture Framework*.

**Domain expert**   Someone involved in the investigation of a business or IT system who can provide expertise in best practice within the industry or sector. The role could be filled by a member of the user community or sometimes by a consultant.

**DSDM**   See *Dynamic System Development Method*.

**Dynamic System Development Method (DSDM)**   One of a family of Agile software development processes, DSDM is an iterative and incremental project delivery framework that emphases continuous user involvement and the importance of delivering the right solution at the right time.

*Note: DSDM was established by the DSDM Consortium in January 1995 and was first published in February 1995 but a major new version called DSDM Atern was launched in April 2007. Since April 2014 the DSDM Consortium has resorted back to using the original name: DSDM.*

**Dynamic testing**   A testing method that involves interaction with the software *program* while it is executed.

**Encryption**   Processing a message sent in such a way that the recipient can only read it if they have the necessary authorisation codes.

**Encryption key**   The code required to read and interpret an encrypted file.

**Enterprise Architecture**   An overall architecture for an organisation that embraces the business structure, data and/or information, applications and infrastructure or technology.

**Entity**   A type of data object represented in data modelling (see *Entity Relationship diagram*). An entity is usually a classification of similar real world 'things' about which the system is required to store and manipulate several items of data. The entity lists the data elements pertinent to that system.

**Entity relationship diagram (ERD)**   A type of *data model* whereby the data objects are represented as *entities* and the logical business connections between them are shown as *relationships*. Additional *semantics* such as multiplicity and optionality of *relationships* and individual *data elements* can be shown in the diagram.

**Escrow**   An agreement between three organisations: the customer, the vendor and a third-party (often the National Computing Centre), often enacted when a software solution is procured 'off-the-shelf'. The agreement allows for the third-party to hold a copy of the source code for the software product and grants permission to the third party to make available this source code to the customer in the event that the vendor ceases trading.

**ETL**   ETL is the three-step process use to extract data held in a source system, transfer the data to the target system, and finally load the data onto the target system. At various points in the ETL, data is modified (or created) to ensure that the final data stored on the target system meets the requirements for processing using the target system. Part or all of the ETL steps are sometimes automated.

**Evaluation**   Reviewing an IT project to see how successful it was. For more detail see *Post-project review*, *Post-implementation review* and *Benefits review*.

**Evolutionary approach (to development)**   An approach to developing information systems whereby parts of the solution are analysed, developed and tested and these evolve in iterations into a complete system.

**Extract, Transform and Load**   See *ETL*.

**Extreme programming (XP)**   An approach to developing and testing *programs* whereby pairs of programmers work together to create software against a tightly-defined timescale.

**Facilitator**   An independent person charged with conduct of a *focus group* or *workshop* whose role is to assist the participants in reaching a conclusion or decision.

**Facilities management**   The control and support of an organisation's IT infrastructure.

**Feasibility study**   A high-level (that is, not detailed) examination of a proposed business initiative or project to establish its objectives, scope, costs and benefits for the purpose of deciding whether a more detailed investigation should be undertaken.

**Financial feasibility**   An aspect of assessing the feasibility of project which considers whether it can be justified in financial terms. See also *Investment appraisal*.

**Focus group**   A group of people brought together with an independent facilitator to discuss a topic.

**Foreign key**   The primary key from one relation (table) that is incorporated as a non-key attribute in another table so as to represent a relationship that exists between the two tables. The foreign key will uniquely identify a single row in the related table.

**Functional model**   A model of the functionality, or processing, within a system will cover. In *UML*, a *use case diagram* can be used to illustrate this functionality.

**Functional requirement**   A *requirement* that defines what a system is to do in functional terms. See also *Non-functional requirement*.

**General requirement**   A high-level *requirement* documenting an important business imperative, for example to comply with some legislation or with organisational policies.

**Generalisation (abstraction)**   Extends the *classification* form of *abstraction* (classification of *objects*) by further classifying groups of *classes* (*sub-classes*) into more general types (*super-classes*). The subclasses are 'a kind of' the superclass and inherit its properties. See *inheritance*.

**Idealisation (abstraction)**   A form of *abstraction* that moves away from a physical model, through a logical model to conceptual and even contextual models. The opposite process, reification or realisation, is the underlying activity through system development, especially Model Driven Engineering.

**IIBA®**   See *International Institute of Business Analysis*.

**Impact analysis**   The identification of impacts within a ***business case***, for example the need to adopt a different management style, which decision-makers need to consider when deciding whether to proceed or not.

**Implementation**   In systems development, implementation is often defined as the stage at which a developed system is placed into live operation and made available to its users. It is worth noting that this definition is somewhat different from that adopted in the ***project management*** community where implementation is the stage of a project where the actual development work is performed.

**Implementation plan**   The implementation plan describes how the tested system will be deployed, installed and transitioned into operational use. The plan contains an overview of the system, a description of the major tasks involved in the implementation, the overall resources needed to support the implementation effort (such as hardware, software, facilities, materials, and personnel), any site-specific implementation requirements, and detailed step-by-step schedule of activities.

**Incremental (development and lifecycle)**   An approach to developing an information system whereby it is analysed and designed completely and then delivered in a series of increments, This allows the most important or urgent elements to be delivered earlier than if the whole system had to be provided in one delivery.

**Inheritance**   An applied form of ***generalisation*** employed by designers and programmers to optimise code by implementing common features once in a group of similar classes. Also allows polymorphism.

**Intangible (costs and benefits)**   In the context of a ***business case***, these are costs and benefits where it is difficult, or impossible, to put credible valuations on them in advance of undertaking a project, for example on 'disruption during implementation' (cost) or 'better staff morale' (benefit).

**Integration testing**   The phase in software testing in which individual software modules are combined and tested as a group.

**Internal rate of return (IRR)**   A simulated valuation of the return on investment on a project, this is defined as the discount rate that would need to be used in a ***net present value*** calculation to get an NPV of zero, that is costs and benefits balance precisely. The IRR can be used to compare projects with each other (the one with the higher IRR being the more attractive investment) and with the cost of capital used in the project, which it should exceed if the project is to be financially viable.

**International Institute of Business Analysis (IIBA®)**   A non-profit professional association founded in Canada in 2003 and which now has chapters in many parts of the world. Its purpose is to promote and support the discipline of business analysis.

**Interview**   A form of ***requirements elicitation*** where a single analyst (usually) talks to a single user to discover their requirements.

**Investment appraisal**   The process of examining the financial case for a proposed project or other initiative to see if, in financial terms, it can be justified.

**Iterative (development and lifecycle)**   An approach to developing an information system which consists of a series of iterations, in each of which a portion of the functionality is analysed, designed, developed and (probably) delivered. This approach allows the most important or urgent elements to be delivered more quickly (and start to provide business benefits) and defers consideration of other elements until later.

**Key**   A unique identifier for data set (such as a row in a table or an entity or class occurrence) within a data structure (Entity, table, Class) comprising one or more data items (attributes). Commonly used with relational databases. Note: Class modelling in an object-oriented sense does not use keys as such but the technique is a valid alternative to ERDs, and hence, keys can be shown on Class diagrams.

**Key performance indicator**   Measures used to assess the performance of an organisation, department or IT system.

**KPI**   See *Key performance indicator*.

**Lean software development**   An approach to developing information systems derived from the principles of lean manufacturing, aimed at cutting waste and doing things 'just in time'.

**Lifecycle**   A series of stages for the development of an information, organised into a logical sequence and used as the basis for managing such projects.

**Linear approach (to development)**   An approach to developing information systems whereby the stages (feasibility study, requirements engineering, design, development, testing and implementation) follow each other in a logical, linear sequence.

**Logical model**   A logical model is a robust model of a system that abstracts out any purely physical element, such as specific technologies, programming languages and so forth. Helps to focus on the underlying requirements and logic rather than a specific solution. See *Idealisation (abstraction)*.

**Malware**   Malware, short for malicious software, is any software used to disrupt computer operation, gather sensitive information, or gain access to private computer systems. It can appear in the form of code, scripts, active content, and other software. 'Malware' is a general term used to refer to a variety of forms of hostile or intrusive software including (but not limited to) viruses, worms, trojan horses, spyware, adware.

**Methodology**   Strictly speaking, the study of methods. However, the term has come to be synonymous with 'method' itself.

**Microfiche**   A sheet of microfilm, six by four inches, holding several hundred reduced images of document pages; read using a microfiche reader or microfilm reader.

**Middleware**   Products that bridge the gap between hardware and software.

**Model**   A representation of a system produced as part of a development or architecture process to aid understanding, communication and aid quality.

**Model driven (software) engineering**   A thread of activity as part of a development approach that produces models at the appropriate level of abstraction for a given point in time, but which show the evolution from requirements to implementation.

**Model Driven Architecture (MDA)**   A specification by the Object Management Group that describes an automated form of Model Driven Engineering through use of appropriate tools and model notation, specifically UML 2.0.

**Modular (design)**   Refers to the design of software using modules (software components), whereby the modules are said to be loosely-coupled and highly cohesive.

**MoSCoW**   An approach to *prioritisation* widely used in *Agile* projects (and elsewhere), whereby requirements are classified as Must have (mandatory, first iteration); Should have (mandatory but may be delivered later); Could have (may be discarded if time and resources do not permit); Want to have but not now (consideration deferred until a later iteration).

**Net present value (NPV)**   The total value of a project, assessed over a period of time, where cash flows in years after the initial one are adjusted to take account of the *time value of money*.

**Non-functional requirement (NFR)**   A *requirement* that defines how a system is to perform or operate or which defines the qualities it should exhibit. See also *Functional requirement*.

**Normalisation**   The process of putting data into third normal form, so that it is organised without duplication or redundancy and is thus very efficient for updating.

**Object**   An instance of a class within a system, with roles and responsibilities defined by its class, which dynamically interacts with other objects to deliver system functionality. Objects can also be dynamically created and deleted from the system as necessary.

**Object-oriented**   An approach to analysing, designing and developing systems (not limited to software systems) that views the system as a set of objects, each with defined roles and responsibilities, that dynamically interact with each other to deliver system functionality, including the representation and manipulation of data.

**Object-relational mapping**   A mechanism for converting data stored in an RDBMS into a set of runtime objects that can be manipulated by an OO programming language.

**Observation**   A form of *requirements elicitation* where a trained observer (for example, a business analyst) studies the work of an individual or group of workers for a period.

**OCR**   See *Optical Character Recognition*.

**Offshoring**   The location of part, or all, of an organisation's systems development operation in another country, usually for reasons of cost or to gain access to skilled resources. See also *Outsourcing*.

288

**OMR**   See *Optical Mark Recognition*.

**OODBMS (Object-Oriented Data Base Management System)**   A specific type of DBMS for object-oriented databases.

**Open source**   Software that has been developed, often collaboratively, and then made available free of charge to anyone who wishes to use it. Often, communities grow up who maintain and enhance such software.

**Optical Character Recognition**   A method of data input where special reading devices can translate written text into data for storage.

**Optical Mark Recognition**   A method of data input where special reading devices can recognise symbols, such as sequences of dots or bar-codes and translate them into stored data.

**Options**   The alternative means of meeting a business need considered in a *business case*, including that of doing nothing and continuing with the existing processes and systems.

**Outsourcing**   The handing over of aspects of an organisation's operations, in the context of this book, systems development, to an external company, usually because of a lack of in-house expertise or because the commissioning organisation wishes to transfer the risk to the service provider. See also *Offshoring*.

**Paradigm**   A world view underlying the theories and methodology of a particular scientific subject. For instance, a software engineering paradigm represents a particular world-view underlying an approach to software engineering, such as the object-oriented paradigm, which is a view that systems can be developed from a series of interacting objects, each encapsulating data and behaviour.

**Parallel run**   With a parallel run implementation, the old and the new system are both used alongside each other, both being able to operate independently. If all goes well, the old system is stopped and the new system carries on as the only system.

**Parameter**   An item of data passed from one program to another. The parameter links the data in the calling program to the program being called (often referred to as a sub-program). Parameters can be used to alter the behaviour of the sub-program to make it specific to the calling program. Also referred to as an 'argument'.

**Pattern**   A known solution to a class of problems. Can apply to functionality, data, structure and other contexts. Recognised and named patterns are often used as a shorthand in discussions over complex issues. There are patterns that may be applied in different contexts; *Analysis Patterns*, (software) *Design Patterns*, *Communication Patterns* to name a few.

**Payback (breakeven)**   A simple method of presenting the investment appraisal for a project or other initiative whereby the initial and ongoing costs and benefits are contrasted over a period of time to find out at what point the cumulative benefits exceed the cumulative costs so that the project has achieved 'breakeven'.

**PDF**   See *Portable Document Format*.

**Perfective maintenance**   'Tuning' a system to make it work better, for example faster or more reliably.

**Phased implementation**   With a phased implementation, changeover to the new system is carried out in a number of stages or phases. If each phase is successful then the next phase is started, eventually leading to the final phase when the new system fully replaces the old one.

**Physical design**   The process of producing a design for a software system that will run on, and exploit the capabilities of, a specific hardware platform.

**Pilot Implementation**   With a pilot implementation the new system replaces the old one in one operation but only on a small scale. For example, it might be tried out in one branch of the company or in one location. If successful, the pilot is extended until it eventually replaces the old system completely.

**PIR**   See *Post-implementation review*.

**Polymorphism**   Run-time behaviour supported by inheritance that allows a group of objects of different classes, but with a common super-class, to be interacted with as though they were of the same super-class type; by using those operations and attributes defined in the super-class and therefore inherited by all the subclasses.

**Portable Document Format**   A file format used to store and present documents in a manner that is independent of the application that was used to create it. PDF is now an open standard, having been made such by Adobe Systems, whose 'Acrobat' product is the leading program to create and read PDF files.

**Post-implementation review**   A review carried out after the completion of a systems development project to find out how well the delivered systems meets the requirements defined for it.

**Post-project review**   A review carried out at the conclusion of a development project to assess how well the project was conducted and to document any lessons for the future.

**Preventative maintenance**   Maintenance taken to anticipate and prevent expected problems with a system.

**Primary key**   A unique identifier for a 'relation' in relational database theory.

**Prioritisation**   The process of placing the *requirements* in a systems development project in an agreed order of importance so that the most valuable requirements are delivered first.

**Program**   A set of instructions prepared to tell a computer system what to do.

**Programming**   The process of developing programs.

**Project management**   The discipline of managing a project so that its objectives in terms of time, cost (or resources) and scope/quality have been achieved.

**Project manager**   One who carries out *project management*.

**Project sponsor**   The person tasked by an organisation with the responsibility for a project as a piece of business (as distinct from its technical aspects which are the province of the *project manager*) and who is ultimately responsible to the organisation for the delivery of the business benefits.

**Prototyping**   A form of *requirements elicitation* whereby simulations of the proposed system are developed and shown to its users to see if it is likely to meet their needs. Prototypes can also be used to explore *non-functional requirements* and in the *validation* of the specification.

**Quality**   'The totality of features and characteristics of a product or service that bear on its ability to satisfy stated or implied needs.' (ISO8402, 199). Other common definitions include 'fitness for purpose' and 'conformance to specification'.

**Quality assurance**   Processes and techniques that ensure that proper standards are in place for the maintenance of quality and that project teams are following these standards. QA is carried out outside of the systems development team.

**Quality control**   The processes used within a project team, including *testing* to ensure the quality of the artefacts developed.

**Questionnaires**   See *Surveys*.

**RAD**   See *Rapid Application Development*.

**Range check**   A form of data validation that checks that an input value is within some pre-defined parameters, for instance that the 'day' in a date field is within the range 01-31.

**Rapid Application Development**   An early empirical approach to software development based around the use of prototyping and collaboration between developers and system users. A precursor to the Agile movement.

**Rational Unified Process (RUP)**   This is an *iterative* approach to software development that was developed originally by the Rational Software Corporation, which was absorbed into IBM in 2003. It provides an adaptable framework which is designed to be tailored by its users to the specific needs of their organisations and their projects.

**RDBMS (Relational Data Base Management System)**   A specific type of DBMS for relational databases.

**Re-testing**   Also known as confirmation testing, this is the test applied to any part of a system that has been changed to check that changes have been made correctly.

**Record searching**   A form of *requirements elicitation* technique where files of records are searched to discover, for example, how many document are produced within a given period.

**Regression testing**   A software testing method that seeks to uncover new software defects, or regressions, in existing areas of a system after changes have been made to new areas of the system.

**Requirement**   A statement of need, condition that must be satisfied, function, constraint (business, user, system, technical, project) or capability.

**Requirements analysis**   The process of examining a set of *requirements* and assessing their completeness, consistency, correctness and relevance to meeting the business needs of the organisation.

**Requirements catalogue**   A repository of *requirements* for a systems development project.

**Requirements documentation**   The set of documents that are used to record the *requirements* for a systems development project, including the *requirements catalogue*, *functional models*, *data models* and often a glossary of terms.

**Requirements elicitation**   The process of using a range of techniques to discover the *requirements* for a systems development project.

**Requirements engineering**   A framework that people can follow and which can be replicated from project to project; a set of techniques that can be used at each stage within the framework; and standards that define, for example, what is meant by 'good' *requirements*.

**Requirements validation**   The process of carrying out a final review of the *requirements* for a systems development project before they are used to build, or procure, the system. See also *Verification* and *Validation*.

**Risk analysis**   The process of identifying, documenting and assessing the risks to a project and devising suitable countermeasures.

**RUP**   See *Rational Unified Process*.

**Scenarios**   A form of *requirements elicitation*

**Scrum**   A lightweight Agile software development framework based around the concepts of Sprints and daily Scrums.

**SDLC**   See *System development lifecycle*.

**Service level agreement**   An agreement between, typically, those building or maintaining an IT system and their customers (external or internal) defining such issues as the time to respond to a request for support.

**Service management**   The management and maintenance of the services provided by IT systems, including facilities management and applications management.

**Service-oriented**   Service-orientation is an approach to creating computer systems by thinking of them in terms of 'services', pieces of functionality that, once built, can be used in a variety of applications. The benefits of this are speed of construction and lowered cost (because most of the services will probably already exist and have been paid for) and greater reliability (because the services should already have been tested and proven in other applications).

**Shadowing**   A form of *requirements elicitation* where an observer follows a worker around to see what they do.

**Shared Source**   The advent of open source software has also encouraged large software corporations, such as Microsoft™, to offer what they call 'shared source' software. Microsoft's Shared Source Initiative was launched in May 2001 and includes a spectrum of technologies and licenses. Most of its source code offerings are available for download after eligibility criteria are met. The licenses associated with the offerings range from being closed-source (allowing only viewing of the code for reference), to allowing it to be modified and redistributed for both commercial and non-commercial purposes.

**SLA**   See *Service level agreement*.

**Software Architecture**   The high level design and specification of a set of software components and modules that interoperate to meet functional and non-functional requirements of a software system. Can be modelled logically and physically.

**Software Engineering**   'The application of a systematic, disciplined, quantifiable approach to the development, operation, and maintenance of software' [Source: IEEE Standard Glossary of Software Engineering Terminology, IEEE std 610.12-1990, 199].

**Software quality**   See *Quality*.

**Software testing**   The process of exercising software to verify that it satisfies specified requirements and to detect errors.

**Solution Architecture**   The high level design and specification of a set of architecture components modules that interoperate to meet functional and non-functional requirements of a solution that delivers a tactical change. May integrate business, software, data and infrastructure components depending on the solution scope.

**Solution requirement**   A type of *requirement* identified by the IIBA® which documents what an IT system is to do and how it is to operate.

**Source code**   The original code written by the developer of a software program. Source code is usually related reasonably closely to normal English and is then translated into the object code that the computer understands and follows.

**Special-purpose records**   Records kept by workers to show how they spend their working time.

**Spiral model**   A model devised by Barry W Boehm which represents the *systems development lifecycle* as a series of iterative stages, each building on its predecessor.

**SSADM**   See *Structured Systems Analysis and Design Method*.

**Stakeholder**   In relation to a systems development project, anyone who has an interest in the project, for example because they have commissioned it or their work will be affected by it.

**Stakeholder concern**   An abstracted summary of stakeholder interests and requirements used in architecture as the basis of determining what viewpoints are needed in an architecture description to ensure that appropriate views are presented that demonstrate that the stakeholder's concerns are being met.

**Stakeholder requirement**   A type of *requirement* identified by the IIBA® which documents the needs of individual stakeholders or of groups of stakeholders.

**Static Testing**   A testing method that involves examination of documents, including software program code but does not require the software program be executed.

**Structured Systems Analysis and Design Method**   An approach to systems development widely adopted in the 1980s and 1990s, especially in the UK public sector, consisting of a structural model, a lifecycle and a set of techniques.

**Surveys**   Also known as questionnaires, these are a form of *requirements elicitation* technique whereby many users are asked to provide answers to a series of structured questions.

**System development lifecycle**   The series of phases, stages, activities or tasks involved in developing an information system shows as a set of logically sequenced elements.

**System lifecycle**   The complete lifecycle of an information system, including its initial development but also its 'life' and sometimes its final decommissioning.

**System testing**   The phase in software testing that uses the complete, integrated system to evaluate the system's compliance with its specified requirements and design.

**Systems architecture**   The development of an architecture for the organisation to support and coordinate its systems and to provide a coherent platform for expansion and development

**Tangible (costs and benefits)**   In the context of a *business case*, these are costs and benefits where it possible to put credible valuations on them (often in financial terms) in advance of undertaking the project, for example 'purchase of new hardware' (cost) or 'staff savings' (benefit).

**Technical feasibility**   An aspect of assessing the feasibility of project which considers whether it is achievable in technical terms, taking into account any constraints in the hardware or software which may be employed to meet the business need.

**Technical requirement**   A high-level *requirement* documenting an important technical imperative, for example to use a specific hardware or software platform to develop a system.

**Test plan**   The test plan defines the test phases to be performed and the testing activities to be conducted within those phases for a particular project.

**Tester**   Someone who designs and performs *testing* on IT systems.

**Testing**   Testing is the performance of a series of structured tests to determine if an IT system operates correctly and does what it was designed to do. For more detail, see *Black box testing*, *White box testing*, *Unit testing*, *Integration testing*, *System testing*, *User acceptance testing* and **Regression testing**.

**Time value of money**   A concept in management accounting whereby money spent or saved today is worth more than a similar sum spent or saved in future years. This is because there is a cost associated with money (for example, interest paid on loans) or the opportunity is lost to earn interest on it if it is invested in a project. The techniques of *discounted cash flow* / *net present value* and *internal rate of return* depend upon this concept.

**TNA**   See *Training needs analysis*.

**Traceability**   The ability to trace a *requirement* back to its source and forward to its resolution.

**Training needs analysis**   The process of identifying the gap between an employee's current skills and competences and the required skills and competences.

**Transition requirement**   A type of *requirement* identified by the IIBA® which documents what needs to be done to make the transition from an existing process or system to a new one.

**UAT**   See *User Acceptance Testing*.

**UML**   See *Unified Modeling Language*.

**Unified Modeling Language (UML)**   UML is a general purpose modelling language that has been created to enable the visualisation and specification of information systems. Version 2 was released in 2003 by the Object Management Group (OMG) and most practitioners and tools comply with that specification, which continues to develop.

**Unit testing**   A software testing method by which individual units or modules application software, together with associated control data, usage procedures, and operating procedures, are tested to determine if they are fit for use.

**Use case**   A description of a required interaction between an actor (user or other system) and the system in focus which is of value to the actor as it helps them achieve a goal. It incorporates multiple scenarios, each telling a whole story, some of which describe the actor succeeding in their goal while others show them failing, usually by not meeting rule based conditions.

**Use case description**   A use case description defines the interaction between an actor and the system.

**Use case diagram**   A diagram showing the boundaries of a business or system, the actors (including other systems) with which it has associations and the *use cases* that these actors will use.

**User (process worker)**   Someone who works within an organisation and who will be expected to work with a new information system.

**User acceptance testing**   The phase in software testing that uses the complete, integrated system to evaluate the system's compliance with its specified requirements. This testing phase is carried out by the users of the system prior to acceptance of the system into operational service.

**User story**   An approach used in Agile software development whereby the needs of system users are captured as 'stories' as a basis for software development.

**V-model (lifecycle)**   A representation of the *systems development lifecycle* that shows the earlier, 'analysis' stages as the left-hand side of a letter 'V' and the later, 'synthesis' (testing) stages as the right-hand side, with the connections between the earlier and later stages.

**Validation**   Checking that an artefact meets the requirements specified for it by its proposed users, in other words that 'the right thing has been done'. Compare with **Verification**.

**Verification**   Checking that an artefact has been created to an appropriate standard, in other words that it has been 'done right'. Compare with *Validation*.

**Waterfall (lifecycle)**   A representation of the systems development lifecycle, where the stages are shown as sequential steps with the work 'flowing' from one stage to another rather like the steps of a descending cascade of water.

**White-box testing**   White-box testing is a method of software testing that tests internal structures or workings of a software application, as opposed to its functionality.

**Workshop**   A form of *requirements elicitation* technique whereby a group of stakeholders are assembled under the guidance of a facilitator to discuss, review and agree the requirements for a system.

**XP**   See *Extreme programming*.

# INDEX